PRISONER
FOR
CONSCIENCE'
SAKE

PRISONER FOR CONSCIENCE' SAKE

The Life of George Reynolds
Bruce A. Van Orden

Deseret Book Company
Salt Lake City, Utah

All photographs courtesy of Grant Reynolds Hardy.

Library of Congress Cataloging-in-Publication Data

Van Orden, Bruce A.
   Prisoner for conscience' sake : the life of George Reynolds /
   Bruce A. Van Orden.
      p.   cm.
   Includes bibliographical references and index.
   ISBN 0-87579-595-1
   1. Reynolds, George, 1842–1909.   2. Mormons – Utah – Biography.
3. Polygamy – Utah.   4. Utah – Biography.   I. Title.
BX8695.R43V36   1992
289.3′092 – dc20
[B]   92-8435
                                                               CIP

Printed in the United States of America
10   9   8   7   6   5   4   3   2   1

Contents

Contents

Preface

George Reynolds (1842–1909) was a leader and writer in The Church of Jesus Christ of Latter-day Saints during a crucial period of its unification and growth. Reynolds was quiet and unassuming and generally did not appear before the public. Nevertheless, he filled numerous callings and assignments that made him one of the most influential people in the Church in the last thirty years of the nineteenth century and the first decade of the twentieth. He served as a secretary to the First Presidency for forty-four years, from 1865 through 1909, and from 1890 to 1909 he was a member of the First Council of the Seventy, or one of the First Seven Presidents of the Seventy, as the calling was commonly designated then.

But it was not as a general authority that George Reynolds made his greatest contribution to the Church. He is particularly remembered for his role in the polygamy test case, *Reynolds v. the United States,* a landmark Supreme Court decision in 1879 that contributed eventually to the abolition of polygamy in the Church. In addition, Reynolds was a prolific author on Church themes and a pioneer scriptural commentator. He began his Book of Mormon commentary work while serving time as a "prisoner for conscience' sake" in the Utah Territorial Penitentiary in 1879–80. In his day he was most beloved by the Saints for his Book of Mormon scholarship and his monumental *Concordance of the Book of Mormon.*

George Reynolds was twice a missionary in England; an emigration agent in the European Mission; a member of the select Council of Fifty; a home missionary; a seventies quorum president; an assistant editor for the *Deseret News,* the *Millennial Star,* the

Journal of Discourses, and the *Juvenile Instructor;* a Salt Lake City councilman; an officer in the Nauvoo Legion, Utah Territory's militia; a regent of the University of Deseret; a member of the board of directors of several businesses; both a local and a general administrator in the Deseret Sunday School Union; a college lecturer; and a polygamous husband and father. This biography will clarify Reynolds's several roles placed in their larger historical settings. His experiences in the vital "Utah period" shed considerable light upon some of the most important events, issues, and individuals in LDS Church history.

George Reynolds was a second-echelon leader in the Church. I define first-echelon Latter-day Saints as the prophets, apostles, and other individuals of such prominence and influence who rival or supersede the effect of many general authorities. Eliza R. Snow and a few other leading sisters would be considered first-echelon Mormons. Second-echelon Church leaders, such as George Reynolds, are lower-level general authorities or individuals whose influence was considerable during their lives but whose names are not easily recognized by most Church members today. Third-echelon Mormons are local leaders who have substantial influence on a community but whose fame does not exist beyond that community. All three types deserve biographical attention but in Reynolds's case, a number of crucial Mormon history issues are addressed in his biography.

I would like to extend appreciation to Professors James B. Allen and D. Michael Quinn for their unwavering support during my graduate school days at Brigham Young University and especially for their help on my study of George Reynolds. Special credit goes to Kathryn Weeks, Linda Hunter Adams, and Val Holladay of the Brigham Young University College of Humanities Publications Center for editing portions of my manuscript and checking the sources cited. I sincerely appreciate the editorial assistance of Suzanne Brady and the design and layout work of Richard Erickson and Craig Geertsen of Deseret Book Company. Thanks also to my friends and colleagues in the Church Educational System and BYU Religious Education for their support, cooperation, and encouragement. I appreciate the willing assistance of the staffs of the LDS Church Historical Archives, Special Collections of the Harold B. Lee Library at Brigham Young University, and the Utah State Historical Archives. Descendants of George Reynolds have been most cooperative. I have enjoyed becoming acquainted with them in two George Reynolds family reunions and being accepted as one of their own. My undying debt of gratitude is acknowledged to Grant Reynolds Hardy, a choice friend and co-laborer.

CHAPTER 1

Youthful Conversion

L IKE SO MANY OTHER LATTER-DAY SAINTS IN THE LATE NINETEENTH century, George Reynolds hailed from the British Isles. More than half of the Mormons living in Utah after 1865, the year of George's immigration, were either British immigrants or their offspring.[1] George was born in 1842, four and a half years after the restored gospel was first taken to his native land. He joined the Church in London in 1856, sixteen years after the English metropolis saw its first Mormon missionaries. He arrived in Salt Lake City in 1865, only eighteen years after Brigham Young first identified the Salt Lake Valley as the new headquarters of Zion.

George Reynolds was born at his parents' home on Regent Street in the district of Marylebone, London, England, on New Year's Day, 1842. London was still in the throes of the Industrial Revolution, which had begun at the turn of the century. Young Queen Victoria had reigned for nearly five years. Sir Robert Peel had just become prime minister in a Tory, or Conservative, cabinet that many did not think would heed the concerns of the working class (including women and children), who labored under appalling conditions. The year 1842 was the fourth consecutive year of meager harvests and heavy unemployment; hence, food prices were high and wages low. Chartism, a movement for social and economic reform, reached its peak, sparking agitation for a repeal of the infamous Corn Laws and

The elder George Reynolds   Julia Ann Tautz Reynolds

for cheaper grain. But these gloomy circumstances would change considerably by 1846 with the help of Peel's government.[2]

Because his was a middle-class family, young George Reynolds was not as adversely affected by these deprivations as most of his countrymen. Indeed, his family's circumstances were improved by the modernization sweeping England. His father, also named George Reynolds, was a master tailor on Regent Street, near the center of London. He ran a lucrative shop because of brisk business from an increasingly wealthy capitalist class. Young George's opportunities for education, both in his homeland and in France, were benefits of the Industrial Revolution.

The elder George Reynolds was born in 1812 in Totnes, Devonshire, a garden spot of England about fifty miles southwest of London. He was a descendent of the brother of the famous painter Sir Joshua Reynolds (1723–1792), who dominated Britain's art world during the middle and late eighteenth century. George's mother was Julia Ann Tautz, born in 1819 in London. She was of German and

2

French middle-class descent.[3] The date and location of the marriage of George and Julia Ann are unknown.

The first Reynolds child, Frederick, born in 1840, lived only a few days. The first surviving child was George, born 1 January 1842. George later had six younger brothers and three younger sisters, the last born in 1860.[4]

George was a favorite of his indulgent maternal grandmother, Amelia Tautz, who lived nearby in the district of Paddington. She encouraged his precociousness and his assiduous desire to learn. Primary education was not universally available in England, so she made it possible for him to attend the North London Collegiate School. There he garnered prizes and certificates of merit for arithmetic, geography, and good attendance. George was also a devoted student of astronomy, history, and literature. "The boy had been trained to think anyone stupid who was not well informed in the subjects of history and geography," wrote his daughter Alice Louise Reynolds.[5]

George also spent considerable time at his father's tailor shop and often observed the tailors and apprentices sitting cross-legged in a circle surrounding a large, upright gas burner on the shopboard. The apprentices treated the intelligent boy as a pet. George, at age seven, overheard the men making cynical comments about supernatural religious claims. George remembered feeling disgust at hearing what was for him a sacrilegious discussion. Among other things, he heard the tailors discussing a young man in America named Joseph Smith who had discovered some buried metal plates that he had translated by means of the Urim and Thummim. George remembered hearing in school that the Urim and Thummim mentioned in the Bible had been carried by Roman soldiers from Jerusalem to Rome and had been lost in the Tiber River. As he sat that day in the tailor shop, he marveled at the discovery of those holy instruments in America.[6] This incident shows that young George was sober, respectful toward sacred and religious subjects, and inquisitive — traits that would prove significant throughout his life.

3

Two years later, in 1851, George chose boys as companions who lived close to a playground near his house. " 'Buttons' was a favorite game: a number of buttons—the big ones called 'two-ers' and the small ones, 'one-ers'—were placed on the ground in a ring and each boy in turn threw at them. The best marksman won the most." George, who was small for his age, often took bright, shiny silver buttons from his father's shop in an attempt to ingratiate himself with his fellows. Eventually he realized that he was stealing, but the boys' praise prompted him to continue. George became annoyed by their constant begging and finally refused to get more buttons for them. He promised himself never to commit this "wrong doing" again. The boys immediately threatened him with a thrashing from the neighborhood bully. Outwardly courageous but inwardly fright- ened of being exposed to his father for fighting, he avoided his usual haunts. Eventually he was forced to defend himself in a scuffle but suffered no lasting injuries.[7]

When telling the story for young readers many years later in Utah, George moralized, "Children, you also can learn one lesson through this short story. If you have been doing wrong, do it no more, leave it off at once and for ever. It is better to face the consequences now, than when your sin has grown worse. Trust in God, plead with him for his aid to strengthen you to do right."[8]

In 1851, at age nine, George met his first Mormon. He often visited his grandmother, Amelia Tautz, and because her home was so large, he fearfully imagined ghosts hiding in the darkness. One day he courageously spoke with a maid. "Mary, are you afraid of ghosts?" Mary, whose real name was Sarah White, took an interest in him. George asked Mary if she went to church and, discovering that she did, obtained permission from his grandmother to go with her. She took him to the Paddington Branch of The Church of Jesus Christ of Latter-day Saints.[9] When George heard the principles of the gospel taught there, he accepted them as truth immediately and applied for baptism, but the elders refused to baptize him without his parents' consent. George's parents, who were nominal adherents

4

of the Anglican Church, refused permission because they considered the Mormon Church an obnoxious American sect. George pleaded again and again for permission but without success. Still, George arranged secretly to attend many meetings of the Saints.[10]

In September 1854, George, then twelve, was sent to Paris to live with his mother's relatives. His grandmother and his parents had two motives for sending him there: they hoped he would forget his foolishness about Mormonism, and they hoped that while in Paris he would have educational opportunities in French and other languages. "The first three months of my life here were wretched in the extreme," George remembered.[11] Homesickness, diarrhea and other sicknesses, his inability at first to communicate in French, and the unkindness of other boys plagued George, but he studied for a year, mastered French, and learned the rudiments of six other languages and of classical literature. Throughout his life George built upon those studies. The secular knowledge he gained as a youth served him well in his later literary contributions to the LDS Church.

In France, George did not forget about Mormonism. Remembering that the missionaries in his newfound faith had preached the imminent return of Christ, George devised an elaborate mathematical calculation that indicated Christ would come again before George reached twenty-one years of age. George was thus afraid he would not have a chance to be baptized. Upon his return to London, and during his frequent visits to his grandmother, George began attending the Somers Town Branch, near his grandmother's new home, where he was unknown by Church members. There, at age fourteen, he applied for baptism and was accepted. He was baptized Sunday, 4 May 1856, by an Elder Hillier and was confirmed the next Sunday by George Teasdale, the branch president. President Teasdale and George developed a friendship that endured throughout their lives. Both eventually worked at LDS Church headquarters, and both became general authorities of the Church. In December, George was ordained a deacon. He reminisced later that he had never magnified any other Church office as well. "[I] took pride in never being absent from meeting, and in being there the very first to open the doors and prepare the rooms."[12]

During his teenage years George participated fully in the LDS Church, despite his parents' learning of his baptism. Some of his father's customers suggested that the elder Reynolds thrash Mormonism out of his son, or that George be committed to an asylum, or that he be taken before a magistrate and confined to prison. Nevertheless, by degrees George's father adjusted to the course his son was taking and took no punitive measures.[13]

George became involved in the Somers Town Branch Sunday School, serving first as teacher and then as secretary. Thus began his lifelong dedication to the Sunday School of the Church.

One year after his baptism George was ordained a priest and appointed an outdoor missionary. Men and boys having this calling preached together at key locations in the city. In his autobiography, George recalled, "This was one of the severest trials of my life, being only fifteen years old, quite small for my age, and very timid and bashful, but, trusting for strength in the Lord, I overcame these difficulties, and from that time for several years I preached in the highways of that huge city on the Sabbath, and when I had opportunity on week day evenings after my work was done." His listeners frequently jeered that he should place "a piece of brown paper under his feet so he might be seen." He wore an Eton jacket when he preached, but he soon decided to wear a man's coat in order to gain respect. Finding no coat that would fit, he purchased one several sizes too large. In time, however, he found pleasure going week after week to the street corners to preach.[14]

Meanwhile, George's father placed him as an apprentice with a dry goods merchant. George did not remain there long, however, and soon undertook eighteen months of cashier's training, which ended abruptly when he was unjustly accused of stealing. He took on another job as a clerk until May 1861, when, at age nineteen, he resigned. The bookkeeping skills he gained as a youth were later

George Reynolds in his late
teenage years

used in many Church businesses and assignments after his emigration to Utah.

George's heart was not in his bookkeeping training. He had been
ordained an elder in the Church the previous August and was await-
ing a promised full-time calling as a missionary. As soon as he
received his call from the British Mission presidency, George happily
bade adieu to both employer and family and entered the ministry.
He was assigned immediately to his home conference in London.[15]
Thus began the diligent and scarcely interrupted full-time service
of George Reynolds in the kingdom of God.

Notes

1. Dean L. May, "A Demographic Portrait of the Mormons, 1830–1980," in
Thomas G. Alexander and Jessie L. Embry, eds., *After 150 Years: The Latter-day
Saints in Sesquicentennial Perspective* (Provo: Charles Redd Center for Western
Studies, 1983), pp. 37–69.

2. George Reynolds Journal, vol. 1, p. 1, Library-Archives, Historical Department of The Church of Jesus Christ of Latter-day Saints (hereafter cited as LDS
Church Historical Archives); "Autobiography of Alice Louise Reynolds," typescript

manuscript, Special Collections, Harold B. Lee Library, Brigham Young University, p. 1; T. Z. [probably a pseudonym of George Reynolds; see Bibliography], "Lives of Our Leaders," p. 285; Goldwin Smith, *A History of England*, 3d ed. (New York: Charles Scribner's Sons, 1966), pp. 506–7, 600–1.

3. Alice Louise Reynolds, "Biography of George Reynolds," unpublished handwritten manuscript, Reynolds Collection, no. 33, Special Collections, Harold B. Lee Library, Brigham Young University, pp. 1–3; T. Z. , "Lives of Our Leaders," p. 385.

4. George Reynolds Journal, vol. 1, pp. 1–2.

5. Alice Louise Reynolds, "Sketch on the Life of Grandfather George Reynolds," typescript manuscript obtained from Joseph Fielding McConkie, p. 1; George Reynolds Journal, vol. 1, p. 3.

6. A. L. Reynolds, "Sketch on the Life of Grandfather George Reynolds," p. 1; A. L. Reynolds, "Biography of George Reynolds," p. 5; T. Z., "Lives of Our Leaders," p. 385; interview with Evelyn Robbins, Provo, Utah, 1 February 1985.

7. George Tautz [George Reynolds], "The Button Thief," *Juvenile Instructor* 3 (15 December 1868): 189–90.

8. Ibid., p. 190.

9. T. Z., "Lives of Our Leaders," pp. 385–86; A. L. Reynolds, "Sketch on the Life of Grandfather George Reynolds," p. 1; A. L. Reynolds, "Biography of George Reynolds," pp. 4–6; "Autobiographical Sketch of George Reynolds," typescript obtained from Grant Reynolds Hardy, p. 1.

10. Ibid.

11. George Reynolds Journal, vol. 1, p. 3; A. L. Reynolds, "Sketch on the Life of Grandfather George Reynolds," p. 6; "Autobiographical Sketch of George Reynolds," p. 1.

12. T. Z., "Lives of Our Leaders," p. 386; George Reynolds Journal, vol. 1, p. 5; A. L. Reynolds, "Sketch," pp. 1–2; A. L. Reynolds, "Biography," p. 7.

13. "Autobiographical Sketch," p. 2; A. L. Reynolds, "Sketch on the Life of Grandfather George Reynolds," p. 2; A. L. Reynolds, "Biography of George Reynolds," p. 7; T. Z., "Lives of Our Leaders," pp. 368–87; George Reynolds Journal, vol. 1, pp. 5–6.

14. Ibid.

15. Ibid., pp. 4–5.

CHAPTER 2

First Mission in His Native Land

GEORGE REYNOLDS BECAME A FULL-TIME MISSIONARY IN MAY 1861 JUST after the American Civil War began. Naturally that conflict engendered great interest among the missionaries, because many elders were Americans and most British Saints planned to emigrate to America. George pondered the importance of this conflict throughout his mission. Coincidentally, his mission concluded in the summer of 1865, just as peace was achieved, bringing an end to the worst human conflict to that point in world history.

Elder George Q. Cannon of the Church's Quorum of the Twelve Apostles, second counselor in the British Mission Presidency and editor of the Church's British magazine, the *Millennial Star*, editorialized on 11 May 1861 that the American Civil War, beginning as it had in South Carolina, fulfilled Joseph Smith's prophecy received twenty-eight years earlier.[1] "We [the Latter-day Saints] knew, therefore, that, negotiate, arrange, and compromise as the opposing parties might please, the war would have to commence at South Carolina, and not in Florida, where Fort Pickens [another potential hotspot] was situate," Elder Cannon explained. "This is the first act in the bloody drama—the precursor of wars that shall spread over all nations, and bring death and misery to many souls, and cause the inhabitants of the earth to mourn."

Elder Cannon warned European Saints to repent when they witnessed such obvious signs of the times:

> The consumption decreed, which is to make a full end of all nations, has begun. It was to commence at South Carolina; but it was to spread until all nations were to be involved in it. The nations of Europe cannot escape from it, if they continue as they are. But the Lord has provided a place of refuge for those who will accept it. All who desire to avail themselves of this place of security [Utah, or the Mormon Zion] can do so, if they be diligent.[2]

Thus George Reynolds and fellow missionaries had a crucial message to declare: Repent of your sins while there is still time, and flee to Zion (Utah) for refuge and peace. There is not and will not be peace in Babylon (most of the United States and Britain). The end of time is near!

Amasa Lyman and Charles C. Rich of the Quorum of the Twelve Apostles served in England as joint presidents of the European Mission beginning in August 1860. In January 1861 they were joined by their younger colleague, the articulate George Q. Cannon. Elders Lyman and Rich departed from Britain in May 1862, leaving Elder Cannon to serve as mission president until July 1864. George Reynolds had started his labors in May 1861, just as most American missionaries were being released to accompany emigrants to Utah. Throughout the rest of 1861 only six new American elders (known as "Valley Elders") were sent to Britain. This sharp decrease was caused by the need for men to lead the "church trains" across the plains, a part of the immigration system that was begun that year. The British Mission, therefore, had to call more native missionaries, Elder George Reynolds being one of them.[3]

Apparently, the increase in native elders threatened missionary harmony. George Q. Cannon wrote in the *Millennial Star*, "We have heard of it [national prejudice] in this country manifesting itself

10

among native Elders, in jealousy of the Elders from Zion. . . . Those who manifested this illiberality have been afraid that their influence would outweigh their own."[4] George Reynolds probably was not one of these grumbling native elders; his surviving papers indicate only profound respect for American missionaries.

Britain's London Conference had three districts in 1861. Elder Reynolds was assigned as a traveling elder to the third district, where he had responsibility under the direction of Elder John Brown, an original Utah pioneer, to supervise five branches in the west and south of London. Elder William C. Staines, an early British convert who before his return to England as a missionary had distinguished himself as a Utah businessman, was president of the London Conference.[5] Elder Staines and George Reynolds began a lifelong friendship.

Shortly before George became a full-time missionary, the Church changed its policy of financing missionaries. For several years, the missionaries in Britain had drawn a small allowance from collective tithing funds. After discovering some abuses in that system, Brigham Young insisted that tithing collections have more supervision from Utah and that the missionaries proselyte "as did the Elders anciently," that is, without purse or scrip. Food and lodging could be obtained from members who were able to provide them. Unfortunately many Church members were suffering themselves on account of the Industrial Revolution, the overcrowding in the cities, and the adverse economic effects of the American Civil War. English factories struggled because of the lack of cotton received from the Southern States.[6]

So, without purse or scrip, George traveled to every branch in his district, preaching the gospel to prospective converts, often baptizing people in local bathhouses. Keeping the Church branches in order brought George both his greatest fulfillment and his deepest frustration. He preached frequently, helped establish productive Sunday Schools, collected and recorded tithes and other donations, organized successful social activities, and helped many of the Saints

11

George Reynolds at age nineteen

prepare to emigrate to Utah. He relished working with other "men of God," both those who were his mission leaders and his local priesthood branch leaders.[7] He drew especially close to the forty-five-year-old president of the Lambeth Branch, Joseph L. Barfoot. Often both men spent long hours counseling over Church and personal matters, and later, when Elder Reynolds labored in Liverpool, the two corresponded as often as twice a week. They both emigrated to "Zion" in 1865 and maintained close ties. Barfoot became curator of the Deseret Museum, where George frequently assisted.

Elder Reynolds became frustrated with some priesthood leaders and even more so with squabbles between members. Occasionally, as presiding officer in "council meetings," as Church disciplinary councils were called then, he ruled on individuals' memberships and excommunicated some for sexual immorality, unruly behavior, or speaking fanatically and erroneously in public meetings. These latter responsibilities wore heavily on the nineteen-year-old missionary. As a result of this stress, he suffered bouts of headaches and diarrhea.[8]

George recorded his feelings about a number of his co-workers after a series of conference meetings in July 1861. Those feelings reveal as much about George Reynolds as they reveal about the subjects. Regarding Elder Amasa Lyman, president of the mission, George said, "When in council [he] can look you through and I

12

believe tell the secrets of your heart. If I had done wrong I feel as though I could not but confess it as it must come out." George observed about Elder Charles C. Rich, first counselor, "He is very conscious, very severe on evil doers, yet kind & affectionate as a husband, father or friend." George's growing admiration for Elder George Q. Cannon was obvious as he noted, "Br Cannon is most homely, affable & pleasing wears a constant smile and you forget the apostle in the friend and brother." He commented about other brethren with whom he worked:

> Br John Brown our district president one of the pioneers is a thorough good man, but with very few striking characteristics. . . . Br Wm. C. Staines is beloved by all from his familiar at-home-everywhere spirit from his preaching being like chatting with the people full of anecdotes and amusing recitals of his experiences in the Church. . . . Br [Francis M.] Lyman [a young elder at the time and future Apostle], a severe commanding spirit, full of the go-ahead Yankee with uncompromising resolutions to overcome evil, a Mormon every inch. . . . Br Barfoot is one of the greatest spirits I have met with. Great in his humbleness and complete subjection to the priesthood.[9]

At the same time, George recorded a perceptive evaluation of himself:

> With regard to myself I find considerable difficulty in presiding, being better able to do as I am told than to tell others what to do, feeling my youth experience and various other things working against me. I sometimes feel bound and broken down with the responsibilities of my position, yet realizing all the time that I have been placed in it by gods servants and to do any less than walk into that position would be dishonoring Him. I know I desire to obey council, yet sometimes find a difficulty in guarding my tongue from telling things that should not be told, and find no difficulty in obeying it, but the difficulty lies in governing controlling and bringing my own feelings passions and desires into complete subjection to my will and of making Gods will my will and his spirit my spirit.

13

George reflected that his quiet disposition often worked against him when he visited the Saints. "I have little to say and let them do the talking. In this respect I expect to change. I try and be as kind as I can and want to see the brethren & sisters live to their positions & callings."[10]

At the end of 1861 George recorded forty-two baptisms in the district and the emigration of eighty Saints. Twenty-six hundred Britons had been baptized throughout Great Britain that year, bringing the Church population to approximately fifteen thousand. Evaluating his own performance to that point in his mission, George wrote: "On the whole during the past year I have learned much of human character gained much experience in the nature of things and the laws of the kingdom of God, & I believe during no year of my life has my character been so changed as during this past finished."[11]

Throughout 1862 Elder Reynolds continued his duties in the London Conference. He lodged at the homes of various members or in the district office. He recorded in his journal numerous spiritual experiences, particularly those in which he felt "free" while speaking. A standard acknowledgment of the time was that one's tongue was loosed with the aid of the Holy Spirit. About once a month he visited his nonmember parents in their London home, where he witnessed the gradual physical decline of his father, who died 17 November 1862. Being the eldest son, George took time at the end of the year to settle his father's estate.

Just as he completed that task in early February 1863, President George Q. Cannon called the twenty-one-year-old Elder Reynolds to be his private secretary and the emigration clerk of the European Mission in Liverpool. George's trustworthiness and untiring devotion to his leaders qualified him for these posts. His first twenty-one months as a missionary were successful in every sense. He had completed his "rite of passage" and now was in a position of trust, working with an illustrious leader in the Latter-day Saint movement. For the rest of their lives, George Q. Cannon and George Reynolds were closely bonded as brothers in the kingdom of God and co-participants in some of the most dramatic events in Mormon history.

Notes

1. This prophecy, known at that time as the "Revelation and Prophecy on War," was given on Christmas Day 1831 in Kirtland, Ohio, and is now found in the Doctrine and Covenants as section 87.

2. *Millennial Star* 23 (11 May 1861): 299–300; see also 23 (28 December 1861): 829–31.

3. Richard L. Evans, *A Century of "Mormonism" in Great Britain* (Salt Lake City: Deseret News Press, 1937), pp. 242–47; *Millennial Star* 23 (17 August 1861): 506–8.

4. *Millennial Star* 23 (1 June 1861): 337.

5. George Reynolds Journal, vol. 1, 8 May–18 May 1861; *Millennial Star* 23 (10 August 1861): 507–8; "Autobiographical Sketch of George Reynolds," p. 2.

6. Richard L. Jensen, "Without Purse or Scrip: Financing Latter-day Saint Missionary Work in Europe in the Nineteenth Century," *Journal of Mormon History* 12 (1985): 3–14; Goldwin Smith, *A History of England,* 3d ed. (New York: Charles Scribner's Sons, 1966), p. 628.

7. George Reynolds Journal, vol. 1, 1861.

8. Ibid.; for a review of reasons why Mormon officials historically have excommunicated members, see Lester E. Bush, Jr., "Excommunication and Church Courts: A Note From the General Handbook of Instructions," *Dialogue* 14 (Summer 1981): 74–98.

9. George Reynolds Journal, vol. 1, 25 July 1861.

10. Ibid.

11. George Reynolds Journal, vol. 2, 31 December 1861 and 5 January 1862. No existing British Mission records give the statistics mentioned here by Reynolds or in his year-end reports later in his mission. Historians have often relied on Reynolds's journal for British Mission statistics. For example, see Richard D. Poll, "The British Mission during the Utah War, 1857–58," in Richard L. Jensen and Malcolm R. Thorp, eds., *Mormons in Early Victorian Britain* (Salt Lake City: University of Utah Press, 1989), pp. 226–27, 240–41.

CHAPTER 3

Emigration Clerk in Liverpool

GEORGE REYNOLDS ARRIVED IN LIVERPOOL ON 17 FEBRUARY 1863 TO assume his new assignment. He was immediately put to work preparing for the emigration season. From February through late June each year no other word described the business of the European Mission office better than *emigration.* Emigration was one of the cardinal commandments of Mormonism. Every baptized member was expected to prepare to leave Babylon behind and gather to Zion.[1]

After the emigration season of 1863, Elder Reynolds became chief clerk of the European-British Mission, a position next in authority to the mission president.[2] As clerk, George oversaw the publication of the *Millennial Star* and the *Journal of Discourses,* helped the mission president follow through with assignments to missionaries and care of the members, and was the right-hand man of the president in supervising emigration. George remained in this vital post until he himself emigrated in May 1865.

While in Liverpool, George maintained close ties with his mother and brothers and sisters, writing them often and visiting them when he could. Several years later his mother, some of his brothers, and a sister joined the Church and emigrated to Utah.

Church authorities considered it an advantage for young English missionaries to be either married or engaged at the time they emigrated to "Zion." For this reason, during his months in Liverpool,

George continued his quest to find a wife. Before his mission George had become engaged to Sarah Burrell, who was five and a half years his senior. She was a daughter of Francis Burrell, who had taken young George to preach on London streets. George had intended to emigrate with her to Zion in 1862 but changed those plans upon receiving his call to the ministry.[3] During his missionary service in London, he visited her several times a week, often walking her home from church meetings. But Sarah demanded more of his attention than he thought reasonable. On 13 December 1861, accompanied by Sarah, George went to a member's home to administer to the sick. He wanted to continue other priesthood work that evening, but Sarah insisted that he accompany her home. In an ensuing quarrel George told her, "If ever such a thing occurs again, I will break off our engagement. The priesthood must with me stand first."[4] The next evening the pair reconciled, but their relationship never recovered. The exact time of the break with Sarah is uncertain because the volume of George's journal that covers August 1862 to May 1863 is missing.

In September 1861 George had become acquainted with a stalwart Mormon family in London, the Tuddenhams. Perhaps because their fifteen-year-old daughter, Mary Ann, had been attacked physically by a Sister Margaret Wright, who often came to church meetings drunk, George felt a sympathy for young Miss Tuddenham, a sympathy that gradually developed into romantic interest. In any event, his journal reveals that on a vacation visit from Liverpool to London in August 1863, he spent considerable time with the Tuddenhams, who lived in the Bayswater district of the city, and with Mary Ann in particular, who by then he frequently called "Polly." After George returned to Liverpool, President Cannon asked him about his relationship with Sister Tuddenham. When George asked him for permission to marry Polly, the mission president replied that he had no objection. Even though George was still receiving letters from Sarah Burrell (to which he did not respond), he wrote

17

letters and poetry to his "sweetheart," Polly, several times a week and started planning their marriage while continuing his mission.

His close friend in London, Joseph Barfoot, informed him that Sarah was terribly bitter; she had no intention of giving him up and even threatened revenge. George counseled with President Cannon about the situation, and President Cannon advised Sarah to forget this lost love. During this time George's mind was diverted from his ministry; his health suffered as he dealt long distance with this problem.

Early in 1864, just before her family was ready to emigrate, eighteen-year-old Polly and her father prepared papers for her prospective marriage to George. But because she was suffering from ill health when President Cannon saw her in London, he counseled her to go to Zion to recover from her infirmities and not to marry at that time. George was heartbroken at first, but respecting President Cannon as he did, he abided by his counsel. Polly left England with her family on 3 June 1864 on the same ship, ironically, that carried Sarah Burrell. George continued to correspond with Polly until he arrived in Utah in July 1865.

But while George remained in England, another young woman entered his life. George wrote in the year-end summary of his journal for 1864:

> I must . . . acknowledge that to an extent I have acted unwisely in my associations with Sis Mary A. Tilley as unperceptable almost to ourselves an attachment has sprung up between us which at present appears to have no honorable solution, as she is engaged to a man out of the church (but of this I have only known a few days) & I to Sis M. A. Tuddenham, which engagement however I have never hidden, which prevented me supposing — until I could no longer be blind to it — that any other girl would "fall in love" with me. How all will end has yet to be proved.

From that point George did not record any more feelings about Mary Tilley, although he did mention several contacts with her and at least three occasions when he accompanied her home from church.

When George emigrated in May 1865, he indicated that Miss Tilley had become engaged to a close friend and Church member in Liverpool, so she and George must have mutually determined to make their relationship platonic.

As mission secretary, Elder Reynolds often, but not always, traveled with President George Q. Cannon until June 1864 and thereafter with Daniel H. Wells. At just twenty-one years of age, George was responsible for the mission's tithing reports, statistical reports, and especially emigration arrangements, funds, and records. President Cannon even entrusted him with some of the negotiations concerning emigrant ships.

The Church publication at Liverpool, the *Millennial Star,* during George Reynolds's tenure reflects the overwhelming interest in the successful emigration of European Saints to Zion. Time and again President Cannon included in the *Star* specific instructions from President Brigham Young and immigration agents telling emigrants how to arrive safely in their new "mountain home." Another who often sent instructions was the prophet's son, Joseph W. Young, who was in charge of the "church trains," the covered wagon teams that lumbered from Utah to Florence, Nebraska, to meet the European immigrants. President Cannon himself usually dictated to George Reynolds weekly editorials and messages on emigration for the *Star.* For example, on 21 March 1863, President Cannon wrote to the Saints, "We wish the Elders and Saints to send up the names and deposits immediately, of those intending to emigrate. *Let not an hour be lost,* for the season is so far advanced that it is imperatively necessary that we should be advised of the number of those who are going, that we may make timely arrangements about vessels, &c." He followed this plea with explicit instructions for signing up and making monetary deposits on proposed emigration.[5] Through Elder Reynolds, President Cannon included numerous instructions that appeared in subsequent editions of the *Star.*

George Q. Cannon was a gifted administrator, and through his and Elder Reynolds's efforts, with the aid of loyal assistants, 3,646

Church members emigrated on six ships from Liverpool in 1863. That was the largest number since 1855, when 4,225 had sailed in thirteen ships. More than half of the Saints who emigrated in 1863 came from Denmark and Sweden.

Beginning in February, when intense preparations for the emigration season began, through July, when he finally finished tabulating statistics and squaring financial accounts, Elder George Reynolds worked unceasingly in the Liverpool office. His only respite was serving as superintendent of the Sunday School in the large Liverpool Branch. Actually, George was happiest when he was teaching children principles of the gospel. At the end of the 1863 emigration season, President Cannon and George Reynolds could, with pleasure, report to the European Saints:

> Six vessels laden with our people, in every instance carrying their full complement of passengers [a feat not usually achieved in previous seasons], have left these shores for New York. . . . By no means the least cheering reflection connected with this matter is that there are very few of them who have not sufficient means to take them as far as Florence, Nebraska Territory, where they will be met by the teams sent from home to carry them across the Plains. . . . We have rejoiced to see so many of the meek and humble sons and daughters of Adam receiving that deliverance from Babylon which they had been commanded to seek, and which many of them had been exerting every energy of mind and body for years to obtain. . . .
>
> . . . Now that the emigration business for this year is finished, we desire to see the Elders and Saints commence immediately to prepare for next year and its claims and duties. The Elders and officers and Saints of every Branch, Conference, District and Mission should exert all their energies to fill up the vacancies created through this year's emigration, by the conversion and baptism of the honest-in-heart.[6]

Brigham Young was likewise pleased with such a bounteous emigration season: "On the ocean, on the railroads, and on the Plains, so far as they have arrived and we learn, the hand of the Lord has been extended with manifest and choice blessings and protection in behalf of this year's immigration."[7]

In October 1863 George devoted himself to gathering statistics on subscriptions to the *Millennial Star* and the *Journal of Discourses,* a periodical published in Liverpool containing discourses of Church authorities in Utah that were drawn primarily from the *Deseret News.* George noted that mission debts were increasing as the circulation of the periodicals was decreasing. This development prompted President Cannon to plead with the European Saints:

> No member of the Church in these lands, who has it in his or her power to subscribe for these periodicals, should neglect to do so; and, whether able to subscribe or not, no member should fail to peruse them. . . . The Saints who pay attention to the instructions contained in the columns of the *Star* and *Journal* have a much better knowledge of doctrine, and the progress and development of the Work of God, and are much more obedient and easily controlled by God's Priesthood, than those who do not read or pay attention to the truths they contain.[8]

At the end of 1863, George wrote in his journal of the previous year's difficulties: settling his father's estate, his transfer to Liverpool, his tedious labor on the emigration projects and records causing ill health, and his hard work in the branch. But he exhibited his usual optimistic faith by concluding, "In all things I can say through this year's experience 'There is a divinity that shapes our ends, Rough hew them how we will' as I have found that all things my perplexities troubles &c &c have all worked for me much better than I could have imagined."

George noted important mission statistics in a year-end journal entry: the year 1863 saw 3,979 baptized in Europe and 3,646 emigrated. The number excommunicated was 1,125 (this high total represents the sincere and continual attempt of leaders to purify the Church and maintain high standards), and 203 members died, making a total of 13,851 in the British Mission and 20,224 in the entire European Mission. The number of Church members in Britain and in Europe was slowly dwindling year by year on account of emigration.[9]

The 1864 emigration season was likewise burdensome, compounded by an increased difficulty in finding suitable and reasonably priced vessels. President Cannon and Elder Reynolds succeeded in finding passage for only 2,223 emigrants on three ships. During the early preparation, Joseph A. and John W. Young arrived in Liverpool to help with arrangements; they announced that the Nebraska outfitting station had been moved from Florence to a small settlement called Wyoming, Nebraska, about six miles from Nebraska City and twenty miles nearer Great Salt Lake City.

Early in 1864 George Q. Cannon learned from Brigham Young that he was to be released after the emigration season and return to Zion. Daniel H. Wells and Brigham Young, Jr., were to be the new mission president and assistant mission president, respectively, in Liverpool. George Reynolds was asked to compile for Brigham Young various reports of European Mission activities during the Cannon years. Elder Reynolds was hard pressed to prepare the necessary records to accommodate an orderly transference to President Wells.

George worked to the last hour, helping his beloved friend and chief, George Q. Cannon. Before leaving, President Cannon presented his protégé with a silver watch. The two even discussed mission matters en route to the ship. After carrying President Cannon's luggage aboard the ship, George bade farewell to this man whom he admired above all other earthly individuals:

> I can scarcely say with what feelings of regret I parted with
> him who had been to me so much of a father, friend & brother,
> as to my own feelings I can say I loved him much & as to others,
> I do not think it too much to say he was universally beloved, his
> kind, tender unassuming disposition, so ready to oblige, so careful
> of others feelings rendered him an object of affection where ever
> he went or whatever circumstances he was placed in, he gained
> friends. One of his most notable characteristics is his love of purity

& hatred for iniquity and as we are told that Jesus was exalted above his fellows, because he loved righteousness & hated iniquity so I believe it to be with his servant, George Q. Cannon. Purity, truth and love seemed to be the element in which he dwelt, but his testimony was none the less forcible, nor his reproofs when required the less bold, he is a man indeed whose whole aim, the end of whose life the motive of whose actions is to glorify the cause of his Father in Heaven.

George Reynolds and George Q. Cannon remained lifelong friends and fellow warriors in the kingdom of God. They assisted one another in numerous endeavors until President Cannon's death in 1901.

Before President Cannon's departure, Elder Reynolds had been called to be Liverpool's branch president, a position he held until his own departure one year later. He enjoyed this responsibility, but, George revealed in his journal, the branch suffered an "over-shadowing" from the mission presidency and frequent visits of general authorities, such as on Pioneer Day, 24 July 1864, when two of them delivered several sermons. "The constant presence of the presidency instead of proving a benefit to [the branch] seemed rather to retard its progress," observed George.

> For these reasons the priesthood had little means of developing themselves in the way of preaching ... the saints being so used to hear these brethren were not willing to give such heed to the teachings of the local priesthood. ... These things caused a dull-ness and carelessness in the saints. Again they were not so united as most branches as they came from almost all parts of the Kingdom English Irish Scotch & Welch.

During the first months of President Daniel H. Wells's admin-istration, George helped with correspondence to missionaries about changes in mission administration and occasionally traveled to other mission areas. While on these trips he was attentive to geographic and social points. He noted, "I had never been in a workhouse before and it was to me a painful though interesting sight to see so many

23

poor & sick creatures wandering about. The building appears to be a very comfortable one, but its not like a home, made me think of boarding school." Though accustomed to hard work George had, nevertheless, been spared the suffering of many of his countrymen that resulted from the Industrial Revolution. He was also more cultured than many of his fellow missionaries and Saints. For a while he tutored Brigham Young, Jr., in French and often went alone to the theatre.

On 21 December 1864 George received an unexpected Christmas gift. Presidents Wells and Young informed him that he was to emigrate the following spring after completing most of the mission emigration responsibilities. George had thought he would be staying at least another year but was pleased to have the opportunity to go "home" to Zion, although he had never been there.

In his annual summary, George reflected on his relationship with Daniel H. Wells: "In Brother Cannons departure I lost a valued friend & advisor, and at the time thought his place could not be supplied in my affections, but Presd. Wells continued & never varying kindness has won my love & esteem so that I do not in the least miss Br. G. Q. C." Regarding his personal progress, George recorded, "As to my private life, I have strived to do right & keep the commandments of the lord, tho' I have occasionally done things that have caused me many sorrowful feelings. Yet I know that my desires are to do God's will & I know he has greatly blessed me. Still I feel that I am far short of what I can see I ought to be."

Among George Reynolds's missionary contributions to Church literature were sixteen doctrinal articles that appeared in the *Millennial Star* between 1863 and 1865. The *Star* invited all missionaries to write articles, and many responded. George's first attempts at writing for publication obviously excited him, because he continued to write after arriving in Utah and for the remainder of his life. Indeed, his writings are his greatest legacy to Latter-day Saints.

George wrote three articles in 1865 that reflect his basic philosophy of life. In a piece he entitled "I'll Ask Counsel," he wrote:

You cannot go to a better source for wisdom than the Lord's servants. Their teachings, inspired by the Spirit of Truth, cannot but be your surest guide. . . . Are you determined to give heed to what you are told? Because if not, you had better not go, for it is a mockery to ask for advice from the Lord and then disregard it — to seek his word and then reject it. . . . To play with the oracles of God in this manner is worse than folly, it is sin; and our Heavenly Father will severely punish those who thus trifle with his Priesthood.[10]

In "The Religion of Every Day Life," George admonished:

All who know anything of the fullness of the Everlasting Gospel, realize it to be an every day religion, that can be lived as well from Monday morning to Saturday night, as during the services of the Sabbath; not consisting alone "in prayer, praise and testimony," but in labor — constant, unflinching, undeviating labor — for the benefit of mankind, and the salvation of the world.[11]

Before departing for "home," George worked tirelessly to make ship and berth arrangements for the emigrants. Twice he sailed to Hamburg to prepare for the emigration of Scandinavian Saints from that port. In all, George arranged passage on three ships for 1,218 more emigrants. These included eight recent British converts from India, who boarded the ship *Belle Wood* at Liverpool.[12]

George sailed from Liverpool on the *Persia*, a new and fast-moving steamer, on 20 May 1865. He was the only Mormon passenger and had a private stateroom, accommodations considerably better than those of the thousands of other emigrants. His journey lasted only twelve days. He was allowed these privileges so that he could arrive quickly in America to continue to assist the immigrants. The *Persia* and the *Belle Wood* arrived in New York Harbor at about the same time, although the *Belle Wood,* which carried 558 Church members, had sailed from Liverpool on 29 April. On 1 June George hired a small boat to carry him aboard the *Belle Wood,* and he spent his first few days in the United States helping to get these immigrant Saints train passage to Wyoming, Nebraska.

George Reynolds in 1865

While in New York, George became acquainted with a leading Salt Lake City merchant, William S. Godbe, who was in the metropolis ordering store supplies. Godbe had joined the Church in England in 1849 and emigrated to Utah in 1851. He subsequently established a profitable "states goods" importing company and became one of the wealthiest men in Utah. Before his 1869 disenchantment with Brigham Young over economic, religious, and political policies, Godbe donated more than fifty thousand dollars to the Church.[13] Godbe invited Reynolds to accompany him west, so beginning on 12 June they traveled by rail through Niagara, Detroit, and Chicago, stopping at each point for Godbe to conduct business.

Reynolds and Godbe reached Saint Louis on 16 June and began a Missouri River voyage to Nebraska City. The river trip was "slow and tiresome" because the vessel was overcrowded with former Confederate soldiers who had enlisted in the army to fight the Plains

Indians. In Nebraska City they were joined by William Shearman, an elder returning from England. They traveled by stage to Fort Kearney, arriving 20 June. After a day's delay, they luckily were able to travel in a doorless coach and arrive in Denver three days later. The Sioux Indians were on the warpath, so the United States cavalry escorted the stage all the way to Denver.

Because of the Indian troubles, the stage company in Denver refused to send more coaches west, so the "irrepressible Godbe" independently obtained a wagon and team of horses. "Trusting in the Lords protecting care & our own vigilance" the three began the rest of the journey alone. They were careful to light no fires and travel at night to avoid being seen by Indians. In the western part of Wyoming they were chased by Indians but safely reached the Green River on 2 July. Because of washed out roads in the mountain passes, the travelers abandoned their wagon and packed into Salt Lake City on mules that they obtained at Little Laramie (now Laramie), Wyoming, arriving at 11:00 p.m. on 5 July 1865.[14]

The next afternoon George Reynolds went to President Brigham Young's office, apparently by previous invitation, to deliver letters. The Mormon prophet happened not to be there, but George was cheered to see many of his friends from the British Mission, including George Q. Cannon, George Teasdale, and William C. Staines. That afternoon he was introduced to Brigham Young and Heber C. Kimball. "I had quite a chat with the president," George wrote to his British friends, "and must say that all the testimonies I have heard by those who first see him and write back to the Saints, I fully agree with. I also like brother Heber, he has been very kind to me."[15]

In the evening he found the Eleventh Ward, where the Tuddenhams resided. "Polly was not in at the time but she shortly afterwards came in then I was pleased to find her well & bearing the same feelings — as I expected — towards me as when she left me in the Old Country." The young couple immediately renewed their determination to be married and made plans for later in the week. "Zion" seemed to be all that George expected.

27

George Reynolds's experiences as a young single missionary in his native land prepared him for his life's work. His superiors found him to be trustworthy, diligent, friendly, and capable of keeping confidences. He had properly selected a wife, as expected by Church authorities. He had gathered to Zion and assisted hosts of others in doing the same. In all things he had abided counsel. Now that he was in Salt Lake City, he was becoming acquainted with the highest Church authorities through leaders he had known in England. He was eager to marry his beloved Polly and "set up housekeeping." George was not so naive as to think that his sacrifices were over, but he probably thought that the sacrifices made thus far had led to the blessings of happiness and peace he now enjoyed. Little did he realize or expect the challenges and responsibilities that awaited him and Polly in the years ahead.

Notes

1. See Philip A. M. Taylor, "Why Did British Mormons Emigrate?" *Utah Historical Quarterly* 22 (July 1954): 249–70; Richard L. Jensen, "The British Gathering to Zion," in Ben Bloxham, et al., ed., *Truth Will Prevail* (Solihull, England: The Church of Jesus Christ of Latter-day Saints, 1987), pp. 165–98.

2. Information for this chapter, unless otherwise noted, comes from George Reynolds Journal, vols. 3 and 4, covering the years 1863–65.

3. George Reynolds Journal, vol. 1, p. 6, and 13 July 1862.

4. Ibid., 13 December 1861 (verb tense and possessive standardized).

5. *Millennial Star* 25 (21 March 1863): 184.

6. *Millennial Star* 25 (20 June 1863): 392–93.

7. Ibid., 25 (31 October 1863): 696.

8. Ibid., 25 (12 December 1863): 792–93.

9. The number of British members who were excommunicated was high for both 1863 and 1864, the years Reynolds kept the records in the British Mission.

10. *Millennial Star* 27 (25 February 1865): 117.

11. Ibid., 27 (15 April 1865): 227.

12. "Church Emigration," in LDS Church Historical Archives.

13. Richard S. Van Wagoner and Steven C. Walker, *A Book of Mormons* (Salt Lake City: Signature Books, 1982), pp. 93–97.

14. "Correspondence," *Millennial Star* 27 (30 September 1865): 621–22.

15. Ibid.

CHAPTER 4

Marriage and Early Career

GEORGE AND POLLY MAY HAVE THOUGHT THEY WERE GOING TO GET married within a week of George's arrival in Salt Lake City, but Sarah Burrell, George's former fiancee, would not hear of it. When she learned that George was in the city, she went immediately to Church headquarters and created "a fuss." Because Brigham Young was out of town, first counselor Heber C. Kimball asked George to postpone his marriage until Brigham returned. Sarah wrote a letter to President Young, insisting that George should fulfill his "covenant" with her because her happiness depended on his truthfulness to her. When Brigham returned, Sarah went to him to plead her case. George Q. Cannon, who also was at the meeting, explained George Reynolds's side of the story, so President Young advised Sarah not to follow George about but rather to marry the first good man who offered himself. "This released me of a great amount of anxiety as I did not know what the push to this affair would be," George recorded in his journal.[1] This event occurred too early in George's Utah experience to be resolved by plural marriage, but when George did eventually enter into plural marriage, he did not marry Sarah.

This untidy matter now resolved, on 21 July 1865 George and Polly went to the Endowment House, the temporary temple in Salt Lake City, and were rebaptized to renew their covenants after their

Mary Ann (Polly) Tuddenham Reynolds,
in her mid thirties

immigration, a common practice for recently arrived immigrants to Zion. The next day, in the same sacred edifice, Heber C. Kimball married them. George was twenty-three and Polly nineteen. Excitedly George recorded in his journal that he was now sealed to his beloved "for time and all eternity" and that he and Polly were offered "every other blessing depending on our faithfulness."

George and Polly were very happily in love. They were not deterred by their lack of means; indeed, they began their marriage with only fifteen cents in their pocket, for earlier in the week they had paid six months' rent on a small house in the Thirteenth Ward near downtown Salt Lake City and "had put in a supply of groceries."[2]

Seven months after moving into the Thirteenth Ward, George was called to the priesthood office of seventy. Most returned missionaries in the Church at that time were seventies, and it is likely that, as was the practice of the period, some members of the sixth quorum of seventies, the quorum to which he was called, had requested that he be called to join their unit. On 18 March 1866, Israel Barlow, himself an original member of the 1835 First Quorum of Seventy and ordained directly by Joseph Smith, ordained George to his new priesthood office.[3] George spent the rest of his life as a seventy, his service culminating in his calling as one of the Seven Presidents of Seventy from 1890 to 1909.

The winter of 1865–66 was unusually severe, and both George and Polly suffered considerable ill health. Because of the fierce weather and their sickness, George and Polly remained mostly confined to their apartment, where the lack of good ventilation perhaps contributed to their sickness. They went out only to visit the nearby Grahams (a couple they had known in England), Polly's family, and the Salt Lake Theatre. Polly became pregnant during that winter, and shortly thereafter she caught a cold that probably turned into pneumonia. For a few days her life hung in the balance. George "administered to her in the name of Jesus while her mother held her," and she recovered.

In the spring, Polly narrowly missed being struck by a collapsing wall on Main Street. This event precipitated her baby's premature birth in May. The baby appeared to have been stillborn, but through the expert attention of the midwife and George's faith, the baby survived. Little George Tuddenham Reynolds, whom the parents called "Georgey," was retarded and frail. He never learned to walk or talk. At sixteen months of age, Georgey died of "canker," some form of infection, and dysentery. George and Polly grieved sorely at the loss of their firstborn. He noted in his diary, "Home seems very lonely without a baby."

Salt Lake City, in mid 1865 when George and Polly were married, enjoyed an optimistic spirit because of the end of the Civil War and the consequent reduction of federal troops under the hostile direction of General Patrick Connor. Before leaving Salt Lake City to fight Indians on the plains, Connor vowed to return to establish mining as a viable enterprise and promote "gentile," or non-Mormon, competition with the Church-dominated economy. The Church, in turn, called for a boycott of gentile merchants to force them out of business and for even stricter economic control.[4]

In this setting George met and was employed by William

31

Jennings, the wealthiest merchant in the territory and a devout Latter-day Saint. He owned the burgeoning Eagle Emporium on Main Street, and having lost his bookkeeper, he hired the highly recommended George Reynolds. George worked at the Eagle Emporium until 2 December 1865, when, through the recommendation of George Teasdale, he was given a post at the Church Tithing Office. Reynolds recorded the following about his first job in Zion: "I left [Jennings], it being a good situation in all respects but one & that was Mr. J's irritable temper caused great unpleasantness to those who worked for him, & his outbursts of passion often scared me & rendered me very nervous." George had worked at the Tithing Office for only a few days when Brigham Young employed him in the Office of the President of the Church, where he remained for the rest of his life. George began working as an understudy bookkeeper with Brigham's son Heber.

In 1866 George enlisted in the Nauvoo Legion, the Utah territorial militia, which was under firm LDS control; it was commanded by General Daniel H. Wells, George's former mission president and friend. He felt invigorated during the four-day training period; the outdoor exercise improved his health. Later George joined the Third Infantry Regiment and was commissioned as a second lieutenant in Company H. In addition, he served as secretary of the regiment. Still later, in November 1870, when Governor J. Wilson Shaffer, who had been appointed by United States President Ulysses S. Grant, challenged LDS control of the militia, George's company participated in the "Wooden Gun Rebellion." Eight officers, not including George, were arrested "for treason and rebellion" and confined for a few months at Camp Douglas.[5]

Meanwhile, George Reynolds continued his writing that he had first tried in England. George Q. Cannon, one of the first pioneers in the Church's Sunday School movement, determined in 1865 that he would fill the void of Church reading material for youth. He enlisted some former British missionaries, including George Reynolds, to assist with this project. Elder Cannon began publishing the

Juvenile Instructor to be used in the Sunday Schools that were being created in Church wards. Despite great difficulty in obtaining sufficient paper, the first issue of the *Juvenile,* as it was affectionately called, came out in early 1866.[6] George kept the books for the periodical, although he remained employed at the Office of the President. He also consented to contribute articles. He wrote thirteen articles as well as several acrostics and charades (riddles) in the *Juvenile's* first year; he wrote more than one hundred more articles before leaving on his second mission to England in 1871. The variety of subject matter of these contributions is impressive: Bible stories, natural history, animals, geography, political history, original stories, essays, editorials, and poems. He readily combined secular with prophetic history. Frequently George's articles were the lead articles and contained the most vivid illustrations. His writings in the *Juvenile Instructor* identified him as one of the most learned and well-read men in Utah Territory.[7]

A few months after Georgey was born in 1866, the family moved across the street into an apartment in the house of a Mr. and Mrs. Shelmerdine. They were now in the Eighth Ward, where George's services were more needed. He was immediately called as a block teacher, an assignment to look after the needs of the families on a city block. When the ward established a Sunday School in the spring of 1867, George was called to teach the boys' Bible class and to be secretary. Once again he was in his happy element as a teacher of the gospel and scripture.

In January 1867 George took sick with chills and fever that brought on violent vomiting lasting twenty-four hours. He wrote in his journal:

> While thus vomiting I lay on one side which caused me to tear or sprain some part of my inside and it was nearly three weeks before I could go to work again. I suffered considerably from rheumatism during this spell and was brought very low, some of my friends fancied I should not get over it but I had no such idea. Bro [George Q.] Cannon in administering to me promised me I should

live to a good old age. The cause of my sickness I ascribe to administering to Bro Shelmerdine when I was unwell myself. He immediately recovered and I commenced to get sick.

In April George received his patriarchal blessing from John Smith, son of Hyrum Smith and patriarch to the Church. Brother Smith promised George that he would be "numbered among the chosen sons of Zion," an appellation that George undoubtedly treasured, considering his loyalty to the work. He was further promised that he would receive an inheritance in the New Jerusalem, that his posterity would be numerous and his sons would sit in council with the just, that he would be an instrument in bringing to the knowledge of the truth many who grovel in darkness, that he would be a savior to many of his kindred dead, that he would travel in foreign lands to preach the gospel, and that many people would flock to him for counsel. George later received an appointment to the select Endowment House prayer circle and to the theological class of the School of the Prophets in 1867.[8]

Beginning in August 1867, George had a small, three-room house built (probably by his father-in-law, John Tuddenham, a contractor) on a large lot he had purchased on the "north bench" of Salt Lake City (now "D" Street in the Avenues section). This location was in the Twentieth Ward, where George's family had many worthwhile experiences for the next several decades. George and Polly moved into their new dwelling in December just as winter was arriving. On 5 January 1868 Polly gave birth to her second child, a daughter, who was small at birth, but nevertheless strong and healthy. They named her Amelia Emily, but she was always known as Millie, the same name as one of George's sisters in England.

George and Polly had much to be happy about. Though small, their house was their own, and the Twentieth Ward was a good place to live. Millie was a strong, beautiful child, who, even though she was having difficulty teething, George wrote in 1869, was "a bright, plucky, mischievous, brave little girl, and we hope to raise her to womanhood, to be an honor in the Kingdom of God." The young parents spent a great deal of time with Millie, teaching her new words and finding delight in everything she learned to say.[9]

George thoroughly enjoyed his associations in the Twentieth Ward after moving there in 1867. Because many of his neighbors were educationally progressive — Bishop John Sharp, the renowned Karl G. Maeser, as well as George Reynolds himself — this ward pioneered several Church programs. The Twentieth Ward ran a successful branch of the cooperative store. As secretary and treasurer of the branch store, George received a small pension.

George served first as Sunday School teacher and librarian and then, in 1869, became superintendent of the Twentieth Ward's Sunday School, a position that demanded considerable attention. Later he was also called to be the tithing clerk. He was assisted in his Sunday School organization by thirteen men and nine women at a time when few, if any, women worked in most other Sunday Schools of the Church. During his first year as superintendent, he worked to increase attendance. One effort was a party, to which he invited mothers of prospective students to help capture their interest. Attendance shot up from approximately fifty to more than two hundred children.

In 1869 George began assisting President Daniel H. Wells in administering sacred ordinances in the Endowment House. A journal entry reads: "I attended the endowment house as a recorder, also taking parts in the endowment. I also assisted Bro Wells."

At the April 1869 general conference, John Tuddenham, George's father-in-law, was called to return to England on a mission. Tuddenham arrived in England in May and was assigned to the London Conference, where he taught George's mother, brothers, and sisters the gospel, hoping to convert them. George's mother became interested, and after some persuasion, she allowed her two youngest sons, Charles and Harry, to emigrate to America and live with George. The boys, aged fourteen and twelve respectively, arrived in Utah in the summer 1870, were baptized, and went to live with George and Polly in their three-room home.

35

George Reynolds in 1870 at age twenty-eight

George, Polly, and daughter Millie were joined by little Heber, born on 12 July 1870. Thus the little house suddenly became quite crowded. "Charley" went to night school and did chores around the house. Harry went to the Twentieth Ward Day School, one of the best in the city, under the direction of Karl G. Maeser. Harry, undisciplined for his age, created frustration for George and Polly, who were now responsible for the boys' upbringing. "Neither [of the boys] are mentally well developed for their age," George recorded.

One afternoon Charley unwittingly placed some bedding on top of baby Heber. Five minutes later Polly went into the bedroom, looking for her baby, and discovered Heber, who was already getting black in the face from suffocation. George felt that the baby had "strained itself" trying to get free and was harmed. After this incident, Heber was always sickly.

George's professional life was varied during the years from 1866 to 1871, when he went to England on his second mission, because Brigham Young frequently rearranged assignments to office personnel. George continued to work in finances until August 1868, when he was assigned to fill Albert Carrington's vacancy as Brigham's confidential private secretary, Carrington having been called as president of the European Mission. At the end of 1868 George was replaced as private secretary by David McKenzie and was assigned as bookkeeper to the general Church accounts. In May 1870 he switched positions with McKenzie again. When Brigham Young returned from Saint George in early 1871, Reynolds was asked to index Endowment House sealings, with McKenzie returning as private secretary. In addition to his work in the Office of the President, he worked as a half-time assistant editor of the *Deseret News* under the direction of George Q. Cannon until May 1870.

During the 1860s Brigham Young was clearly the most influential person in political, economic, social, and spiritual aspects of life in Utah Territory. He guided the economic affairs of the Church as it delved deeply into numerous self-sufficiency enterprises. President Young's fervent desire was for the Church to be totally economically independent of all gentile influences. His secretaries and clerks were assigned both ecclesiastical and secular tasks, all of which were interchangeable in the minds of Church leaders. Secretaries did not have prescribed duties and could easily rotate assignments.[10] Perhaps Brigham did that purposely to avoid giving any one secretary too much authority or depending exclusively on any one.

They performed staff responsibilities and, in the Office of the President, did not exercise any priesthood or ecclesiastical authority. After Elder Cannon was relieved of secretarial duties in 1868 to perform other apostolic responsibilities, the dichotomy between "priesthood" and "staff" became even more pronounced. Yet the First Presidency hired only trusted priesthood holders as secretaries and clerks where confidential and highly significant documents, discussions, and decisions were involved. Each secretary held his own ecclesiastical calling apart from his office work. George Reynolds, for example, was a seventy and Sunday School worker.

Out of his close association with the Church hierarchy in the Office of the President, George received appointments throughout his life to responsible positions in education, government, and church-run businesses. In territorial Utah, Brigham Young and his advisors in private councils determined who should fill these important posts, although the appointments formally came from the appropriate government agencies. George received his first appointment in February 1869 at age twenty-seven when he was elected unanimously by the territorial legislature as a University of Deseret regent. Soon he was functioning as executive committee secretary of the board of regents. He continued in that position for several years, being released only temporarily during his second mission. In 1870 he was also appointed as secretary to the Utah statehood committee.

George Reynolds had obviously risen in the estimation of the First Presidency as one who was reliable, versatile, and trustworthy. At the end of 1869, he noted wryly in his journal, "It will thus be seen my hands were full in having so many honorary callings."

George was excited in late 1870 to buy a modern Singer sewing machine for his wife. That turned out to be a good investment, for in just a few months George was called to go to England on his second full-time mission and Polly was able to take in sewing to help sustain the family in his absence.

In an 1870 letter to his father-in-law, George revealed his feelings about current Salt Lake City events. George repudiated the "Godbeite" faction that had begun to attract attention. George had known key figures of this "new movement," but he was not persuaded. At this time the "gentile Ring," a group of anti-Mormon businessmen and lawyers, banded together to oppose Mormonism through the legal system. United States President Ulysses S. Grant

38

supported this faction and made appointments to territorial offices that annoyed the Mormons. George wrote: "We do not feel like being pissing posts for every hell hound that is sent here as governor, judge, marshall &c. But we should all, I hope, be on hand to do just when the Lord requires, be it in accord with our feelings or not. Perhaps the Lord is preparing a scourge, on account of our unbelief, lukewarmness &c."[11] Little did George realize that in a few years his name would be in the center of this controversy between the Mormons and the gentiles.

George Reynolds, twenty-nine years old in 1871, had become a trusted lieutenant in the Mormon kingdom. As a secretary in the Office of the President, he was near the seat of power. Still, in his humility, which came naturally to him, he sought neither position nor honor. He felt deep allegiance to the anointed prophets and apostles of God.

Notes

1. Information in this chapter, unless otherwise noted, is drawn from George Reynolds Journal, vol. 4, 1865–71.

2. Alice Louise Reynolds, "Biography of George Reynolds," p. 9.

3. First Council of Seventy Index to Seventies Ordinations, 1839–1971, Reel 12, LDS Church Historical Archives; Ora H. Barlow, ed., *The Israel Barlow Story and Mormon Mores* (Salt Lake City: Publishers Press, 1968), pp. 106–21, 205–7, 437, 446; George Reynolds's seventy's certificate and an accompanying note: "Geo. Reynolds ordained a Seventy by Prest Barlow, who was ordained by the Prophet Jos Smith," in possession of Jane Reynolds, Salt Lake City, Utah (hereafter cited as Jane Reynolds Collection).

4. Thomas G. Alexander and James B. Allen, *Mormons and Gentiles: A History of Salt Lake City* (Boulder, Colo.: Pruett Publishing Co., 1984), pp. 67–70.

5. B. H. Roberts, *A Comprehensive History of The Church of Jesus Christ of Latter-day Saints*, 6 vols. (Salt Lake City, Utah: Deseret News Press, 1930), 5:353–57; Alexander and Allen, *Mormons and Gentiles*, pp. 93–94.

6. Lawrence R. Flake, "The Development of the *Juvenile Instructor* under George Q. Cannon and Its Functions in Latter-day Saint Religious Education," master's thesis, Brigham Young University, 1969, pp. 17–19, 32–34.

7. See Appendix A for a complete bibliography of George Reynolds's published writings.

8. Information about prayer circles is found in D. Michael Quinn, "Latter-day Saint Prayer Circles," *BYU Studies* 19 (Fall 1978): 79–105. Information about the School of the Prophets is found in Leonard J. Arrington, *Great Basin Kingdom*

(Lincoln, Neb.: University of Nebraska Press, 1958), pp. 145–51; John R. Patrick, "The School of the Prophets: Its Development and Influence in Utah Territory," master's thesis, Brigham Young University, 1970.

9. George Reynolds to "Dad" (John Tuddenham), 7 April 1870, letter in possession of Emily Jensen, Provo, Utah.

10. Leonard J. Arrington, *Brigham Young: American Moses* (New York: Knopf, 1985), pp. 336–41.

11. George Reynolds to "Dad" (John Tuddenham), 7 April 1870.

CHAPTER 5

Second Mission to Britain

In April 1871 George was unexpectedly called on another mission. Shortly before April conference, 1871, Elder Albert Carrington of the Quorum of the Twelve Apostles had been called to serve a second term as president of the European Mission. The call included the editorship of the *Millennial Star*. Carrington suggested to the First Presidency on 9 April that George Reynolds accompany him to England to be the associate editor of the *Star*. The next day the First Presidency approved the call and notified George, as they did so many other missionaries, by reading his name in general conference. The day after conference, Elder Wilford Woodruff set George apart, blessing him to be inspired to write "for the benefit and comfort and edification of the Saints of God" and promising that he would return to his family in safety.[1]

During the ensuing month George put his financial affairs in order so that Polly, their two children, and his two brothers would be cared for in his absence. He helped set up Polly's home sewing business. He sold a part of his lot, on which there were trees, to a friend and neighbor, Septimus W. Sears, for sixty dollars. With the money he bought his wife a washing machine and a sack of sugar. He arranged for Polly to pick up flour as needed from the George Q. Cannon family farm. He obtained jobs for his brothers: Charley began work in the construction trade with George's father-in-law,

John Tuddenham, and Harry obtained employment in the Deseret Museum under Joseph Barfoot. George was sincerely grateful to his friends for helping him get ready for his mission. "I left home clear of debt to all men," he noted in his journal.

George also resigned from most of his positions — Sunday School superintendent in the Twentieth Ward, secretary to the Twentieth Ward Cooperative Store, clerk to the ward bishopric, secretary to the North Bench Water Ditch Company, member of the executive committee of the University of Deseret Board of Regents, and officer in the territorial militia. He did not resign from his job in the Office of the President. Carefully he calculated how much pay he had drawn since he was hired in December 1865: $8,902.41, or $1,618.62 per year.[2]

Before his departure, the Twentieth Ward Sunday School children presented George with a silver pen holder, a gold pen, and an engraving of Brigham Young framed in walnut. The presentation of these gifts touched him deeply. He recorded the name of each child who had contributed to the gifts.

George arrived in Liverpool 21 May 1871, almost exactly six years after he had emigrated from that port. He confided in his journal, "Everything in England looks strange, the high houses, the narrow streets, the cumber of dark children & particularly the office the rooms there only look half their proper size." George went immediately to London to visit his family and former friends.

This mission was an opportunity to strengthen family ties. His mother had missed him, and, now in her advancing years, she was in need of George's attending to family matters. Recently she had turned for assistance to the next oldest son, Arthur, who was now married and a father. George found his mother to be "a little cranky" and noted that her "head is full of all sorts of notions." He was pleased that his twenty-three-year-old sister Julia had converted to the Church. He arranged for Julia to emigrate and then to reside with his wife in Salt Lake City. After three weeks in London, George returned to Liverpool with his brother, nineteen-year-old Walter, who had also joined the Church and who would serve as a printer's assistant in the mission office.

Throughout his mission, George kept in close contact, either in person or by mail, with his mother, brothers, sisters, and some aunts and cousins.[3] He counseled his sister Millie about what to expect in her prospective marriage. He helped Arthur settle the Reynolds family estate in Devonshire. Of immense satisfaction to George was his obtaining vital data about his ancestors on both paternal and maternal lines when he went to numerous villages to gather records.

George was patient, but frustrated, with his mother. He yearned for her to emigrate, feeling that in Utah she would convert to the Church, transform her life, and drop her traditional attitudes. He succeeded in helping her quit drinking beer so that she would not miss it after she emigrated.

In the Liverpool office, George busied himself editing the *Millennial Star,* which was published weekly, and the *Journal of Discourses,* which was usually published monthly. Every Monday he made a journal entry saying he "got out" such and such a number of the *Star.* That referred to his work of proofreading and final editing, for the magazine was dated as of every Tuesday. George continued to aid his friend George Q. Cannon with the *Juvenile Instructor,* writing fifteen articles and procuring and sending to Utah numerous engravings and woodcuts.

About a month into his calling, George described his new routine and his feelings about it:

> The work in this office is very much like any other kind of work, one day's labor very much resembles that of its fellows. It is like laying up adobies. There is a great sameness, it lacks the interest of going round visiting the saints, proclaiming the gospel, visiting fresh scenes and forming the acquaintance of new faces, particularly here in Liverpool, where the work of the Lord has for several years been at a standstill. It is not considered wise to preach in the open air, we have no week night meetings, and we only get about twenty five saints even to the Sunday evenings

meetings. So you see there is not much society or exchange. Still I am well satisfied with my calling and am striving with the aid of the Lord to do my duty and make the "Star" interesting and instructive, and in that I have much pleasure.

In time President Carrington invited George to represent him at various conferences, thus allowing him to visit paternal relatives in Devonshire and to obtain more genealogical information. While on a trip to Manchester in late August 1871, he contracted a severe case of smallpox; a number of other missionaries were also ill. Twenty-three thousand people died of the disease in Britain in 1871. For several days George lingered between life and death before beginning to recover. George later described his illness for George Q. Cannon:

> In my sickness I remembered your promise made to me when sick at Sherlmardines in the 8th ward [in 1866], that I should live to a good old age, also my blessing when set apart that I should "go in peace and return in safety." But I can assure you when the disease was at its height I cared little about this world or anything else. I knew I was an individual called George Reynolds, and that this individual had the smallpox and that was all. I was in a state of dreamy stupor much of the time, caused I believe considerably by the sleeping draughts I had given me. I can understand now something of the "Reveries of an Opium eater" for my mind was always terribly active, thinking in pictures, often strange and beautiful, sometimes shocking and horrible.

George was embarrassed to be seen in public because of the unsightly pock marks on his face, and he was slow to regain his strength. To speed his full recovery, it was eventually decided he should return to Utah earlier than he had originally planned.

The following item was published in the *Juvenile Instructor* relative to George Reynolds:

> We [George Q. Cannon and company] were grieved to learn from the Millennial Star, and also from private correspondence, that Elder George Reynolds now on a mission to England, and a

very constant and valued writer for the Juvenile Instructor, was attacked with that loathsome and dangerous disease, small-pox, on the 27th of August. The Star said that strong hopes were entertained of his recovery.

The friends and family of Brother Reynolds were anxious, after this news reached here, to learn more respecting his condition, so a dispatch was sent by telegraph from here to him in England, inquiring how his health was. An immediate reply was received, dated Liverpool, September 26th, by Brother Septimus W. Sears [George's neighbor and former missionary companion], in which Brother Reynolds stated that he had quite recovered. This good news relieved the anxiety of his family and friends. They all felt thankful for the use of a telegraph wire, by which news could be sent from one continent to another, thousands of miles distant, in so brief a space of time. The reply of Brother Reynolds left Liverpool on the 26th and reached this city in time to be published in the Deseret Evening News on the same day.[4]

Soon after George returned to the mission office, the missionaries were shocked when a telegram came from Salt Lake City summoning President Carrington immediately; no reasons were given. He departed on 29 September, after appointing Elder George Reynolds as acting head of the European Mission.[5] George functioned in that position until Carrington returned nearly eight months later.

One unfortunate task that George had to assume responsibility for during President Carrington's absence was caring for the remains of Elder Caleb W. Haws, who succumbed to smallpox, leaving a wife and three children in Utah. George purchased silk and linen to have burial clothes made, dressed the body in temple robes, and arranged for the burial.

President Carrington had been called back to Utah because of a rapidly festering conflict between extremist gentiles and the Mormon hierarchy. Territorial Chief Justice James B. McKean had been threatening the Church leaders with arrest since early September. A few days after summoning President Carrington, Brigham Young and Daniel H. Wells were arrested for "lewd and lascivious cohabitation and adultery for living with their polygamous wives." Later they were arrested again, this time on murder charges arising from rumors dating back to the Utah War. The Mormon leader was forced to spend the months from September 1871 until 25 April 1872 under house arrest before McKean's indictments were dismissed by the United States Supreme Court.[6]

As George Reynolds learned of events transpiring in Utah, he informed the European Saints through the *Star*. Speculation was rampant in Britain that Brigham Young would be hanged by United States officials. The news of President Young's arrest caused great persecution in England, particularly by the press. Reynolds wrote to George Teasdale, "Our newspapers here are pretty much filled with the 'End of Mormonism.' "

As acting mission president, Elder Reynolds wrote weekly editorials in the *Millennial Star*. Some titles were "The Decline of Mormonism?" "Hints to Emigrants," "Signs in the Heavens," "Be Not Discouraged," "Train Up a Child in the Way He Should Go," "Our Amusements," "The Weight of Our Calling," and "Tithing a Privilege and Blessing." As an experienced Church leader, he sincerely strived to teach the less mature European converts. Straightforward in style, he also seemed somewhat condescending. His correspondence with family and friends in Utah shows his frustration with the lackadaisical attitude of the British Saints who had not yet decided to gather to Utah. Those thoughts are also reflected in this editorial:

> The interest of "the kingdom of God and His righteousness" should be, at all times, the first great consideration with every Latter-day Saint. All personal, selfish or inferior considerations should be subservient to this one great object. No motive which falls short of this should inspire the life of a Saint. . . . He who considers he has interests apart from those of God's kingdom has interest in which there is no satisfaction, no salvation; interests in which truth and righteousness have no part, but in which death, hell or the grave will claim co-partnership.[7]

46

The European Mission over which Elder Reynolds temporarily presided included England, Scotland, Ireland, Wales, Holland, Switzerland, Germany, Sweden, Norway, and Denmark. He did not visit the missionaries and members on the continent but kept informed about them through frequent correspondence. He visited the Saints in the British Isles regularly and was not always pleased with his observations:

> "Things are not as they used to be some years ago." Many of the folks have degenerated into good old singsong sectarians. Apparently not a spark of the true living spirit of the gospel with them. They would make mighty good Methodists perhaps. They are always glad to see an elder, will give him something to eat, live good moral lives etc, but there's not the true ring about them, they are so fast asleep you can't wake them up. They have been preached to so much that they are tired of it.

At the end of 1871 George recorded that in Britain that year there had been some 7,206 British members, 594 baptisms, and 593 emigrations; in Scandinavia, 4,907 members, 1,020 baptisms, and 467 emigrations. The Swiss-German Mission had 597 members and 40 baptisms, and Holland had 31 members. The European Mission was but a shadow of its former self because of massive emigration and also because proselyting was less successful.

During this time George renewed ties with a former fellow worker in the Office of the President. Elder George Gibbs had returned to his native Britain to oversee the mission's financial affairs. On 27 October 1871 Elder Gibbs measured Elder Reynolds: he was five feet, six and one-quarter inches in height; thirty-six inches around the chest; and thirty-three inches around the waist.

Throughout his mission, Reynolds paid close attention to what was occurring with his family in Utah. He wrote his beloved Polly more than one letter per week, and each was several pages long and filled with much news and kind words. In the early months he gently chided her for not writing more often to him. He yearned for her letters, and his days were bright only when he received a letter from his "sweetheart." He was apologetic when he learned that caring for little Heber, who seemed to be crying all the time and needed much attention, so sapped her strength that she could do little else. He fretted about her situation. Did she have enough money, enough milk, enough flour, enough help? He wrote to others in the city, asking them to look out for her in various ways where they had some specialty. In one letter he referred to friends of the family who were having marital problems. "Heaven preserve me from such a life," he said. "I think one of the greatest blessings pronounced upon my head by the Patriarch was that I should have *peace* in my family."

Frequently he closed his letters to Polly with such sentiments as the following:

"May God preserve you from all evil, may the wicked have no power over you. May your joy be full in the Lord Jesus, and may God grant that when we meet it may be in happiness, in health and in satisfaction and may our love forever increase for each other is the prayer of your loving husband."

Once he was revelling in memories of the old days a few years previous in the British Mission but quickly added, "I was never happier than now. My married life has been its happiest days."

George referred to his wife with many terms of endearment. "My dear girl" seems to have been his favorite. At the end of the year 1871, George felt especially homesick for Polly:

> I have been thinking of you, Polly, all this day long, of many little incidents of our past wedded life and before we were "one flesh." Of the "Yes, George" in Florence St, the parting on the "Hudson," the 22 July 1865 [their wedding date], of many endearments, of much love, of the pleasures of house, of the fondness of a wife, of the happiness of trust and faith in those who to us are more than all the world beside, and of many other things that fond recollections will no doubt bring to your mind as to mine. Of these joys, I may say with the poet — "Oh had I the wings of a dove, how soon I would taste them again." But it cannot be so, so I must not think too much of home, wife and babes, but wait

patiently until that day dawns which in the providence of the Lord will restore us to each other.

George took great interest in his children, Millie and Heber. He sent Millie many books, most of which were well illustrated, and he hoped that she would learn to read as well as to look at the pictures. He also sent her other mementos and Christmas presents from England. Millie responded by telling her Aunt Julia what she wanted to say in return letters to her "papa." Once Julia held Millie's hand with the pen and helped her write a letter to her father. For her fifth birthday, George wrote Millie a special letter, one that she cherished all her life. He asked her all kinds of things, about the house, about her learning, about the pets and chickens. He expressed his wish for her: "May you grow to be a good and wise woman and live long on the earth to be loved and cherished. I hope now, that you are a good girl. Mamma tells me you are getting to be a big girl, so I hope you are also kind and truthful."

In his letters George expressed deep sorrow to Polly about the deteriorating condition of their little Heber. He fasted and prayed for the benefit of his son and counseled Polly to do the same and also to look to her father and kind brethren in their neighborhood for counsel and comfort. Finally, in May 1872, after George had been gone a year, little Heber died. Several Church and civic dignitaries attended the infant's funeral. The news of his son's death brought George considerable grief and contributed to his returning home somewhat early from his mission.

George's sister Julia and his brothers Charley and Harry continued to live with Polly. Julia was a tremendous help in every respect, and Charley seems to have behaved maturely, but Harry was a source of trouble for Polly and nearly anyone else with whom he came in contact. He had troubles in school. He was fired from the Deseret Museum. Septimus Sears hired him at the Twentieth Ward Co-op Store, but Harry also caused trouble there.

George formed definite opinions about members of his family.

He liked working with Walter in the Liverpool office and commended him for his progress. Nonetheless, he reported to a cousin, "He is a queer stick. So are most of the Reynolds'." To his wife he wrote, "It seems to me there are two races in our family, one of which will make Latter-day Saints and the other have no affection or sympathy for the gospel. On the one side are myself, Julia, Walter, and Charley, on the other Arthur, Milly, Ned & Harry. I hope the result will be higher than my expectations."

Albert Carrington returned to Liverpool on 21 May 1872, and on the following day, George learned of little Heber's death. During the early months of 1872 George had often mentioned in his journal and letters the incessant rainy weather that was adversely affecting his health. Because of his declining health, George was to be sent to London for a month's "holiday" to recuperate, but after further consideration, President Carrington released George to go home. On 26 June Elder Reynolds sailed for America on an emigrant ship carrying Scandinavian Saints.

The voyage lasted thirteen days. After seven more days by railroad, he arrived in Salt Lake City, where he was greeted by an anxious family on 17 July. George and Polly had sorely missed each other and were grateful to be together again. He was also pleased to be reunited with his daughter Millie and his sister Julia.

Notes

1. Information for the paragraphs about Reynolds's mission preparation and arrival in England are drawn from George Reynolds Journal, vol. 4, 1871.

2. These figures, compared with other evidences of income for residents of Salt Lake City at the time, indicate that Reynolds earned about an average wage. An examination of the tax rolls for Salt Lake City indicate that Reynolds's property holdings were also average to slightly less than average. Later in life he supplemented his income by writing, publishing, and investing in Mormon-owned businesses.

3. Reynolds kept a letterpress book of his correspondence during his mission of 1871–72. That is now in the hands of Vessa Hood Johnson, a granddaughter of Reynolds, in Springville, Utah. A photocopy is labeled as No. 32 in the Reynolds Collection in Special Collections, Harold B. Lee Library, Brigham Young University. Reynolds wrote more than once weekly to his wife and frequently to others in his extended family. Information and quotations in the rest of this chapter, unless other-

wise noted, come from the many letters in the letterpress book or George Reynolds Journal, vol. 4, 1871–72.

4. "Editorial Thoughts," *Juvenile Instructor* 6 (30 September 1871): 156.

5. *Millennial Star* 33 (3 October 1871): 632.

6. Thomas G. Alexander and James B. Allen, *Mormons and Gentiles: A History of Salt Lake City* (Boulder, Colo.: Pruett Publishing Co., 1984), pp. 94–95.

7. G.R., "Our Highest Interest," *Millennial Star* 34 (25 June 1872): 408–9.

CHAPTER 6

Home Again

ALTHOUGH HE WAS VERY PLEASED TO BE HOME AGAIN, GEORGE STILL continued to suffer from fever and nervousness; likewise, Polly remained ill. But a month later, in mid August, they were feeling much better. George's sister Julia accompanied them to the Endowment House, where they officiated in numerous baptisms for the deceased relatives George had learned about while in England.[1]

On 27 August 1872 George returned to work as a recorder of baptisms and sealings in the Endowment House. That assignment lasted only two days, for Brigham Young asked George to act as treasurer of the Salt Lake Theatre. Later that year Brigham promoted George to be general manager and theatre supervisor as well.

George enjoyed his assignment with the theatre because of his interest in drama, but he experienced difficulty as a manager because of conflicting advice from previous managers and the sheer mass of duties. During the winter, attendance suffered from foul weather, a smallpox scare, and an epidemic afflicting horses, which caused fewer people to attend because they could not ride in their buggies. George later arranged for his daughters Millie and Alice to act in bit parts in dramatic productions, even after he no longer worked in the theatre. George continued as manager until June 1873, when Brigham Young sold the theatre to a private group. George then returned to the Office of the President and worked as a clerk on Church records.

In late 1872 the Reynolds family received word that George's mother and two more brothers had joined the Church and would emigrate to Utah the next spring. Knowing his house could not hold three more people, George contracted with his father-in-law to build a substantial addition, which was ready when his mother and brothers arrived on 24 July 1873.

Meanwhile, George was called anew as superintendent of the Twentieth Ward Sunday School and secretary of the ward cooperative store. He was also reelected to the board of regents of the University of Deseret. George Reynolds was back in the mainstream of Utah and Church affairs.

George Reynolds loved the Sunday School cause. He agreed with his mentor George Q. Cannon that Zion would not flourish unless her youth were properly trained in the principles of the gospel. Just before Reynolds returned from his second mission in the summer of 1872, Elder Cannon had brought all of the emerging ward Sunday Schools in the Church, most of them still in Salt Lake County, into a centrally administered Deseret Sunday School Union. Every ward in the Church was charged to start a Sunday School. Elder Cannon's *Juvenile Instructor* served as the semiofficial organ for the Union, and teachers often drew material for their classes from it. Before his mission, George had written 144 articles for the magazine, mostly either Bible stories or descriptions of various animals. Now he assisted Elder Cannon by compiling the editorials, particularly when the apostle went to Washington, D.C., as Utah's territorial delegate.

As superintendent again of his own ward's Sunday School, George sought ways to create student interest and rapport. He pioneered an idea that soon caught on in other wards. He devised an out-of-class activity and fund-raiser on Pioneer Day, 24 July 1873, at a beach on the Great Salt Lake. More than seven hundred students and parents attended.

53

Exactly a year later the Deseret Sunday School Union hosted a "Juvenile Jubilee" in the Salt Lake Tabernacle in honor of the twenty-fifth anniversary of the first Sunday School in Utah. George Reynolds was one of twenty-three executive committee members who planned the event. He was in charge of the finances. Nearly ten thousand Sunday School children from four counties—Salt Lake, Utah, Davis, and Weber—crowded into the Tabernacle, filling the aisles. Numerous choirs and bands organized for the occasion. George eventually left his ward Sunday School program, but he remained with the general Deseret Sunday School Union his entire life.

Professionally, George continued as a clerk, cataloging Church records for the First Presidency. In 1873–74, Brigham Young spent the first of several winters in "Utah Dixie" at his new home in Saint George. Reynolds helped keep the work current in the Office of the President in Salt Lake City. In 1874 President Young returned to Salt Lake City, exuberant about renewing the united orders in Zion, based loosely on the economic program introduced by Joseph Smith in the 1830s. He commenced organizing city wards into separate united orders, beginning with George's Twentieth Ward. George was elected secretary of his ward's order on 29 April 1874. In a letter to Joseph F. Smith, counselor in the First Presidency, George bore witness of the united order:

> When President Young . . . proclaimed to us the necessity of entering into the United Order of Zion, I received a testimony of its truth, I realized that it was the only means by which we could be saved from the evils that were encompassing us around and taking deep root in our midst. . . . The further we hold off from this the greater openings we give for wrong doing, and the longer shall we be at arriving at the unity of the faith.

For several years after his immigration to Utah, George remained monogamous. But because he worked closely with Church leaders, who in public and private frequently advocated that most worthy and loyal Mormon men enter what was known as the "principle," George inevitably considered marrying a second wife. No doubt George involved Polly in the decision, for he would have been fully conversant with the "law of Sarah,"[2] which provided that the first wife agree to the second marriage and help select the second wife.

By January 1873 George had concluded to enter polygamy. He wrote to Amelia Jane Schofield, daughter of the Church's branch president in Manchester, England, asking her to become his second wife. Amelia immediately accepted his proposal and would have emigrated that year to America if Albert Carrington had not objected to the match and delayed her emigration. Carrington may have objected because by now he disliked or distrusted Reynolds. In private correspondence, George had shown that he was put off by Carrington's obvious pompousness, so there probably was mutual antipathy.

Meanwhile George entered plural marriage in another way that was becoming common: he was married by proxy to deceased women. On 24 February he was sealed in the Endowment House to Rosalie Cundle, a second cousin and his "childish sweetheart," and to distant cousins Alice Tautz, Kate Tautz, Eliza Ann Tautz, and Henriette Francis Tautz. George's sister Julia acted as proxy for these women in the ceremonies. George firmly believed that he would have claim to these women in the hereafter.

George and Polly were blessed with two more daughters during this period: Alice Louise, born 1 April 1873, and Florence Mary (Florry), born 13 July 1874. Both were premature births and the girls were small, but both fortunately became healthy children.

In early 1874 Amelia Jane Schofield chose to emigrate to Utah in spite of any protests and marry George. On 3 August President Daniel H. Wells married George and Amelia in the Endowment House. George took this step "most thoroughly convinced that Plural marriage was the Law of the Lord, to fulfil that law and escape condemnation and His displeasure." He added, "This I did consci-

55

Amelia Jane Schofield
at the time of her marriage

entiously and to carry out my most deep seated religious convictions."[3]

Amelia moved into the Reynolds household, which consisted of George, Polly, their three daughters, George's mother, his sister, and his four brothers. Once again the house was bursting at the seams with three adult men, four adult women, two teenage boys, and three children. Obviously there would have been some strain. Another addition was started on the house.

In October 1874, just as George Reynolds was settling into his new domestic arrangements, he suddenly became an important public figure in Utah: the First Presidency of the Church called upon him to be the polygamy "test case." Before this case played itself out, George would suffer through three court trials, his name would become a household word nationwide as *George Reynolds v. United States* was argued and decided before the United States Supreme Court, and he would be imprisoned for eighteen months.

Notes

1. Unless otherwise noted, information for this chapter is drawn from George Reynolds Journal, vol. 5, 1872–74.

2. See Doctrine and Covenants 132:34, 61–65; Orson Pratt, *The Seer* 1 (March 1853): 41; Richard S. Van Wagoner, *Mormon Polygamy: A History* (Salt Lake City: Signature Books, 1986), pp. 246–47.

3. "Autobiographical Sketch of George Reynolds," p. 3.

CHAPTER 7

Chosen as the
Polygamy "Test Case"

THE "POLYGAMY QUESTION" HAD BEEN HEATING UP BETWEEN THE federal government and the Latter-day Saint hierarchy for several years. Beginning with the first notice taken of the Mormon marriage practices in the early 1850s and the Church's official acknowledgment of the practice by Orson Pratt in 1852, antagonism increased in America. Throughout the 1850s the Saints defended their practice of polygamy on religious, moral, and political grounds, while national politicians mounted an offensive against it. The Republican Party, in its 1856 presidential platform, and immediately thereafter the Democrats, launched an antipolygamy propaganda campaign. The "institution of polygamy, and the temporal power of the Church which insured its survival, became the focal points of attack in the federal crusade to 'americanize' the Mormon community."[1] Although the Morrill Anti-Bigamy Bill, signed by President Abraham Lincoln on 8 July 1862, was designed to punish and prevent the practice of polygamy in Utah Territory, President Lincoln did not enforce that law during the rebellion of the southern states. And Mormons responded to the law by performing numerous new polygamous marriages.[2]

After the Civil War, federal officers found it useless to make arrests for polygamy offenses; the Utah Territorial Legislature had extended criminal jurisdiction to the territorial probate courts and appointed trusted Mormon leaders as probate judges. Furthermore, plural marriages were performed secretly: no public records were available. Consequently, no convictions were obtained under the 1862 law, and there would be none as long as Mormons retained control of the courts through the elective and appointive processes.

This church-state issue received national publicity in 1869 when United States Vice President Schuyler Colfax visited Salt Lake City. There a member of the Church's Quorum of the Twelve Apostles, John Taylor, engaged Colfax in public debate. Colfax insisted that Mormons were defiantly breaking the law; Taylor asserted that they were practicing a religious belief protected under the first amendment to the Constitution. The debate ended in a stalemate, each side believing he had convincingly stated his case.

Meanwhile, several bills strengthening the Morrill Act of 1862 were introduced in Congress. Though none was enacted, the 1870 Cullom Bill came close. This legislation would have empowered the president's choice of governor to appoint local judges, notaries, and sheriffs. Polygamists would have been barred from naturalization, voting, and holding public office. Wives would have been permitted to testify against husbands. Furthermore, the president could have employed the military to enforce this law's provisions. And because the bill echoed recent measures to reconstruct the South, it aroused nationwide attention.

To the surprise of Eastern Mormon-watchers, three thousand Mormon women, including George Reynolds's wife Polly, gathered in the Salt Lake Tabernacle to draft a protest against the Cullom Bill. Even though the House of Representatives passed the bill, it was kept off the Senate floor by an outcry in leading newspapers against a repeat of the Utah War fiasco and by the lobbying of those with transcontinental railroad financial interests.[3]

Throughout his term, President Ulysses S. Grant, frustrated by the failed Cullom Bill, continued to push the Congress to act. He appointed General J. Wilson Shaffer as governor of Utah and James B. McKean as chief justice. Shaffer died after a few months, but not before challenging Mormon control of the territorial militia. McKean, a New York lawyer associated with the earliest Republican opposition to polygamy, launched what he considered to be a holy crusade against plural marriage. He proceeded to adjudicate as if the Cullom Bill were indeed the law. By allowing the United States marshal to impanel juries, he made possible numerous convictions. He indicted Brigham Young for "lascivious cohabitation" in 1871 and announced that the case was really one of "federal authority versus polygamic theocracy."[4]

Judge McKean was encouraged by zealous Utah anti-Mormons, who were collectively labeled the "gentile ring"[5] by Church leaders. McKean's crusade was temporarily derailed, however, when the United States Supreme Court ruled in April 1872 that juries had been illegally drawn. McKean was ridiculed in the nation's press. It was during this tense time that Albert Carrington was recalled from the European Mission presidency, leaving George Reynolds to serve in his stead as acting president.

McKean's failure emphasized the necessity of congressional support if there were to be a successful attack on the Mormon theocratic dominion. Representative Luke Poland of Vermont introduced compromise legislation in 1874 that gave United States district courts exclusive civil and criminal jurisdiction; it also provided that jury lists be drawn by the district court clerk (usually a "gentile") and the judicial district probate judge (usually a Mormon), thus assuring equal representation. The bill passed and was signed by President Grant in June 1874.[6] In October Judge McKean organized a grand jury under the provisions of the Poland Act.

William Carey, United States prosecuting attorney for Utah, began seeking indictments against polygamists. He threatened arrest and trial of several leading Church authorities. The lack of public records of polygamous marriages and the fact that most prominent polygamists had entered the practice before the passage of the 1862

Morrill Act stifled Carey. The matter came to a head on 21 October 1874 when George Q. Cannon, Brigham Young's counselor and Utah Territory's delegate to the United States House of Representatives, was arrested on charges of polygamy. If Cannon had been required to go to trial, he would have been prevented from returning to Congress.[7] Federal harassment once again hit close to home. Church officials had to act quickly to avoid additional embarrassment as well as the difficult court cases involving the hierarchy, as had occurred in 1871 and 1872. Their solution lay in establishing a "test case" of the 1862 Morrill Act.

As early as 1866 Brigham Young had discussed with federal officials the possibility of deciding the constitutionality of the 1862 Morrill Act. Church officials were confident that if they could plead their position before the United States Supreme Court, the anti-polygamy law would be ruled unconstitutional.[8] George C. Bates, who preceded Carey as United States district attorney in Utah, had advocated in 1872 that three or four leading Mormons be indicted for polygamy so that the question could be settled through the courts.[9] After negotiating with Mormon authorities in the summer of 1874, Carey agreed that if a test case were provided, other proceedings would be dropped.[10] These secret negotiations were successful, and on 21 October 1874, the evening of George Q. Cannon's arrest, Cannon, representing the First Presidency, asked his friend and protégé George Reynolds to act as the test case for the Church.

In his autobiographical sketch written two years later, George wrote:

> In October 1874 it was agreed between the U.S. Prosecuting Attorney [William Carey] and the Presidency of the Church that a case should be gotten up, to test the constitutionality of the law of 1862 (the Anti-Polygamy Act) and that other prosecutions should be stayed in the mean time. I was asked to step to the front. I willingly complied and afforded the prosecution such information with regard to my marriages and the names of important witness as I thought could prove the facts desired.[11]

The myth persists that George Reynolds volunteered to stand in as the test case. In reality he "volunteered" only in the sense of willingly accepting the desires of his leaders in the Church. Loyalty to Church leaders was always one of George's chief attributes. He wrote of how he was approached:

> On the evening of Wednesday Oct. 21st, I, accompanied by my wife Amelia visited bro Edwin Dowden, on my return, whilst passing the south side of the temple block I met bro Cannon, who informed me (in substance) that it had been decided among the brethren of the Presidents Council to bring a test case of the law of 1862 (Anti-Polygamy Act) before the court and that it had been decided to present my name before the grand jury.[12]

Selecting Reynolds was President Cannon's idea,[13] and since he was intimately acquainted with the thirty-two-year-old Church employee, it was he who approached Reynolds. So responsive was George Reynolds to the brethren's desires that he provided President Cannon with the names of witnesses by early the next morning. By prearrangement, on Friday, 23 October 1874, the district attorney examined George Reynolds and the designated witnesses; Reynolds was indicted for bigamy, a felony. On Monday, 26 October, George pleaded not guilty and was released on a twenty-five-hundred-dollar bond provided by Salt Lake City businessmen.[14] According to historian Orson Whitney, both the bond and the bail were established by previous agreement between United States Attorney Carey and the defendant's counsel, one of the few Mormon lawyers, J. G. Sutherland.[15]

The Reynolds trial would have perhaps proceeded quietly if it had been held immediately, but an extremely tense situation had developed by the time George's trial began on 31 March 1875, five months later. During those months George Reynolds changed from a cooperative defendant, willing to risk conviction so that the law might be tested in the courts, to an uncooperative defendant, anxious to be acquitted. Private discussions and decisions in the Office of the President of the Church during this time are not available, so the reasons for a change of tactic on the part of Church leaders can only be surmised. But it is obvious that numerous provocative acts by the district attorney's office and by the federally appointed judiciary contributed to the Church leaders' change.

First was the continued harassment of George Q. Cannon. Despite the agreement to drop charges against other Church leaders after the indictment of George Reynolds, Carey, influenced by the "gentile ring," arranged for the arrest and indictment of George Q. Cannon on 12 November 1874. When Cannon and his attorneys asked that he be given a speedy trial so that he would be able to serve in the Congress that December, Carey claimed that the docket was filled and he would be unavailable for a few weeks. Even though Cannon was freed on bail to serve in the Congress during winter term, he and other Church leaders undoubtedly smarted over the violation of their agreement with the district attorney.

Second was the persecution of Thomas E. Ricks of Logan. Ricks, a leading Mormon in Logan and former Cache County sheriff, had been impanelled on McKean's October 1874 grand jury. Probably having learned of Ricks's polygamous marriages through their contact with him on that jury, Carey and his associates indicted him for polygamy. While searching for bondsmen, Carey "resorted to a ruse" and had Ricks arrested for first-degree murder. In 1860 Ricks, as sheriff, had killed a renegade horse thief, according to Ricks, while the prisoner was trying to escape. Ricks was held in the Utah penitentiary without bail to await trial, which did not come up until March 1875, just before the Reynolds case. In early November, Ricks and his attorneys sought abatement (annulling or quashing) of the charges against him on the grounds that the grand jury that had indicted him had been improperly impanelled, but Judge McKean refused to grant the abatement.[16]

By early December, Church leaders determined to try to obtain abatement of the charges against George Reynolds as well, and on identical grounds as those of the Ricks case.[17] This effort marks the change in attitude of George Reynolds and Church leaders in the "test case." Thereafter, no cooperation existed between the prosecution and the defense.

Because of this ordeal, Brigham Young transferred George out of the Office of the President to the accounting office of ZCMI (Zion's Cooperative Mercantile Institution), the Church's cooperative retail store. George had first been offered the position of tithing clerk in Logan, but after consulting with his family, he decided to remain in Salt Lake City.

Life was stressful for the Reynolds family during the period between October 1874 and March 1875. There was considerable strain with two wives, one óf them, Amelia, having just joined the family, and many in-laws living in the same house. Amelia suffered through her first pregnancy during this public furor. George's mother became increasingly difficult.

Through it all, George did not complain, at least not publicly nor in his private journal. His first loyalty was to God and the Church's leaders. He was obedient, even if the costs were heavy.

Notes

1. Gustive O. Larson, *The "Americanization" of Utah for Statehood* (San Marino, Calif.: Huntington Library, 1971), p. 59.

2. Ibid., p. 60.

3. Ibid., p. 65; Gustive O. Larson, "Government, Politics, and Conflict," in Richard D. Poll, et al., eds., *Utah's History* (Provo, Utah: Brigham Young University Press, 1978), pp. 250–51.

4. Thomas G. Alexander, "Federal Authority versus Polygamic Theocracy: James B. McKean and the Mormons, 1870–75," *Dialogue* 1 (Autumn 1966): 85–100; Larson, *"Americanization,"* pp. 73–74; Larson, "Government, Politics, and Conflict," pp. 251–52.

5. Mormons may have given the pejorative term *ring* to their gentile enemies consistent with the negative usage of the term throughout the United States, as in the "Tweed Ring" in New York at the same time (1871) and the "Whiskey Ring" in Saint Louis in 1875.

6. Larson, *"Americanization,"* p. 77; Larson, "Government, Politics, and Conflict," p. 252.

7. Scott G. Kenney, ed., *Wilford Woodruff's Journal*, 9 vols. (Midvale, Utah: Signature Books, 1983–85), 7:202; *Salt Lake Daily Herald*, 22 October 1874, p. 2.

8. Orson F. Whitney, *History of Utah*, 4 vols. (Salt Lake City: George Q.

Cannon and Sons, 1898) 3:45–46; B. H. Roberts, *A Comprehensive History of The Church of Jesus Christ of Latter-day Saints*, 6 vols. (Provo, Utah: Brigham Young University Press, 1965), 5:468–69; Junius F. Wells, "A Living Martyr," *Contributor* 2 (February 1881): 154.

9. Bates was interviewed by the *Omaha Herald*, and the resulting article was reprinted in the *Salt Lake Daily Herald*, 19 June 1872, p. 2.

10. Whitney, *History of Utah*, 3:46; Wells, "A Living Martyr," p. 154; Richard S. Van Wagoner, *Mormon Polygamy: A History* (Salt Lake City: Signature Books, 1986), pp. 110–11.

11. "Autobiographical Sketch of George Reynolds," pp. 3–4. Here Reynolds clearly stated contemporaneously that his case was considered a "test case" by all important principals. The contemporary newspaper accounts dating from his indictment by the grand jury bear out the same contention. Nevertheless, Robert N. Baskin in his *Reminiscences of Early Utah* (n.p., 1914) argued that Orson F. Whitney was wrong in stating in his *History of Utah* that *Reynolds* was a test case. My research leads me to a middle ground. *Reynolds* was considered a test case in the beginning, but that idea was soon abandoned by both the prosecution and the defense. Later, when Reynolds was convicted, he and the Church leaders again brought up the idea that *Reynolds* was a test case in order to get him pardoned or have his sentence reduced.

12. George Reynolds Journal, vol. 5, 16 October 1874.

13. Letter of George Q. Cannon to President Hayes, as cited in George Reynolds Journal, vol. 5, March 1879.

14. Utah District Court Records, Record Group no. 21, United States of America, District of Utah, papers and files in case nos. 1631 and 2148, *United States of America v. Geo Reynolds*, located in National Archives-Denver Branch (hereafter referred to as Reynolds Case Papers); *Salt Lake Daily Herald*, 17 October 1874, p. 3; George Reynolds Journal, vol. 5, 26 October 1874.

15. Whitney, *History of Utah*, 3:47.

16. *Salt Lake Tribune*, 2 April 1875, p. 3; Whitney, *History of Utah*, 2:769–73; George Reynolds Journal, vol. 5, February 1875.

17. George Reynolds Journal, vol. 5, January 1875; Reynolds Case Papers.

CHAPTER 8

On the Defense

By March 1875 animosity had risen to fever pitch between Mormon officials and federal appointees Judge James B. McKean and United States Attorney William Carey. Church leaders, who once had wanted to cooperate with a test case, now wanted to get George Reynolds off the hook. Concurrent circumstances that drew considerable national attention to Utah contributed to the ill will and the circus atmosphere.

First was the hostility between George C. Bates, the non-Mormon district attorney previous to Carey, and Robert N. Baskin, Salt Lake City attorney and chief intellectual leader of the gentile ring. In 1872, when Bates became frustrated with Judge McKean's zeal to embarrass Brigham Young in the courts, he had traveled to Washington to consult with the United States attorney general. McKean followed Bates to assert his side. President Grant favored McKean's view, and when Bates would not resign, he was fired and replaced by William Carey on 10 December. When Bates returned to Utah, the Church hired him to defend those indicted as a result of McKean's crusade.

Robert N. Baskin, a lawyer who had come to Utah in 1865, was as eager as McKean to rid Utah of theocracy and polygamy. Baskin desired peace in Utah so that he could help develop Utah's vast mineral wealth. He was a staunch advocate of the separation of church and state and of *laissez faire*. He was a coauthor of the Cullom Bill and served as an assistant district attorney under Bates. When Bates became sympathetic to the Mormon cause, however, the two men became inveterate enemies. Unquestionably, their mutual distrust contributed to the pervasive tension that existed when Reynolds came to trial. Both Bates and Baskin played key roles in the Reynolds case.[1]

Two other trials involving Church leaders and affecting their reputations were taking place about the same time as the Reynolds case. The first was the divorce case between Brigham Young and Ann Eliza Webb, one of his plural wives. Unknown to Brigham, Ann Eliza was still legally married to her first husband when she and Brigham married in 1868. In 1873 she filed for divorce in Judge McKean's court, thus creating sensational national news, especially because she asked for alimony. On 25 February 1875, McKean ordered President Young to pay Ann Eliza ninety-five hundred dollars for attorney's fees, alimony, and the education of her children. The case was appealed to the Supreme Court of the territory. Brigham Young legally should not have been required to pay until the appeal was decided, but McKean charged Brigham with contempt of court when he failed to pay the fee by the appointed date. McKean sentenced President Young on 11 March to twenty-four hours imprisonment and fined him twenty-five dollars. President Young submitted to the overnight stay in the penitentiary along with hundreds of armed disciples to ensure his safety. Members of the Church did not want another Carthage.

The nation's press ridiculed McKean's decision, and even President Grant lost patience with this overzealousness. Within days the chief justice was removed from office. "Glory Hallelujah the Lord has heard and answered our Prayers," exulted Mormon apostle Wilford Woodruff. "McKean has been the most unjust tyrannical Judge ever sent to Utah and we have prayed for his removal for a long time."[2] Thus Judge McKean was discharged before he had a chance to preside over the Reynolds trial. Associate Justice Philip

H. Emerson, from Michigan, who over the years had developed a reputation for fairness, presided instead.

The second related trial took place in the Second District Court in Beaver immediately after Reynolds's Salt Lake City trial. John D. Lee, who had participated in the Mountain Meadows Massacre in 1857, had finally been found and arrested. The case obviously was important to the anti-Mormon judicial crusade because of its national propaganda value. Lee's trial was postponed until Carey and Baskin finished with the Reynolds case so they could go to Beaver as prosecuting attorneys; George C. Bates was Lee's defense attorney, as he was for Reynolds.

Hence, the Reynolds trial took place in the midst of a verbal war between the adamant and politically influential gentile ring and the Mormon hierarchy, represented now by George Reynolds, a relatively unimportant employee in the Office of the President. George's trial lasted two days: Wednesday, 31 March, and Thursday, 1 April 1875. President Grant sent General Benjamin R. Cowen, assistant Secretary of the Interior, to be an observer at the trial. Attorneys for the defense were J. G. Sutherland, George C. Bates, and Zerubbabel Snow.

During the first morning a jury of seven Mormons and five non-Mormons was selected, but not without some labored discussion with prospective jurors. Some Mormon jurors indicated their belief that the 1862 antipolygamy law was unconstitutional, but that if the court ruled the law constitutional and if the evidence warranted it, they would return a guilty verdict.[3]

The calling of witnesses for the prosecution began in the afternoon. The prosecution naturally had a full slate of close friends and relatives of George Reynolds because of the voluntary list given the district attorney in October when Reynolds was indicted. Carey indicated that his purpose was to prove that Reynolds married Mary Ann Tuddenham in 1865 as his first and lawful wife and that he married Amelia Jane Schofield while still married to his lawful wife. Fourteen witnesses were called and each was "unfriendly" to the prosecution, as Carey tried to elicit definitive information about George Reynolds's marriages, particularly his second one.[4]

Each witness said as little as possible and avoided giving proof of George and Amelia's marital relationship. Indeed their testimonies bordered not merely on evasion but on lying. For those devoted Latter-day Saints, the welfare of the Church was the most important consideration. For example, George's sister Julia testified that she lived in the Reynolds household and that there was another woman besides Mary Ann (Polly) in the house, but that she did not know if the defendant and the other woman cohabited as husband and wife. Another witness, George's neighbor James Evans, reported that he had seen another woman in the house but had never heard the defendant speak of her as his wife. Daniel H. Wells, Reynolds's friend and officiator of his marriage to Amelia in the Endowment House, testified that he could not remember performing a marriage for George Reynolds on the third of last August and that he had no record. When Orson Pratt was asked if he knew whether marriage records were kept in the Endowment House or in the separate branches of the Church, he answered that he did not know and, furthermore, he did not know whose duty it was to keep such records.[5]

During Daniel H. Wells's examination, Baskin, Carey's unofficial aide, quietly discussed with the United States marshal that Reynolds's second marriage was not being proved. At this point Baskin obtained a subpoena for Amelia Reynolds and instructed Arthur Pratt, a deputy marshal who had apostatized from the Church, to procure a buggy and bring the witness to the courthouse immediately. In the meantime, the prosecution had exhausted its resources and Carey appeared befuddled. Mormons in the courtroom jubilantly leaned over the railing, congratulating Reynolds on his easy victory. Baskin then indicated to Carey that Reynolds's second wife was en route. Carey requested and received a short recess.[6]

The marshal soon escorted the obviously pregnant Amelia in by the side door where she could be easily seen. General Cowen, the government observer, wrote, "As the marshal stepped aside from the door and revealed the person of Mrs. Reynolds No. 2 framed in the doorway, the consternation of the Mormon crowd was startling. The ghost of Joe Smith would scarcely have produced a more profound sensation."[7] Because Amelia had not been previously subpoenaed, she had not been instructed on how to evade giving the prosecution relevant information. Amelia calmly testified that she had been married to George (pointing to him) the previous August by President Daniel H. Wells.[8] Following her testimony, the court adjourned in pandemonium.

During the intervening hours prior to the next morning's session, Church leaders apparently decided to concede without further argument that George was plurally married and to make a case that the principle of plural marriage was a religious rite and that Reynolds entered into his second marriage as a religious duty. When the court convened, William Carey of the prosecution rested his case. Defense Attorney J. G. Sutherland explained that Daniel H. Wells, who was not present in the courtroom, could now remember marrying George and Amelia on 3 August, and that this admission established two marriages. Sutherland then read a lengthy statement discussing the history of plural marriage as a principle in the Church, including:

> They [the Mormons] believe it [polygamy] to be a divine institution, and they will be indebted for their highest happiness in another life to their fidelity and obedience to it in this; that this defendant holds their faith ... and [is] a sincere believer in the verity of said revelation [about plural marriage], and that it was his solemn duty to obey it. . . . They [the Mormons] are willing to bear [pains and penalties of the law] rather than lose the high estate in another life to be gained by celestial marriage.[9]

The prosecution objected to the testimony as irrelevant, and Judge Emerson sustained the objection. The defense offered no further evidence. Judge Emerson charged the jury, indicating that Congress had the constitutional right to pass the Morrill Anti-Bigamy law and that a person's religious belief "can have nothing to do with this case." He explained that "religious liberty is not violated when the citizen is called upon to answer for his external acts, which are in violation of a valid law of the land."[10]

The jury then retired and returned thirty minutes later with a verdict of guilty. The defense counsel moved that the court set aside the verdict on grounds of a mistrial, the defendant not having been arraigned or given opportunity to plead to the indictment. For a few moments, confusion reigned. The judge then determined that Reynolds, indeed, had not been allowed to plead either guilty or not guilty. Judge Emerson ruled that the verdict be set aside. District Attorney Carey then insisted upon a new trial immediately. Once again, there was confused discussion. Finally Reynolds approached his counsel, whispering. Sutherland withdrew his motion and requested that the defendant now enact the irregularity of pleading not guilty so that the case could eventually be heard by the Supreme Court of the United States. The court took the question of the validity of the proceeding under advisement until the next Tuesday, 6 April.[11]

Immediately after this trial, the more famous George Q. Cannon was brought to trial in the same Third District Court. Following arguments, the court dismissed his case because of the United States statute of limitations.[12]

On Tuesday, 6 April, George Reynolds learned that the prosecuting and defense attorneys had altered his court documents to avoid holding a new trial.[13] Judge Emerson did not make a judgment against Reynolds, however, because, in his opinion, the Poland Law did not require such judgment. But Carey and Baskin, chagrined by their mismanagement of aspects of Reynolds's trial and their loss of Cannon, pressed the court for a judgment against Reynolds, asking that he be imprisoned pending the appeal to the higher court.[14]

Judge Emerson called Reynolds into court on Saturday, 10 April, and sentenced him to one year of hard labor in the territorial penitentiary, commencing that day, and the payment of a three-hundred-dollar fine. When Reynolds's attorneys made an appeal to the territorial supreme court, the judge accepted Reynolds's bonds and the prisoner was given liberty. In this tense atmosphere, rumors spread that George had been taken to the penitentiary and had been rescued by a body of Saints.[15]

On the following Wednesday and Thursday, Reynolds's case unexpectedly came before the court again. George was apprehended in the Office of the President and was taken to the courtroom, but he later received an apology from the judge. Carey and Baskin continued their insistence that Reynolds serve his prison term. Judge Emerson finally ruled that Reynolds would remain free until his appeal came before the territorial supreme court.[16]

At last, temporary peace came to George and his family. The stress had had a telling effect upon them. Later that month, April, George was transferred from the ZCMI accounting office to the store's new building as cashier in the retail department.[17]

By June George's mother had had enough of Utah and decided to return to her homeland, taking Ned and Harry with her. "Neither of the three had any comprehension of the gospel and my mother could not reconcile herself to the difference of the surrounding of Salt Lake City as compared with what she was used to in London," George confided in his journal. He added that Harry was actually opposed to the Church. Yet both boys spoke of returning to Utah.[18] George's mother died six years later in London. Both young men returned to Utah after her death, with Ned dying a year later himself. Harry never became an active member of the Church.

Soon the Utah Supreme Court, consisting of the three federally appointed district judges in Utah Territory, were to rule on the appeal. George, his family, and his friends awaited the outcome.

Notes

1. Robert N. Baskin, *Reminiscences of Early Utah*, pp. 5–22, 156–58; Orson F. Whitney, *History of Utah*, 4 vols. (Salt Lake City: George Q. Cannon and Sons, 1898), 2:674–77, 731.

2. Scott G. Kenney, ed., *Wilford Woodruff's Journal*, 9 vols. (Midvale, Utah: Signature Books, 1983–85), 7:221.

3. *Salt Lake Daily Herald*, 1 April 1875, p. 3.

4. *Salt Lake Tribune*, 1 April 1875, p. 4.

5. Ibid.; *Salt Lake Daily Herald,* 1 April 1875, p. 3.

6. Baskin, *Reminiscences of Early Utah,* pp. 62–63, 66.

7. As cited in ibid., p. 66.

8. *Deseret News,* 3 April 1875, p. 3; *Salt Lake Daily Herald,* 1 April 1875, p. 3; *Salt Lake Tribune,* 1 April 1875, p. 4.

9. *Salt Lake Daily Herald,* 2 April 1875, p. 3; *Salt Lake Tribune,* 2 April 1875, p. 4; *Deseret News,* 3 April 1875, p. 2.

10. Ibid.

11. Ibid.

12. *Salt Lake Daily Herald,* 3 April 1875, p. 3; *Deseret News,* 6 April 1875, p. 2; Whitney, *History of Utah,* 2:773–74.

13. George Reynolds Journal, vol. 5, April 1875.

14. Ibid.; Junius F. Wells, "A Living Martyr," *Contributor* 2 (February 1881): 154–55.

15. George Reynolds Journal, vol. 5, April 1875; *Salt Lake Daily Herald,* 11 April 1875, p. 3; Reynolds Case Papers.

16. Ibid.

17. George Reynolds Journal, vol. 5, April 1875.

18. Ibid., June 1875.

CHAPTER 9

Awaiting the Decision

On 7 June 1875, the Utah Territorial Supreme Court, consisting of the three district judges, convened to hear the appeal of *Reynolds v. the United States*. Reynolds's lawyers, this time better prepared, successfully argued that the grand jury of the original indictment was illegally constructed of twenty-three men. Territorial law required fifteen. On 19 June, the court ruled in favor of Reynolds and set aside his indictment,[1] causing joy among faithful Latter-day Saints. "The result of the opinion is a signal triumph for Territorial law, and oversees the pet schemes of the ring of over-riding all laws passed by the [Mormon-dominated] Territorial legislature when it suited their purpose in persecuting the people of God," reads Reynolds's journal.[2]

Carey, Baskin, and their friends of the gentile ring were angered by this ruling of the court and immediately vowed to bring Reynolds to "justice." Throughout the summer, there was surface calm and joy among the Saints.

On 6 July 1875, George's second wife, Amelia, gave birth to her first child, a boy named Sidney. On 5 August, George Reynolds, as part of a general Church reformation movement, was invited to join a united order branch of fifteen men who worked closely with Brigham Young on business matters. Then, on 23 August President Young asked George to return to his office to serve as private secretary, replacing Albert Carrington, who was returning to England as European Mission president.[3] George was rewarded for having served as the Church's sacrificial lamb. All now seemed normal in the Reynolds household; George's two wives took separate summer vacations. The future seemed secure. But this calmness did not last.

In October 1875 a new grand jury was created that conformed to the legal guidelines of fifteen men (seven Mormons and eight gentiles). Abandoning compassion for Reynolds, who one year previously had voluntarily submitted to indictment as a "test case," United States attorney William Carey brought a new indictment on 30 October. Two days later George was arrested as he was working in the office of President Young. He pleaded not guilty and was admitted to bail until his trial in the United States Third District Court came up on 7 December.[4]

George, meanwhile, became more closely connected with the Church's hierarchy. On 5 November 1875 he recorded in his journal, "I was rebaptized at the Endowment House, in accord with the general reformation in the Church. Elder Geo Q Cannon baptized me and Elder John Taylor was mouth at my confirmation."[5] He accompanied Elder Cannon to Pleasant Grove, establishing a united order according to the Church's reformation principles then in effect.

On 20 November, George was appointed to a vacancy on the Salt Lake City council occasioned by the resignations of Theodore McKean and Feramorz Little.[6] Appointments to local governmental positions, including placement on the ticket of the People's Party (the Church's political party), were decisions of Brigham Young and leading Church councils. The irony of appointing a person to governmental leadership whom the federal government considered a lawbreaker was undoubtedly not lost on George Reynolds and Church leaders. In addition, George Reynolds was called, on 4 December, to be one of seven presidents of the Twenty-fourth Quorum of Seventies and was set apart by members of the First Council of Seventy.[7]

By December Alexander White of Kansas had arrived in Utah

to replace Judge McKean as chief justice and justice of the Third District Court, but his appointment had not yet received Senate confirmation. White replaced Philip H. Emerson as judge for the Reynolds trial. Later, in a reminiscence, Reynolds offered his opinion: "I have always considered that the Judge [White] thought that convicting a polygamist would secure his confirmation to his office by the U. S. Senate, which, however, it did not do; he was not confirmed."[8] In preparation for Reynolds's second trial, Church leaders employed different legal counsel: P. L. Williams, distinguished attorney for the Oregon Shortline Railroad Company and two prominent non-Mormon (but not unfriendly) Salt Lake City attorneys. Realizing that the prosecution intended to show criminality and demand punishment for Reynolds, the defense determined to prove innocence.

When the trial commenced on Tuesday, 7 December 1875, Williams attempted to have Reynolds's case dismissed on grounds of irregularities surrounding the formation of the latest grand jury. The court then recessed until the next morning to give Carey time to answer the allegations. After lengthy arguments Judge White ruled against each of the defense pleas and ordered Reynolds's trial to proceed.

On Thursday, 9 December, jurors were selected while the deputy marshal sought in vain to locate the prosecution's prime witness, Amelia Reynolds, who had gone into hiding. The court recessed in the late afternoon. At 7:00 P.M. the court reconvened. The prosecution had no difficulty proving George Reynolds's first marriage but offered to prove through testimony of the first trial's court reporter that George was married to a second wife, Amelia Jane Schofield. The defense objected to such novel procedure, and Judge White indicated that he would hear arguments the following morning as to the admissibility of the absent witness's testimony.[9]

Both sides anxiously awaited White's crucial decision. White allowed the prosecution to introduce the evidence, and after hearing the objections of the defense, ruled that such evidence was valid.

Deputy Marshal Arthur Pratt testified that while he was searching for Amelia Reynolds, he encountered the defendant (George Reynolds), who told Pratt that he could search anywhere but he would not find Amelia and she would not testify. With additional cooperative rulings from the court, the prosecution then closed its case.[10]

Daniel H. Wells took the stand as the defense's first witness. He testified at length of the doctrinal nature of plural marriage and of the importance that entering polygamy had for someone like Reynolds. Wells said that "when male members came to a thorough understanding of the revelation on and principle of plural or celestial marriage, and other circumstances being favorable, if they failed to obey it they would be under condemnation, and would be clipped in their glory in the world to come."[11]

Orson Pratt then testified "that he knew by the revelations of the Holy Ghost that Joseph Smith, the man through whom the Lord revealed the doctrine of celestial marriage, was a prophet of God."[12] John Nicholson, a close friend of George Reynolds since their childhood in England, testified that he had heard George favorably preach of plural marriage, that he was a "practical polygamist," and that "an honester man to his convictions of right did not exist."[13] Reynolds's bishop, John Sharp, indicated that he had given George a certificate indicating that he was worthy to marry a second wife.[14] After this witness the defense rested its case.

In their final arguments, Reynolds's attorneys took turns arguing that the essential element rested upon the defendant's criminal intent: that Reynolds did not have such intent but was impelled to act under potent religious conviction; that if he refused to enter polygamy, condemnation awaited him hereafter; that polygamy was not a crime but a religious practice; and that the Constitution guaranteed religious freedom to all.[15]

Judge White then gave a charge to the jury, reminding them that the first trial testimony was valid. He insisted that the central issues to the case were whether Reynolds was married and whether he took a second wife. The jurists' personal opinions as to whether marrying a second wife was a "crime" or not had no relevance. Moreover, White continued, the issue of "criminal intent" was invalid. On the issue of religious freedom, White asserted that there "must be some limits to this high constitutional privilege."[16]

Some years later, in 1879, in looking back on this experience, George Reynolds insisted that he did not have a fair trial, that prosecuting attorney Carey "was a very poor lawyer, and Judge White turned in and helped him to prosecute."[17]

The jury returned in two hours with a verdict of guilty. Reynolds's lawyers asked for a ten-day stay of judgment to allow time for preparing an appeal.[18] On 21 December 1875, Judge Alexander White sentenced George Reynolds to two years of hard labor at the federal house of corrections in Detroit, Michigan, and to pay a five-hundred-dollar fine.[19] The "hard labor" penalty went beyond the full extent of the law, a judgment that undoubtedly pleased William Carey and Robert Baskin. In his last journal entry for 1875, Reynolds wrote in characteristic understatement, "This year has been one of the most eventful of my history."[20]

After the verdict was rendered but before the sentencing, Elder John Taylor respectfully took issue with Justice White regarding White's arguments on religious freedom and more particularly on comparing the evils of Hindu suttee with Mormon polygamy. "It is absurd to compare the suttee to polygamy; one is murder, the destruction of life; the other is national economy and the increase and perpetuation of life. Suttee ranks truly with *infanticide,* both of which are destructive of human life. *Polygamy* is salvation compared with either and tends, even more than monogamy, to increase and perpetuate the human race."[21]

George's appeal did not come before the Territorial Supreme Court until 13 June 1876. Meanwhile George was nominated by the People's Party caucus and elected to the Salt Lake City Council. ZCMI shareholders elected him as a director, and Brigham Young appointed him to handle business affairs while he went to Saint George, Utah, for his health.[22]

Reynolds v. United States was argued before three federally appointed justices of the Utah Territorial Supreme Court in the June term. After hearing arguments from both sides on 13 June, the Court sustained the guilty verdict. The bench ruled that Reynolds was not required to provide witnesses for the state, such as his second wife Amelia, but since he had tried to conceal her, her initial testimony could be admitted as evidence. Antipolygamy bias, typical of the United States at large, was also evident in the territorial supreme court. The original court was not held in error in explaining that polygamy was a crime, "especially too when we remember that this crime has a blighting and blasting influence upon the consciences of all who it touches, as is everyday and everywhere witnessed throughout the Territory."[23]

George Reynolds and his counsel appealed to the United States Supreme Court in October, but more than eighteen months passed before the case came up. During that time George remained close to Church affairs. When Brigham Young was in Salt Lake City, George was usually at his side. While President Young was staying in Utah's Dixie, he entrusted George with major business responsibilities. George accompanied the prophet on his last trip to Brigham City and on his last carriage trip. When Brigham died on 29 August 1877, George was at his bedside.

George Reynolds then became clerk to the Quorum of the Twelve Apostles.[24] This body led the Church until 1880 under the leadership of John Taylor, quorum president. George grew close to President Taylor, as he had to President Young. George continued other assignments: member of the city council, a director of ZCMI, regent of the University of Deseret, superintendent of the Twentieth Ward Sunday School, Deseret Sunday School Union treasurer, a director of the Deseret Telegraph Company, secretary to the board of Zion's Savings Bank and Trust Company, and *Omaha Bee* special correspondent. He resumed writing articles for Sunday School children in the *Juvenile Instructor.* At the October 1877 general conference, George was called as a home missionary, a calling that required him to address a different ward each Sunday.[25]

In his own home, George Reynolds presided over a young, rapidly growing plural marriage household. Each wife gave birth to two more children: Polly to Amy on 16 April 1876 and Eleanor (Nellie) on 21 September 1878, and Amelia to Marion (May) on 7 November 1876 and Charles (Charlie) on 6 June 1878. In all, eight young children were in the household: six girls and two boys. Four adults still lived in the home: George, his two wives, and his sister Julia. George wanted to build another house to divide the two families. He had the property but not the funds to construct the dwelling. And his complicated legal battles diverted his attention from his domestic needs.

Sickness also plagued the Reynolds household during this trying period. Little Florry was stricken with pneumonia during the 1875 court trials and did not grow properly during that period. In 1876 everyone in both families came down with serious coughs and colds. Polly suffered from inflammation of the womb and Amelia from inflammation of the bowels. Later the same year all the children caught the measles. This was not a time for optimism in the family. Then, during the height of their dismay in late summer, Polly rallied and became more healthy than she had ever been during her married life. The others also recovered, although Florry remained "quite delicate."[26]

In 1878 the children all contracted whooping cough and later scarlatina. In 1877 Amelia had a bout of rheumatism. In 1878 Polly had "dropsy" (swollen legs and feet caused by retaining too much water) during her pregnancy and severe pneumonia after the delivery. More than half the time there was some kind of serious sickness in the house.[27]

These difficulties did not hamper the intellectual development of the children, however. George was eager to give his children the best education available. He had enrolled Millie in Brigham Young's private school along with Young's children. This elite school employed private tutors from England.[28] When President Young died in 1877, the school was closed, but George worked relentlessly to provide his children with a strong education. Alice Louise recounted her first educational experiences:

> My first school was a private school, taught by Miss Izzie Calder, daughter of David O. Calder. I was only four years of age at that time [1877]. My father being English, believed that children might be sent to school very young if the right sort of training was given them. I was wheeled to school in a baby buggy by my mother's maid. This thing did not last very long, for I had only been in attendance three months when the teacher married, and that was the end of the school. Then I was at another private school taught by Hyrum Barton. Neither did this school last long, the only definite recollection I have of it is that the teacher took me in his buggy to see the circus. At six I started regularly to public school [the Twentieth Ward District School].[29]

The children received a first-rate education at the district school. Professor T. B. Lewis, a well-educated Virginian and one of Utah's most respected educators, was the teacher. Alice expressed her gratitude for the love of literature and good books instilled in her by Lewis. George Reynolds was not as pleased with the Twentieth Ward School after the departure of Professor Lewis in 1885.[30]

George's sister Julia took a major role in caring for the children during the 1870s. Alice Louise reminisced:

> My childhood was exceptionally happy for I had the constant care of my father's sister, Julia A. Reynolds, who lived in my mother's home for thirteen years before her marriage. My father's sister was very fond of children, and seemed to anticipate most of my wishes. Consequently, I spent much time roaming the hills, picking wild flowers, and watching city creek, in the Canyon, go bubbling down into the heart of Salt Lake. We always had in our home many house plants with which I was familiar.[31]

Alice's experiences were probably typical of those of the other children in the family during this period. Theirs was a loving home, but one under great stress from the drawn-out legal process leading to a momentous decision that would affect the future course of The Church of Jesus Christ of Latter-day Saints and America's doctrine of separation of church and state.

Notes

1. George Reynolds Journal, vol. 5, June 1875; *Salt Lake Daily Herald,* 20 June 1875, p. 3.

2. George Reynolds Journal, vol. 5, June 1875.

3. Ibid., July-August 1875.

4. Ibid., October-November 1875; Reynolds Case Papers.

5. George Reynolds Journal, vol. 5, November 1875.

6. Ibid.; *Salt Lake Daily Herald,* 24 November 1875, p. 3; seal of George Reynolds appointment to the Salt Lake City Council, Reynolds Collection, no. 11.

7. George Reynolds Journal, vol. 5, December 1875.

8. "Interview of W. Cox with George Reynolds," handwritten manuscript in Reynolds Collection, no. 25.

9. Reynolds Case Papers; *Salt Lake Daily Herald,* 10 December 1875, p. 3.

10. Reynolds Case Papers; *Salt Lake Daily Herald,* 11 December 1875, p. 3.

11. *Deseret Weekly News* 15 (December 1875): 732.

12. Ibid.

13. Ibid.

14. Ibid.

15. Ibid.; Reynolds Case Papers.

16. Ibid.

17. "Interview of W. Cox with George Reynolds."

18. Reynolds Case Papers; *Salt Lake Daily Herald,* 11 December 1875, p. 3.

19. George Reynolds Journal, vol. 5, December 1875; Third District Court, 21 December 1875, sentence of Alexander White upon George Reynolds, Reynolds Collection, no. 18.

20. George Reynolds Journal, vol. 5, December 1875.

21. *Salt Lake Daily Herald,* 19 December 1875, p. 4.

22. George Reynolds Journal, vol. 5, February to June 1875; election certificate of George Reynolds as director of ZCMI, 5 April 1876, Reynolds Collection, no. 23; election certificate of George Reynolds to City Council of Salt Lake City, 14 February 1876, Reynolds Collection, no. 17.

23. George Reynolds Journal, vol. 5, June 1876.

24. Ibid., 1877.

25. Ibid.; election certificate of George Reynolds to be director of Zion's Savings Bank and Trust Company, 29 July 1878, Reynolds Collection, no. 22; election certificate of George Reynolds to City Council of Salt Lake City, 14 February 1878, Reynolds Collection, no. 17.

26. George Reynolds Journal, vol. 5, 1875-76.

27. Ibid., 1877–79.
28. Interview with Emily Jensen, Provo, Utah, 29 November 1985.
29. Alice Louise Reynolds, "Autobiography of Alice Louise Reynolds," p. 2.
30. Amy Brown Lyman, *A Lighter of Lamps: The Life Story of Alice Louise Reynolds* (Provo, Utah: Alice Louise Reynolds Club, 1947), pp. 11–12, 15.
31. Ibid., p. 1.

CHAPTER 10

The Supreme Court Decides

GEORGE REYNOLDS EAGERLY AWAITED THE DAY HIS CASE WOULD reach the United States Supreme Court, as did the Church hierarchy. Surely, they thought, he would be vindicated, because the divinely inspired Constitution[1] guaranteed freedom of religious expression. The Supreme Court justices would not be as bigoted as Utah's federal appointees, they reasoned.[2]

In February 1878, the *Reynolds* case was unexpectedly advanced on the Supreme Court docket, being ruled a criminal case.[3] This event alarmed the members of the Quorum of the Twelve Apostles, presided over by President John Taylor. Elder George Q. Cannon, a member of the Twelve and also Utah Territory congressional delegate in Washington, wrote to President Taylor on 11 March, discussing possibilities of postponing the case. "The case is of such importance that we should do all in our power to carry it in our favor, and therefore we should have strong council."[4] Elder Cannon continued working for a delay to obtain competent eastern counsel. On 19 March, he informed President John Taylor that government officials, while respectful and polite, continued to press for a late March-early April trial in the new Supreme Court schedule. Elder Cannon also pointed out that first-class lawyers commanded "very large fees."[5]

On 29 March, the case was called up before the high court. The

United States solicitor general called for an early trial, but the court learned that the Reynolds people were unprepared and agreed to hear the case 15 October 1878.[6] George Q. Cannon employed George M. Biddle, from Philadelphia, as senior counsel and Benjamin Sheeks of Salt Lake City, a gentile who had assisted in the second trial, as junior counsel. Sheeks gathered the necessary Utah documents and prepared the argument's technical portions.[7]

On 7 April 1878 Elder Cannon made a fervent plea before the Twelve Apostles in behalf of the Reynolds cause. Elders Erastus Snow and Franklin D. Richards were thereupon appointed to see that legal technicalities of the case were attended to.[8]

In the intervening six months before his case came before the Supreme Court, George Reynolds's family suffered excessive ill health. George used some of his time to conduct research on the biblical history themes of the house of Israel and Abraham and his contemporaries. He desired to place a unique Latter-day Saint theological imprint on these two subjects. He noted in his journal that he studied outside "authorities" on these subjects. He prepared two series of articles for publication in the *Millennial Star,* entitled "Are We of Israel?" and "The Book of Abraham—Its Genuineness Established."[9] Thus, even as George Reynolds was gaining notoriety in America through his Supreme Court case, through his writings he was further establishing himself as one of the Church's well-known and trusted writers.

When 15 October finally arrived, eight of the nine members of the court were prepared to hear the famous polygamy case. Reynolds's senior attorney, George Biddle, wrote to Elder Cannon, "We found that Justice [Stephen J.] Field would be detained in California until the close of the month, and knowing his great ability and desiring his presence, and not wishing besides to run the risk of the judgement being affirmed by a divided court, we asked postponement of the case until judge Field should be present."[10] The case was thus postponed until 14 November. Arguments were heard over two days, 14 and 15 November 1878. The defense presented five arguments:

1. The grand jury that indicted Reynolds the second time consisted of fifteen persons when a new federal law required no more than twenty-three and no fewer than sixteen.

2. The trial jury was not impartially selected.

3. The testimony of Reynolds's second wife, Amelia Schofield Reynolds, from the first trial was improperly admitted into evidence.

4. Reynolds should have been acquitted; he married the second time out of religious duty.

5. The court erred by improperly charging the jury on the consequences of polygamy.[11]

Chief Justice Morrison R. Waite's papers reveal that in a private preliminary vote on 16 November, five justices voted to uphold Reynolds's conviction, while four, including the chief justice, disagreed. Waite indicated that "it is almost certain that the four votes to reverse cast on November 16 were motivated by doubts that the Reynolds trial had violated federal law."[12] But, by the time Waite issued his now famous official opinion on 6 January 1879, the justices had resolved their doubts and the vote was unanimous against Reynolds.

In Chief Justice Waite's lengthy and classic decision, he paid little attention to the defense's issues, but chose, instead, to speak primarily to the First Amendment issue of religious freedom. He held that marriage is a relationship created, regulated, and protected by civil authority. Since the monogamous family was the basis of western societal life, the government had the power to preserve this system by prohibiting polygamy. Polygamy had always been viewed as an "odious" practice among northern and western Europeans and was almost exclusively a practice of backward Asian and African civilizations. That the defendant's religious convictions required him to practice polygamy no more immunized him from the operation of the law than would a person's religious belief in human sacrifice immunize him from the operation of the laws against homicide. According to Waite, to permit religious beliefs to justify polygamy would be to make the professed doctrines of religious belief superior to the supreme law of the land—the Constitution—and would, in effect, permit every citizen to become a law unto himself. Since the Constitution did not recognize a higher authority than itself, neither would the court.

Waite cited Thomas Jefferson as his authority on the proper exercise of religion. Jefferson wrote that government had the right to rule against religious expression if it resulted in "overt acts against peace and good order." Waite considered polygamy to be "subversive of good order and a violation of one's social duties."[13] Waite's handling of the religious question was influenced by the opinions and research of his close friend and prominent period historian George Bancroft.[14]

Robert G. Dyer, a present-day attorney, has argued that the high court allowed itself to be swayed by popular opinion and prevailing social attitudes when it ruled that polygamy was an "odious" institution instead of referring to "detailed social science and psychological studies that often accompany briefs today."[15]

The major eastern newspapers strongly favored the Supreme Court's decision. The *New York Times* called the Reynolds decision "a decided victory" and a "great gain" for the nation. The *New York Tribune* branded polygamy an "abomination" that "stands on the same level with murder."[16]

Leaders of the Mormon community at first reacted with horror. Elder Cannon wrote to President Taylor that the Supreme Court justices "appear willing to leave us to our fate, or the fate our enemies would mete out to us. Now it is up to the Lord to preserve us."[17]

A federal official, O. J. Hollister, asked President John Taylor if perpetuation of polygamy was worth the continued antagonism. President Taylor replied, "Our revelation given in August, 1831, specifically states that if we keep the laws of God we need not break the laws of the land. Congress has since, by this act placed us in an antagonism to what we term an unconstitutional law, and now it becomes a question of whether we should obey God or man."[18] The implication was clear that President Taylor and the Church would obey God.

Eliza R. Snow sarcastically wrote in the *Deseret Evening News:* "Let us chase thousands of honorable, loving wives to be stigmatized as prostitutes, and their offspring as bastards. Let us immure in prisons those brave men, who, for the sake of worshipping God according to the dictates of their own conscience, left their homes and graves of their noble ancestors, and sought refuge in the sterile American Desert."[19] In an interview with an eastern reporter, George Reynolds responded, "I regard [the decision] a nullification of the Constitution, so far as religious liberty is concerned. To say the Constitution simply grants freedom of religious opinion but not the exercise of that opinion is twaddle." He added, "I should never have taken a second wife had I not considered that in so doing I was obeying a law of God, which I could not evade without just condemnation."[20]

The Saints gradually returned to their normal lives. In a letter to the English Saints, Mormon journalist John Jaques reported:

> There is no particular excitement in this city. Of course the people are not oblivious to passing events, nor insensible to the importance of that decision, and its possible influence upon them, and upon the country at large. But there is no uncommon excitement. Most of the people know well that God has overruled many times in the past, and that they readily and calmly trust in Him to do the same in future exigencies, should any arise.[21]

But what of George Reynolds? The Supreme Court had not responded to the issuance of his two-year sentence of hard labor. On 20 January 1879, Biddle, Reynolds's eastern attorney, filed a petition for a rehearing, on grounds that the sentence included "hard labor," which exceeded the law and the authority of the judge.[22] The Supreme Court did not consider setting aside the verdict but eventually ruled on 5 May 1879 that the Utah territorial supreme court should set aside the sentence and establish a new one.

Meanwhile, in Washington, D.C., George Q. Cannon was laboring on two projects—a scholarly rejoinder to the *Reynolds* decision[23] and an organized campaign to urge President Rutherford B. Hayes to pardon Reynolds. Cannon wrote John Taylor on 7 March that he had had an interview with President Hayes and had outlined the Reynolds case. President Hayes took careful notes and appeared concerned. Elder Cannon explained to him: "While I had no wish to go to prison, I would almost as soon go myself, in view of what I had done to get Bro. Reynolds to submit to be the test case, as to have him go."[24]

When Elder Cannon returned in April for general conference, he collected a "monster petition" asking President Hayes to pardon Reynolds on the grounds that his was a test case. Two petitions were circulated: a general one to the public and another one to mayors, city councilors, and judges throughout Utah Territory. In all, 31,168 people signed the general petition and 922 signed the official petition. Both were forwarded to Cannon in late May.[25] A counter petition was circulated by the gentile ring. Regarding the latter, an angry editorial in the *Millennial Star* stated, "Inspired by the diabolical passion of religious hate, [the counter-petitioners] malignantly desire that a conscientious man . . . should be afflicted with pains and penalties."[26]

In May, Reynolds wrote William Carey, requesting him to share his affidavit that the case was a test case. Reynolds recorded the following regarding Carey's response: "In his letter he denies that the case was a test case, ignores the fact that I supplied the witnesses, and actually states that he could not give the affadivit because it would not be true. Mr Carey is a coward and a liar."[27] While understandably upset with Carey, Reynolds did not mention that he himself discouraged the test case idea initially.

On 5 June, Cannon presented the petitions to President Hayes, who responded kindly and said such a petition deserved his attention.[28] Although considerate to Cannon, like most other Republican Party leaders, Hayes was an inveterate enemy of Mormon theocracy and polygamy. For example, six months later, in a diary entry dated

13 January 1880, Hayes wrote, "Now the Territory [of Utah] is virtually under the theocratic government of the Mormon Church. The union of Church and State is complete. The result is the usual one—the usurpation or absorption of all temporal authority and power by the Church. Polygamy and every other evil sanctioned by the Church is safe. To destroy the temporal power of the Mormon Church is the end in view. This requires agitation. The people of the United States must be made to appreciate, to understand the situation."[29]

On 13 June 1879, President Hayes's cabinet met in Washington to discuss the Reynolds situation. Four cabinet members were against the pardon and three favored it. One member argued that since Reynolds employed every known means to break the prosecution and cause government expense in securing his ultimate conviction, he should suffer the law's full penalty. General administration policy toward polygamy was also considered. The president decided during the meeting not to issue the pardon.[30] The next day the Utah supreme court issued a corrected two-year sentence, meaning no hard labor, and a five-hundred-dollar fine. George Reynolds's fate as a prisoner was fixed.

In the more than one hundred years since the *Reynolds* decision, this case has remained a basic guide for understanding the First Amendment's free exercise clause, but the interpretation has been significantly qualified. In fact, the critical element in *Reynolds*—the distinction between action and belief as a test for First Amendment protection—has been largely amended. Since the *Wisconsin v. Yoder* case (1972), which ruled that the Amish have a right to educate their children apart from public education, "courts require the law to survive a strict balancing test in which the state interest must be of sufficient magnitude to override the interest claiming protection under the free exercise clause." Genuine religious conduct must now be afforded state deference. The government must demonstrate compelling evidence that serious social injury is caused by religious practice. Hence, under current Supreme Court rationale, for George

Reynolds to have been convicted, the state would have had to prove conclusively that polygamy caused great harm to society.[31]

In a late twentieth-century legal case, and one that referred to *Reynolds,* Royston Potter was fired from the Murray, Utah, police department following his polygamous marriage to a second wife in 1980. Potter's was one of approximately ten thousand families in Utah in which the father was polygamous. He sought reinstatement to the police force on grounds that the city was violating his First Amendment rights to practice his religious beliefs, although The Church of Jesus Christ of Latter-day Saints had excommunicated Potter for practicing polygamy. The Denver 10th United States Circuit Court of Appeals upheld Potter's dismissal, thus upholding Utah's antipolygamy law. In October 1985, the United States Supreme Court refused to hear Potter's case, denying a chance for *Reynolds* to be overturned. Hence *Reynolds* still governs in related cases.[32]

George Reynolds's name is remembered, if for no other reason than that he was the defendant in such a landmark Supreme Court decision. George would have preferred otherwise. He never sought nor enjoyed the limelight. But he was also willing to suffer any indignity or sacrifice to help move forward the cause of Zion. Now he was required to go to prison as the sacrificial lamb of Mormonism.

Notes

1. Doctrine and Covenants 101:77, 80.
2. George Reynolds Journal, vol. 5, 27 October 1878.
3. Ibid., February 1878.
4. As cited in ibid.
5. As cited in ibid., March 1878.
6. Ibid.
7. Ibid.
8. Ibid., April 1878.
9. Ibid., 1878; see Appendix A under *Millennial Star* for publication information on these series.
10. As cited in ibid.
11. "The Reynolds Case, Supreme Court of the United States, No. 180 – October Term, 1878, George Reynolds, Plaintiff in Error, vs. The United States," a pamphlet in Special Collections, Harold B. Lee Library, Brigham Young University, Provo, Utah.

12. C. Peter Magrath, "Chief Justice Waite and the 'Twin Relic': *Reynolds v. the United States,*" *Vanderbilt Law Review* 18 (1965): 523.

13. Reynolds Supreme Court Case.

14. Magrath, "Chief Justice Waite and the 'Twin Relic,' " pp. 525–27. Ironically, the most influential associate justice of the Supreme Court for this period, Stephen J. Field, agreed with Waite's interpretation of freedom of religion. Field became renowned during the 1870s for advocating natural law and natural rights and declaring that the inalienable rights mentioned in the Declaration of Independence had been incorporated into the Constitution by means of the Fourteenth Amendment.

15. Robert G. Dyer, "The Evolution of Social and Judicial Attitudes towards Polygamy," *Utah Bar Journal* 5 (Spring 1977): 35–45.

16. See James L. Clayton, "The Supreme Court, Polygamy and Enforcement of Morals in Nineteenth Century America: An Analysis of *Reynolds v. United States,*" *Dialogue* 12 (Winter 1979): 54.

17. As cited in ibid., p. 53. See also Richard S. Van Wagoner, *Mormon Polygamy: A History* (Salt Lake City: Signature Books, 1986), pp. 111–12, 249.

18. "Interview with John Taylor and O. J. Hollister in the President's Office 13 June 1879," pamphlet in Special Collections, Harold B. Lee Library.

19. *Deseret Evening News,* 21 January 1879, p. 2.

20. "Interview of W. Cox with George Reynolds," handwritten manuscript in Reynolds Collection, no. 25.

21. "Correspondence," *Millennial Star* 41 (3 May 1879): 142–43.

22. Junius F. Wells, "A Living Martyr," *Contributor* 2 (February 1881): 155.

23. George Q. Cannon, *A Review of the Decision of the Supreme Court in the Case of Geo. Reynolds vs. the United States* (Salt Lake City: Deseret News Printing and Publishing Establishment, 1879).

24. As cited in George Reynolds Journal, vol. 5, March 1879.

25. Ibid., vol. 5, May 1879; Wells, "A Living Martyr," p. 155; petition to President Hayes, 14 May 1879, Reynolds Collection, no. 24.

26. "The Petition for Clemency," *Millennial Star* 41 (16 June 1879): 378.

27. George Reynolds Journal, vol. 5, June 1879.

28. George Q. Cannon to John Taylor, 5 June 1879, cited in ibid.

29. Charles R. Williams, *The Life of Rutherford Birchard Hayes,* 2 vols. (New York: Da Capo Press, 1971), 2:225.

30. George Reynolds Journal, vol. 5, June 1879; Christian August Madsen to George Reynolds, 21 June 1879, Reynolds Collection, no. 14; *Omaha Bee,* 14 June 1879, p. 2.

31. Edwin Brown Firmage and Richard Collin Mangrum provided a thorough summary of "the legal contributions of *Reynolds*" in their *Zion and the Courts: A Legal History of The Church of Jesus Christ of Latter-day Saints, 1830– 1900* (Urbana, Ill.: University of Illinois Press, 1989), pp. 151–59. See also Jeremy M. Miller, "A Critique of the Reynolds Decision," *Western State University Law Review* 11 (Spring 1984): 165–98, and Richard S. Van Wagoner, *Mormon Polygamy: A History* (Salt Lake City: Signature Books, 1986), pp. 221–22.

32. Van Wagoner, *Mormon Polygamy,* pp. 219–20; *The [Provo, Utah] Herald,* 8 October 1985, p. 5.

CHAPTER 11

Prisoner for Conscience' Sake

JOHN TAYLOR, GEORGE Q. CANNON, AND OTHERS OF THE CHURCH hierarchy felt deep sorrow that their friend George Reynolds would be required to suffer in prison. They were certain that he would be pardoned or released early and not have to serve the full two years of his sentence, but they also believed that his sacrifice would benefit the entire Church. Throughout his eighteen-month incarceration, George was recognized by other Latter-day Saints as a "living martyr to the cause of Zion" who served as "a representative prisoner suffering for the conscientious faith of the whole people." The Morrill Act, under which he had been indicted, posed little legal threat to his brethren: the law required proof of a second marriage, and federal officers found witnesses scarce indeed among the Saints. Most Mormons believed that once the *Reynolds* case was over and George had successfully sacrificed himself for the sake of the kingdom, there would be few, if any, further prosecutions for polygamy.[1]

Throughout George's imprisonment, Congressional delegate George Q. Cannon worked tirelessly to commute or reduce his two-year sentence. At length an act of Congress reduced his sentence by six months. The Church provided George's family with every needful resource in his absence; in fact, his family members realized that they would not "fare as well" financially after his eventual release.[2] Moreover, the Utah Sunday School children donated nickels to pay George's five-hundred-dollar fine.

Church members, especially children, offered regular prayers in his behalf during worship services. Leading Church and community officials visited George frequently after he returned to Utah to complete his sentence in the Territorial Penitentiary. He also received countless encouraging letters from friends and admirers. When he was released in January 1881, George was hailed as a returning champion and honored with reporting his "mission" in the Assembly Hall on Temple Square.

Despite attempts by the Church and its members to mitigate the severity of George's confinement, prison life for him was not an easy cross to bear. His family missed him, and several family members, including his first wife, Polly, suffered from ill health. Two of his children died during his imprisonment. George himself endured primitive and extremely unpleasant conditions in the vermin-infested Utah penitentiary in Sugar House, four miles from the heart of Salt Lake City. Ironically, George suffered worse conditions in the penitentiary in Utah than he did in Nebraska. In the long run, however, George's stint as the sacrificial lamb for the Church firmly entrenched him as a hero among the Latter-day Saints and helped set the stage for further service in the Church he loved.

As soon as it was obvious that George would not be pardoned by United States President Rutherford B. Hayes, Church head John Taylor directed on 14 June 1879 that George instruct L. John Nuttall in the responsibilities of chief secretary in the Office of the President.[3] George's association with Nuttall, begun under such unhappy circumstances, remained close throughout the rest of their lives. Later the same day President Taylor and Elder Franklin D. Richards of the Quorum of the Twelve laid their hands on Reynolds's head and pronounced a blessing upon him:

> Bro. George Reynolds, in the name of Jesus Christ and by authority of the Holy Priesthood, we lay our hands upon thy head

to bless thee under the peculiar circumstances under which thou art placed at the present time, having offered up thyself as a substitute of the Church of Jesus Christ of Latter-day Saints in this test case.... We bless thee and ask our Heavenly Father to cause his Holy Spirit may rest upon thee to enlighten thee and enlighten us and all who are interested in the interests of the church and kingdom of God and pertaining to those great revelations which he has given to us for our guidance in our social relations.... That thou mayest have dreams and visions and the manifestations of the Spirit of the Lord to be with thee daily, and that thou mayest feel to rejoice that thou has been accounted worthy to place thyself in jeopardy because of the wickedness and corruption of the world (being in conflict with the laws of God).... And set thee apart to this office, as a sacrifice in behalf of Israel.[4]

Some of the promised blessings came during George's prison stay.

After spending a last Sunday on his own recognizance with his family (some of the rabid anti-Mormons had demanded that he be put in chains until Monday), George bade his saddened family farewell early on Monday morning, 16 June. His household consisted of Polly and her five children, Amelia and her three children, his sister Julia, and his brother Charles. By this time George had added two rooms to the back of the house for Amelia and her children, but obviously there was still insufficient room for such a large household. Sadly George trudged alone the mile to the Union Pacific depot, arriving at 7:00 A.M.[5]

George surrendered himself to two federal marshals at the depot. A large group of Saints gathered to send him off "with a hearty God bless you."[6] Then, in special sleeping berths provided by his bishop, John W. Sharp, who was the Utah superintendent of the Union Pacific Railroad, George and the two federal marshals began their comparatively pleasant journey to the Nebraska State Penitentiary in Lincoln, where he had been ordered by the United States Department of Justice and where federal prisoners from the territories were housed. George wrote to his loved ones from railroad stops in Cheyenne and Omaha. Several newspaper reporters interviewed him in

Omaha about his recent Supreme Court case. George also wrote his friend John Nicholson, then serving as assistant editor of the *Millennial Star* in Liverpool: "I am here in Omaha, a prisoner, bereft of liberty for Christ's sake. The issue is direct; for it is for obeying what I most assuredly know to be a revelation from God," he explained. "I feel proud (not too proud, I trust,) and happy to think that I have been deemed worthy to represent His word and will in this important particular."[7] The prisoner arrived at the Nebraska State Prison on the outskirts of Lincoln on 19 June 1879.

Prison officials took George to a room for a bath at once. They took all his possessions from him and gave him a prison suit, consisting of a striped tick shirt, a pair of shoes, a cap, and a striped jacket and pants. Reynolds bemoaned, "I had not a stitch or a thread to remind me of home." But he received his worst indignity when at the cellhouse a barber shingled his hair and cut off his beard.[8]

Rules were strict, and life was difficult in Lincoln. Letters could be written only once every two weeks and then only to family. Inmates were not allowed paper and pencil in their cells, a situation that was greatly disappointing to him. No prisoner was allowed to talk outside of his cell, not even to the guard, without permission. At six each morning officials marched the prisoners out of their cells, each man placing his right hand on the shoulder of the man in front of him, closing up as near as possible and keeping his eyes to the left. In this manner the inmates were marched around the food table and back to their cells where they ate their food in solitude. The same process was repeated for lunch and supper. Each prisoner was assigned to a branch of work that he pursued for ten hours a day, so George was grateful to be assigned as a bookkeeper for the foreman of the prison knitting shop. On Sundays the prisoners stayed in their cells most of the day, except when they attended an abbreviated Episcopal service in the prison chapel. "Its brevity is its great excellence in the eyes of the convicts," George reported.[9]

Shortly after George was settled in Lincoln, he reported to his family, "Yesterday I was made very happy by receiving my garments.[10] I feel myself again now; it is no part of the policy of the prison to interfere with a man's religion." George also indicated that he was treated with respect as long as he abided the prison rules. Since he could write only once every two weeks, he asked that his two families pass his letter around and then show it to President John Taylor and other authorities. In this letter he also apparently coined a phrase that for the next ten years was used as a refrain by future Mormon polygamous prisoners: "Be assured there are many worse places in the world than in prison *for conscience' sake.* It cannot take away the peace which reigns in my heart." But he added, "The day of deliverance, however soon it may come, will be gladly welcomed, with exceeding joy."[11]

Time passed slowly for George in Nebraska, but he felt that he was treated fairly there. "I will say that I never had a word of derision or contempt offered to me from anyone, from the time I left Utah to the time I returned," he told John Nicholson. "One gentleman, as I left the prison, told me that though I had been a prisoner in their charge there was none of them that could regard me as a criminal." George left a good impression with the foreman at the knitting shop, for during the time he was in the prison in Lincoln he straightened out the man's books and accounted for the finances to the moment he left.[12]

Reynolds received numerous letters from family, friends, and general authorities, and lamented that he could not return the favor. In the letters he was allowed to write to his family, he reported his own good health, his homesickness for his family, and his confidence that there was a "bright side" to his confinement. He asked how the new kitchen was working and how the summer garden was progressing.

During the first week of George's confinement, United States Attorney General Charles Devens, who was personally vindictive toward the Mormons, nearly sent George to the federal prison in Detroit, Michigan. But through the efforts of George Q. Cannon, Reynolds was assigned to spend the remainder of his prison term

97

in the Utah Territorial Penitentiary.[13] George's stay in Lincoln, Nebraska, lasted only one month.

He wrote and urged his family to meet him at Ogden and take with them portraits of all the family members to help him recollect the children through his extended stay in the Utah penitentiary.[14] Accordingly they met at the Ogden depot the afternoon of 17 July 1879. Bishop Sharp had sent a special railroad car to carry George's family and friends to collect him. It was a bittersweet reunion because some of the younger children did not recognize their father without his beard. "I don't wonder at it," he remarked. "The lower part of my face is marked with much stronger lines than I expected. Florry [five years old] was very distant. She was very anxious to see her Pa, but when she did see him he did not look like the Pa she expected."[15] Reynolds was taken that same evening to the Utah Penitentiary, usually referred to as the "Pen," at Sugar House, some five miles from the Reynolds residence on the north bench of the city.

During the summer the federal government attempted to transfer him back to Lincoln. On 16 August 1879, about a month after he arrived in Utah, he received a copy of the *Omaha Bee,* for which he had been an occasional contributing correspondent. The newspaper stated that President Hayes and his cabinet had decided to send him back to Lincoln on the grounds that he was only nominally imprisoned in Utah, that he often went home to see his family, and that he rode around town with the federal marshal.[16] Apparently the Hayes administration believed these false rumors from Utah. Major Willard Chase, the government prison inspector from the Justice Department, was sent to investigate before sending Reynolds back to Nebraska. The United States marshal and the Utah prison warden, annoyed at the rumors, gave affidavits to Chase that Reynolds had never been home and had not been driven around town, which was the truth.

Chase made two visits, one in late August and another in late September to check on the visits Reynolds was receiving. Because of Chase's report and the work of George Q. Cannon in Washington, Reynolds was allowed to stay in Utah. George concluded that it would be wiser to receive fewer visitors than before and noted, "All that can truthfully be said about me is that I have seen more visitors than the other prisoners, but the visits of my friends have been strictly under the prison regulations, and if any other man in this penitentiary had as many friends to come see him as I have, they would have had the privilege of seeing him."[17]

For three weeks in August 1879, George was joined by three other Mormon notables in the territorial prison. Judge Jacob Boremen, who, like Judge McKean, used his position on the bench to crusade against polygamy and theocracy, ordered George Q. Cannon, Albert Carrington, and Brigham Young, Jr., to the penitentiary on charges of contempt of court relating to their acting as executors of the Brigham Young estate. While in prison, these brethren, especially Cannon, continued to conduct Church business. The outgoing Cannon seemed to enjoy himself as he entertained many visitors and responded to inmate requests to "preach to the spirits in prison."[18] On 28 August the Utah Supreme Court overturned Boreman's order and released the three. George Reynolds settled back into the sameness of his routine at the Pen.

Notes

1. Junius F. Wells, "A Living Martyr," *Contributor* 2 (February 1881): 154; George Reynolds Journal, vol. 5, June 1875; Alice Louise Reynolds, "Biography of George Reynolds," pp. 18–19.

2. A. L. Reynolds, "Biography," p. 19.

3. L. John Nuttall Journal, typescript, 4 vols., vol. 1, p. 198, in Special Collections, Harold B. Lee Library.

4. George Reynolds Journal, vol. 5, June 1879.

5. George Reynolds Journal, vol. 5, June 1879.

6. L. John Nuttall Journal, vol. 1, pp. 299–300.

7. "Imprisoned for Conscience' Sake," *Millennial Star* 41 (14 July 1879): 444.

8. George Reynolds to his family, 22 June 1879, in George Reynolds Journal, vol. 5, June 1879.

9. "Correspondence," *Millennial Star* 41 (18 August 1879): 518; *Biennial Report of the Warden of the Nebraska State Penitentiary for 1879 and 1880* (Lincoln,

Neb.: Journal Company, 1881), pp. 47–63, in the Nebraska State Historical Society, Lincoln, Nebraska.

10. "Garments" refer to the underclothing worn by faithful Mormons after participating in temple rites.

11. George Reynolds to his family, 22 June 1879; italics added.

12. "Correspondence," *Millennial Star* 41 (18 August 1879): 518.

13. L. John Nuttall Journal, vol. 1, pp. 300, 303–4, 312; George Reynolds Journal, vol. 5, June 1879; "Imprisoned for Conscience' Sake," p. 445.

14. George Reynolds Journal, vol. 5, June-July 1879.

15. "Correspondence," *Millennial Star* 41 (18 August 1879): 518; L. John Nuttall Journal, vol. 1, p. 312.

16. George Reynolds Journal, vol. 5, 16 August 1879.

17. "Correspondence," *Millennial Star* 41 (29 September 1879): 621; "Correspondence," *Millennial Star* 41 (20 October 1879): 668.

18. Richard S. Van Wagoner and Steven C. Walker, *A Book of Mormons* (Salt Lake City: Signature Books, 1986), p. 52; George Reynolds Journal, vol. 5, August 1879.

CHAPTER 12

Life in the "Pen"

CONDITIONS AT THE PENITENTIARY WERE FAR FROM PLEASANT. FOR the first four months of George Reynolds's confinement, the prisoners were kept in iron cages until a lumber bunkhouse was completed. Even when that was finished, there were still many cracks between the boards. The summer of 1879 was hot, dry, and dusty. The Jordan River was at its lowest known point since 1847. "One's eyes are begrimed with dust, mouth parched, nostrils choked up, clothes and body coated, whilst the face and hands tingle and smart as shower after shower of grit and small pebbles are blown against them," George recorded. "At those times reading is a vexation, and writing twice as bad; sleep is out of the question, and walking a laborious perplexity."[1]

The winter of 1879–80 in Utah was also severe. The thermometer dipped to thirty degrees below zero Fahrenheit during the Christmas season. No fire was permitted, for fear that prisoners might burn down the building. Although he was supplied with plenty of bed clothing and blankets by his friends, he still suffered from the bitter cold. Frequently morning found his beard, now regrown, frozen into a solid mass of ice. As the weather finally grew warmer, George recorded in his journal that the winter was "generally observed to be the longest and most disagreeable winter ever experienced in Utah."[2]

George soon became accustomed to the prison routine in the Pen and tried to make the best of it. Unlike in the Nebraska prison, there were generally no work projects for the prisoners in Utah. George quickly got into the daily habit of reading and answering letters, exercising, reading in the scriptures, and writing articles for Church periodicals. He kept a daily account of who visited him and to whom he wrote letters. Prison food, principally bread and beef, was monotonous and poorly cooked. Friends and family supplied Reynolds with delicacies to relieve the monotony of prison fare.

In his frequent letters to his families and in his journal George faithfully reported the state of his health. During the first summer his health improved somewhat from being in the open air. He admitted, however, that outdoor life made him sleepy and, in his view, lazy. But laziness to the diligent workaholic was failing to do something productive for perhaps an hour or two. Beginning in the fall of 1879 George experienced tooth problems. Many of his teeth were pulled while he was in prison. George wryly noted the "first class tooth puller" who was employed at the Pen: "He's always nigh, nigh at hand."[3] George also complained of being "bilious," meaning that he was suffering from stomach disorders or irregularity. Once, because of food poisoning, all the prisoners suffered from the "skitters." George had to get up only twice in the night; the others were worse off. He also suffered an occasional sty on one of his eyes from the dust storms.[4] George was careful to guard his good health and usually got plenty of sleep. According to his journal, his worst month for health was December 1880, his next-to-last month in confinement.

Some believed that he physically suffered unduly in prison, but the existing evidence indicates that other than losing so many teeth, he suffered no worse ill health at this time than he had in the years that preceded or followed his stay in prison. His severe health problems twenty-four years later cannot be traced directly to his prison experience. Indeed, George's only complaint, and it was infrequent and mildly stated, was the monotony he had to endure in the Pen.

On average, fifty prisoners were held in the Utah penitentiary at that time. The ranks swelled manyfold during the next decade when hundreds of George's compatriots followed him as prisoners for conscience' sake. Some of his fellow prisoners became interested in his good advice and example. Beginning on 16 March 1880 a prison school was established with George as the teacher. Even with the continual difficulty of bad weather, he taught reading, writing, arithmetic, grammar, and geography to the men. Those prisoners who were considered wild avoided engaging in their propensities in the presence of George Reynolds. The prison warden stated, "Reynolds was worth more than all the guards in preserving good order among the prisoners."[5]

George maintained a positive and even, at times, humorous attitude about his confinement. In a letter to John Nicholson, he quipped:

> An acre of bare ground, enclosed by four adobe walls is the limit of my present "paradise." (Paradise must here be understood to mean not only for spirits but also for bodies.) Its pleasures are those which each man brings with him, and as Zion is "the pure in heart," and "a contented mind is a continual feast," so, it is a Zion blessed with a continual flow of good things to those only who bear that spirit with them.

George also told Nicholson that he was doing as much good in prison as elsewhere, "preaching a sermon in a somewhat strange manner."[6]

The privilege of seeing his family and many friends did much to mitigate the distress of confinement. He recorded in his journal every visitor that came to see him. In the second half of 1879 (having come to the Utah penitentiary on 17 July of that year) he was visited nearly every day by someone, frequently by from five to ten people. Through 1880 the number of visitors tapered off to about half. He expressed his disappointment in his letters to his family on the days when no visitors came. His journal reveals his disappointment — when no letters arrived or no visitors were received, a long slash was entered in the empty space.

103

In addition to his immediate family, visitors included his in-laws; his siblings who were in America; Twentieth Ward members; friends from the mission field and from his early days in England; Sunday School groups from various wards; such government officials as Territorial Governor George W. Emery, Major Willard Chase from the Department of Justice, and Salt Lake civic officials; workers in the Church offices; leading Mormon women; his bishop, John Sharp; his stake president, Angus Cannon; newspapermen such as Charles Penrose; and numerous Church authorities. Nearly all the members of the Quorum of the Twelve Apostles, including President John Taylor before he was sustained as president of the Church in 1880, visited him, some of them many times. These visitors never failed to assure him that he was often in their thoughts and prayers and that his sacrifice for the rest of Zion was appreciated. On 27 May 1880, Wilford Woodruff, Charles C. Rich, and Erastus Snow left Church headquarters and rode out to the penitentiary to visit their friend, but the goodwill of the visit was clouded by a rumor that Elder Woodruff had been taken to the prison by force.[7] George especially remembered the visit of Church Patriarch John Smith on 13 June 1880 to give him a blessing.[8]

George kept a thorough record of the letters he wrote and the correspondence he received. He repeatedly told members of his family how he longed for their letters and said in a letter to the *Millennial Star:* "Solomon wrote, 'As cold waters to a thirsty soul, so is good news from a far country' (Prov. xxv, 25). If you were in prison you would know Solomon was right. Believe my testimony and write often."[9]

Many of the letters Reynolds received in prison have been preserved. They reveal a sensitivity and a sympathy for the prisoner's plight and a desire to encourage him. While still in Nebraska, George received a tender letter from President John Taylor, urging him to be of good cheer and reminding him that he was continually in the remembrance of the brethren.[10] An example of feelings expressed in letters from close friends is from Bishop Christian August Madsen from Gunnison, Utah:

> The Comforter, I believe, had administered of its most sublime enjoyments inside prison walls. If they had comprehension and could speak, they might say: We can do nothing with George Reynolds, he is outside of our jurisdiction, notwithstanding it appears as if we held him in our grasp. . . .
>
> May the God of Heaven fill you with joy and delight, in your confinement, and your heavenly associates administer to you.[11]

At the end of George's confinement, Bishop Madsen wrote, "In regard to your memory, I hope that your prison life shall not affect you any more than a passing shudder once in a while."[12]

George Teasdale, a future apostle engaged at the time in Church railroad business in Nephi, wrote:

> I do not think there is a man in Israel for whom prayer is offered up, that receives more fervent prayers offered up for him than yourself. In our Sabbath School, our primers where the sweet prayer of purity and innocence is uttered, you are remembered and fervent blessings are invoked upon yourself and your family. I heard a lady remark the other day, she was sure that Brother Reynolds was blessed because of the fervent prayers of her dear [Sunday School] children.[13]

One thing can be said with certainty about George Reynolds and his confinement in prison: he was disciplined in his use of time. On most days of his imprisonment, except when prevented by adverse weather or health conditions or severe family disruptions such as the death of two of his children, George busied himself with a reading or writing project. Through the last two decades of the nineteenth century, Church members recognized him as one of its leading scriptural authorities. The mass of his published writings on scriptural themes drawn from the Old and New Testaments, the Book of Mormon, the Doctrine and Covenants, and the Pearl of Great Price, is mind-boggling.[14]

105

No other Latter-day Saint writer of the nineteenth century wrote as much commentary on specific scriptural subjects as George Reynolds. From his teenage years onward he had been interested in getting to the bottom of questions related to scripture, including questions about history, biography, chronology, and geography as well as doctrine. But not until his imprisonment does it appear that he had sufficient time to formulate many of his ideas in writing and then see them into publication.

During the early part of his confinement, George usually read one or two whole books of scripture (such as Numbers or the Epistle of James) daily. His surviving records reveal that he read the Doctrine and Covenants during his stay in the Nebraska prison. In the Utah penitentiary he commenced the Old Testament, leaping through the books at the rate of two or three per day. He did not necessarily read the books in the order of their appearance in the Old Testament, but he finished them all in twenty-six days. With an eye to writing a series of articles for the *Juvenile Instructor,* he next began reading the Book of Mormon, which he finished in thirty-nine days. His "slowness" can be attributed to his writing many articles for publication concurrently. The following week he studied the Pearl of Great Price and moved on to the New Testament. He then returned to the Doctrine and Covenants as well as reading some theological works of earlier Latter-day Saint writers. By the time he began teaching the other prisoners in March 1880, he had read through all the standard works and was rereading portions again.

George Reynolds's writings on the Book of Mormon, begun in the penitentiary, gradually became a hallmark of his ministry. Before becoming a prisoner, George had not written on Book of Mormon themes but had confined himself to Bible stories and doctrines. His early writings reflected the general Church disposition toward using the Bible more than the Book of Mormon. Throughout the pre-Utah period, the Bible was preferred in Church literature to the Book of Mormon in a ratio of nineteen to one. That general trend continued for several decades following the Saints' settlement in the Great Basin.[15]

Elder George Q. Cannon had appointed George chairman of publications for the Deseret Sunday School Union before his incarceration. The two men recognized the need for more Book of Mormon instruction for the Church's youth; so while in prison George researched and then wrote about the Book of Mormon's contents. Coincidentally, not long after arriving in prison, he received Orson Pratt's 1879 edition of the Book of Mormon, which was divided into more chapters than had existed in previous editions and, for the first time, was further divided into verses. Elder Pratt supplied numerous footnotes for cross-referencing. Reynolds was thrilled with what he saw. To the British Saints he exclaimed, "It is wonderful to me how much more interesting the study of the Book of Mormon has become since it has been divided into chapters and verses. I seem to get hold of the sense so much better than when it was in such long paragraphs."[16]

While in prison George also began his pathbreaking study of the origins of words and names in the Book of Mormon, which he later incorporated in his writings. His scientist friend Joseph Barfoot assisted him. George learned from Barfoot of recent "important discoveries" of a German professor linking the ancient South American language Ayamara to Hebrew and Arabic.[17]

His first article on the Book of Mormon, "The Zoramites," appeared in the *Juvenile Instructor,* in the 1 December 1879 issue, five months after his arrival at the Utah penitentiary. Over the next thirteen months, George submitted twenty-one additional articles on Book of Mormon history to the same publication. Titles included "Personal Appearance of the Nephites," "Agriculture among the Nephites," "Domestic Life among the Nephites," "Lands of the Nephites," "Proper Names of the Nephites," and "Science and Literature among the Nephites." He cited page numbers in the 1879 edition for the reader's benefit. For the *Contributor,* a new publication of the Young Men's and Young Ladies' Mutual Improvement

Associations, George wrote thirteen biographical sketches of Book of Mormon personalities and three articles on the Nephites during the reign of the judges. He also wrote fifteen biographical sketches and a series of six historical articles on the Lamanites for the *Millennial Star.*

During his eighteen months in prison, George wrote approximately eighty articles, which appeared in the *Juvenile Instructor,* the *Woman's Exponent,* the *Contributor,* the *Millennial Star,* the *Deseret News,* and the Provo *Enquirer.* In addition to the historical, geographical, and ethnological pieces pertaining to the Book of Mormon, which drew specific praise from George Q. Cannon in Washington,[18] Reynolds also wrote children's stories, lessons for the *Second Reader* (for children of the Deseret School Union; he was still functioning as chairman of the publishing committee), editorials, and articles on education and economics in Utah. He also revised his *Are We of Israel?* that he had previously written in serial form for the *Millennial Star.* That his writings were enthusiastically accepted is evidenced by Bishop Madsen's comment to George: "Your literary works have been read with great interest both for the writing themselves, and because you was the writer."[19]

By the summer of 1880 Reynolds had finished his writing projects. Out of psychological desperation a brainstorm hit him on 28 August 1880 that led to his best-known undertaking: a concordance to the Book of Mormon. He patterned his effort after Alexander Cruden's famous *Complete Concordance to the Old and New Testaments.* With renewed vigor he pressed on with this new endeavor each day until he was released from the penitentiary. He occupied nearly all his free time with preparing and transcribing passages from the Book of Mormon, copying as many as 350 per day. On 15 October 1880 prison officials granted him the special privilege of working on his project in the guards' dining room during the day. That enabled him to work in more comfort and at a more rapid pace. By the time of his release in January 1881, George had completed twenty-five thousand entries in his concordance.[20]

George's prison writings did not come at an easy price, because living conditions at the Pen were far from ideal. Until he was given special privileges late in his confinement, he was forced to nail his copy onto the prison wall, sit with a small stool facing it, and write on a lapboard. Often cold benumbed his fingers or dust blinded his eyes. Occasionally gusts of wind flurried his papers over the prison yard.[21] He often noted in letters and in his journal the difficulties of writing during cold or stormy weather.

If George's writings were his most important contribution to the Church arising out of his imprisonment, his most unhappy experiences relating to his confinement were concerns over his family, including ill health and death. Early in his incarceration, George often felt compelled to comfort family members who were distressed about the unsettled circumstances of whether he would remain in Utah or not. To his second wife, Amelia, he wrote, "I am much less troubled than you are on these matters. It is the Lord's business where I am; he knows best what he requires to accomplish His Holy work."[22]

Once he was settled in the Utah prison, George and his wives organized a regular routine of visiting and sending letters. He got into the habit of writing separate letters to each wife, realizing that they preferred it that way. He usually wrote two letters a week to each, and he generally received from both a visit and a letter per week. Visiting him was not easy, since they had to ride with a neighbor or friend who would convey them by team and wagon. Often Polly and Amelia brought one or more of the older children to visit as well. George yearned for their visits and their letters. The older children, when they reached adulthood, often retold stories of visiting their father in the Pen. Alice recorded, "I have another memory of those days. It is of Father with his watch in his hand saying to mother as she sat visiting him, reluctant to leave. 'Now my girl, you had better be going.' He was trying to save her from seeing him turned into the prison yard, so he kept close watch on the time."[23] Alice also recalled visiting her father on her seventh birthday:

> Father looked at me and then picked me up and held me in his arms for a few moments. Then putting me down on the floor, he took from his pocket a leather purse, which was somewhat worn. From it he took fifteen cents, and as he gave it to me he said, "This is for your birthday; it is all the money I have!" As I have matured, I think I have grown to feel that was the most precious birthday gift I ever received.[24]

In his letters, George counseled his wives about their domestic duties and difficulties, almost as if he were home with them. Life was not easy for them, especially with two wives and two families in relatively tight quarters. Inevitably some jealousies arose. Patiently George tried to calm each wife with her cares and complaints. To Amelia he wrote on 9 October 1879:

> You have two or three times of late intimated that I write oftener to Polly than I do to you. I have never paid any special attention to the matter, but since I returned from Lincoln I have kept a memorandum in my pocket book of all letters I receive and write. So last night after receiving your letter I counted up and find I have written in that time (not including this one) twenty letters to you and sixteen to Polly, or five to you to every four to her. So you see your complaints on that score are not just. Some weeks you have got the most, some weeks she has. But in the total you are ahead.[25]

Of prime concern to George was the health of his wives and children. Both Polly and Amelia were pregnant when he went to prison, and he expressed anxiety about them, particularly when they traveled to visit him in inclement weather. Any ailments of his children also distressed him.

George learned in October 1879, two months after arriving at the Pen, that his and Amelia's one-year-old son, Charlie, had contracted typhoid fever. By the end of the month the little boy had not improved, so George in deep grief fasted for his son on 30 October. He learned the next morning that Charlie had passed away during the night. He received permission to go home for the funeral. On 2 November his bishop, John Sharp, and a deputy marshal took him home for the brief service, at which his friend George Teasdale and the stake president, Angus Cannon, spoke. While at home, Reynolds blessed his wives, received the sacrament from his fathers-in-law, and met privately with George Q. Cannon, L. John Nuttall, and George Teasdale. He returned to the penitentiary by 4:30 p.m.[26]

George had found Amelia terribly despondent. Back in prison, he wrote her:

> As I reminded you yesterday the future must be considered as well as the past. The past cannot be recalled, the future is measurably in our hands. So for many considerations take care of yourself. Don't lose your faith, or your hope, or omit your prayers, all things are with the Lord, trust in his goodness. Strive to feel, if you cannot say it aloud, "The Lord giveth and the Lord taketh away, blessed be the name of the Lord." May He bless and comfort you, and preserve you and yours from all evil is the prayer of your affectionate Husband.[27]

A week later he wrote: "Don't rebel against the providences of God, remember you have two children left, give them your care, they are as precious as the one that's gone for a while to a brighter and better home, where we shall one day follow."[28] Amelia remained despondent over the loss of Charlie, but in February, when she gave birth to a new baby, her sorrow was eased.

About a month after Charlie's death, George's first wife, Polly, gave birth prematurely to a little girl. The territorial marshal allowed George to go home a second time, for an hour and a half, to see his wife and newborn daughter, named Julia. Polly suffered a severe and nearly fatal illness, probably pneumonia, for several weeks after the delivery; consequently little Julia received little nourishment and was very small.[29]

On 9 February 1880 Amelia delivered her "fat healthy girl."

111

Ironically, prison officials allowed him to go home on the occasion of the birth, legally speaking, of an "illegitimate" child. George went home for a third visit on 10 February to meet his new daughter, Susanna Alberta (Bertie). He spent most of the day at home this time.[30]

In July 1880 two young Reynolds daughters took very sick with the measles but recovered. Weak little Julia took ill and died. George walked all the way home and back, a round-trip distance of ten miles, to see Julia buried. That was his fourth visit home.

During his last two months in prison, the rules of George's confinement were relaxed, with federal officials recognizing that he would soon be released. He was allowed to go home six times during those two months, including two days over Christmas.[31] The gentile population of Utah may have been generally disposed unkindly toward him during his two trials, but now, in his imprisonment, the gentile judges proffered him kindness and respect.

George's family fared quite well financially during his absence. President John Taylor saw to it that sufficient money was sent every month to them. "I recall Mother and Aunt Amelia saying to us on more than one occasion," wrote Alice Louise, "you will not fare as well when your Father is released."[32]

As George's prison term drew to its end, the Church leaders began preparing for his return and continued to assure him of their appreciation for his sacrifice. Elder Lorenzo Snow of the Twelve wrote George:

> I suppose that a great number of people will obtain their salvation and some kind of glory without making very little, if any, what is called personal sacrifice. But to gain a Celestial crown and be exalted to the fulness of the Godhead, I believe one and all will have to pay one time or another, a big price, all he is able or capable of paying. . . . It has fallen your lot in the progress of the work of God to be cast into a penitentiary: which may be considered your part to fulfill as you move forward in your path to the fulness of the Godhead. Do you regret it now? When you shall have been

seated upon the throne of your glory will you then regret this part
that has been allotted you?[33]

When George was released on 20 January 1881, friends took
him directly to the office of Church president John Taylor, where
he was presented a sum of $1,415.28, which had been gathered in
small and large amounts from Church employees and other members.[34] This sum represented approximately what George would have
earned in one year. He quickly put this money into building a new
house for Amelia just north of his first house.

Three days later George was asked to address the weekly Sunday services in the new Assembly Hall on Temple Square in Salt
Lake City. He solemnly stated that he felt like a missionary reporting
his labors (these meetings often included reports from recently returned missionaries), for he regarded his imprisonment as a mission,
though admittedly a peculiar one. He was thoroughly convinced that
his mission had contributed to the building of the kingdom of God.
He expressed his trust in God and testified that his experience
proved that if one placed his trust in God, he would not be forsaken,
no matter what the circumstances. He claimed it was as possible
for a man to be happy in a prison cell and to hold sweet reflections
on the dealings of God with his children as under more advantageous
circumstances. As to whether he would have done the same thing
again, he insisted that he would, realizing that this experience was
valuable to him both in this life and throughout eternity. He hoped
that his sacrifice "would be of some use to his brethren and sisters."
George claimed that in the history of the world, it had long been
proved that men could not stamp out religious belief by penalties,
persecution, prosecution, or even martyrdom. He urged the Saints
"not to be intimidated into doing that which was contrary to their
knowledge." If God was with them, they could afford to bear the
persecutions of men; but they could not afford to turn away from
the truth.[35]

George Reynolds's contribution as a "sacrificial lamb" for the

Church he loved was not a lasting one. After the *Reynolds* case was decided in the Supreme Court, the church-state battle in Utah left the pulpit and took place in the Congress and the courts. In 1882 after a bitter battle, the Congress narrowly passed the Edmunds Act, which defined unlawful cohabitation and penalized it, disfranchised polygamists, nullified their eligibility for office and jury duty, and placed territorial elections under the control of the Utah Commission, which had power to disqualify polygamous candidates. Federal judges were empowered to launch a sustained offensive against the polygamists. United States marshals and their deputies hounded and arrested hundreds of Mormon men accused of being "co-habs." Gentile juries convicted nearly all of them under the new law and sent them to prison. Hundreds of other Mormon men, including the First Presidency, went on the "Underground," dropping from sight.[36]

Even so, George Reynolds's imprisonment for conscience' sake remains significant in Mormon history. While not in the least approving his treatment in the courts nor desiring to serve a prison sentence, George, meekly and without complaining, submitted to the law. He was a model prisoner and accomplished several remarkable achievements in confinement, the most important of which were his voluminous writings expounding the scriptures. His model of endurance through severe weather, primitive prison conditions, and suffering of family members probably served to steel the Latter-day Saint prisoners who followed to endure their ignominy well and to make good use of their time while in prison. Even though subsequent prisoners were likewise hailed as heroes, their families could not receive as much favored attention as did those of Reynolds, although in many cases members of the Church did come to the aid of families of other prisoners for conscience' sake. George Reynolds had served his Church well.

Notes

1. "Correspondence," *Millennial Star* 41 (29 September 1879): 621; *Omaha Bee*, 14 July 1879, p. 1.

2. George Reynolds Journal, vol. 5, 30 April 1880; Alice Louise Reynolds, "Biography of George Reynolds," p. 20.

3. "Correspondence," *Millennial Star* 41 (29 September 1879): 621.

4. George Reynolds to Polly Reynolds, 10 October 1879, in Reynolds Collection, no. 32.

5. Junius F. Wells, "A Living Martyr," *Contributor* 2 (February 1881): 157; see also George Reynolds Journal, vol. 5, 31 March 1880.

6. "Correspondence," *Millennial Star* 41 (29 September 1879): 622.

7. Scott G. Kenney, ed., *Wilford Woodruff's Journal*, 9 vols. (Midvale, Utah: Signature Books, 1983–85), 7: 572.

8. George Reynolds Journal, vol. 5, June 1880.

9. "Correspondence," *Millennial Star* 41 (29 September 1879): 622.

10. John Taylor to George Reynolds, 3 July 1879, in Reynolds Collection, no. 5.

11. Christian August Madsen to George Reynolds, 21 June 1879, in Reynolds Collection, no. 14.

12. Christian August Madsen to George Reynolds, 17 December 1880, in Reynolds Collection, no. 14.

13. George Teasdale to George Reynolds, 6 September 1879, in Reynolds Collection, no. 8.

14. See Appendix A, "Identifiable Writings of George Reynolds."

15. Grant Underwood, "Book of Mormon Usage in Early LDS Theology," *Dialogue* 17 (Autumn 1984): 35–74; see also Gordon Irving, "The Mormons and the Bible in the 1830s," *BYU Studies* 13 (Summer 1973): 473–88. A scholarly study similar to Underwood's has not been conducted for the 1850–80 period. Nevertheless, a perusal of the contents of Mormon periodical literature during that time suggests a pattern similar to that of the pre-1850 period. The only person before George Reynolds to describe systematically the contents of the Book of Mormon was James A. Little, a historian and writer from Kanab, Utah. He wrote "Book of Mormon Sketches," a series that appeared in thirty-six issues in 1878–80 in the *Juvenile Instructor*.

16. "Correspondence," *Millennial Star* 41 (20 October 1879): 669.

17. Ibid., p. 668.

18. George Q. Cannon to George Reynolds, 13 February 1880, in Reynolds Collection, no. 7.

19. Christian August Madsen to George Reynolds, 17 December 1880.

20. George Reynolds Journal, vol. 5, August 1880–January 1881.

21. Wells, "Living Martyr," p. 156.

22. George Reynolds to Amelia Reynolds, 16 August 1879; photocopy in possession of this writer.

23. Alice Louise Reynolds, "Biography of George Reynolds," p. 24; interview with Emily Jensen, 29 November 1985, Provo, Utah; interview with Haroldeane Rasmussen, 29 November 1985, Provo, Utah.

24. Amy Brown Lyman, *A Lighter of Lamps: The Life Story of Alice Louise Reynolds* (Provo, Utah: Alice Louise Reynolds Club, 1947), p. 11.

25. George Reynolds to Amelia Reynolds, 9 October 1879, in Special Collections, Harold B. Lee Library, Brigham Young University, Provo, Utah.

26. George Reynolds Journal, vol. 5, November 1879; L. John Nuttall Journal, vol. 1, p. 361.

27. George Reynolds to Amelia Reynolds, 3 November 1879, in Special Collections, Harold B. Lee Library.

28. George Reynolds to Amelia Reynolds, 10 November 1879, in Special Collections, Harold B. Lee Library.

29. George Reynolds Journal, vol. 5, December 1879–April 1880.

30. Ibid., February 1880.

31. Ibid., July 1880–January 1881.

32. A. L. Reynolds, "Biography of George Reynolds," p. 19.

33. Lorenzo Snow to George Reynolds, 11 January 1881, in Reynolds Collection, no. 4.

34. "Gifts to George Reynolds," manuscript in Reynolds Collection, p. 26.

35. Journal History, 23 January 1881, p. 1.

36. See Gustive O. Larson, *The "Americanization" of Utah for Statehood* (San Marino, Calif.: Huntington Library, 1971), pp. 115–206.

CHAPTER 13

Secretary to
President John Taylor

GEORGE WAS PLEASED BEYOND EXPRESSION TO BE BACK WITH HIS WIVES
and children after his incarceration. He now had funds to build a
new house and separate his two families. Finally they were beginning
to accrue some of the comforts of life. Indeed, his polygamous households at this point took on a semblance of normalcy.

Construction began immediately on a new house for Amelia's
family just north of George's existing house in the Twentieth Ward.
By summer Amelia and her children had moved in. With several
renovations and additions, this large dwelling still stands at 316 North
D Street in the Avenues section of Salt Lake City. For the next
several years, Amelia's house was the "north house" and Polly's
the "south house."

When George returned to work in late January 1881, President
Taylor informed him that he was needed to help finish some writings
that the prophet had been working on. Since October 1880 a new
First Presidency had led the Church; the Quorum of the Twelve
was no longer the presiding body. John Taylor, the Church's third
president, had selected Elders George Q. Cannon and Joseph F.
Smith as first and second counselor, respectively. George Reynolds

117

was already a protégé and close personal friend of President Cannon. In future years he also drew close to Presidents Taylor and Smith.

George Reynolds was first hired to work in the Office of the President of the Church in December 1865, five months after immigrating from England. Except for his thirteen-month mission in his homeland (1871–72) and the eighteen months he spent in prison, he was employed continuously for nearly forty-four years as a clerk to the First Presidency. He labored under five presidents: Brigham Young, John Taylor, Wilford Woodruff, Lorenzo Snow, and Joseph F. Smith. At various times he functioned as confidential secretary to Presidents Young, Taylor, and Woodruff and was privy to intimate Church hierarchy discussions and business. As one who helped draft important documents and letters for the First Presidency, he helped mold and affect policy.

During George's service, secretaries and clerks, even confidential ones, were never given any publicity. Nevertheless, the First Presidency depended heavily on their devotion, trustworthiness, and reliability. Without their production and allegiance, the Mormon leaders could not have performed their tasks efficiently. Secretaries and clerks became intimate associates with one another and with Church leaders who frequented the Office. On the strength of their work as secretaries, they can be regarded as second-echelon Church leaders. That was especially true of L. John Nuttall and George F. Gibbs, two other prominent secretaries during this period. George Reynolds was prominent in other ways as well—as scholar and writer, the first prisoner for conscience' sake, Deseret Sunday School Union general board member, and eventually a general authority.

Reynolds was a natural secretary. His teenage apprenticeship in London was as a bookkeeper. He valued order and neatness, even becoming disturbed when his projects or papers were disorderly. His penmanship, excellent anyway, improved after being a Church employee. Dependable, punctual, and trustworthy, he did not mind working long, tedious hours.

George had considerable training in England as a secretary before emigrating to Salt Lake City. No sooner had he joined the Church than he was assigned to be secretary of the Somers Town Branch Sunday School. His daughter Alice Louise later referred to that first calling: "From that time on until his death, he was secretary [of] from one to a half-dozen things all his life. Golden Kimball [a close colleague on the First Council of Seventy from 1892 to 1909] tells us that once when he was walking up the steps with him, Father said, Golden I fancy that when I am entering the pearly gates someone will call out here comes Brother Reynolds, let's make him secretary."[1]

As a teenager George served simultaneously as secretary to the Sunday School, the branch tract society, and eventually the Somers Town Branch (probably comparable to a branch clerk). In 1861 he became a full-time missionary and one year later London Conference secretary. In 1863 George Q. Cannon transferred him to the Liverpool mission office to work as emigration clerk. A few months later he became chief clerk, remaining as such until he emigrated in 1865.[2]

George Reynolds proved himself an efficient secretary in the Office of the President under Brigham Young from 1865 until Brigham's death in 1877. George served alternatively as financial bookkeeper, editorial assistant with Church periodicals, secretary to Church businesses, and confidential secretary as President Young rotated the assignments of the approximately five men who were serving as clerks at any one time.

When Brigham Young died, George became confidential secretary to John Taylor, president of the Quorum of the Twelve, over the next two years until the Supreme Court decided his polygamy test case in 1879. At that time, Taylor summoned his son-in-law L. John Nuttall, stake president in Kanab, to take over for Reynolds, should the latter not receive executive clemency. In June, after all of George Reynolds's petitions to President Rutherford B. Hayes failed, George turned his duties over to Nuttall. Among other things, he had to explain the details of the embarrassing battle over the estate of Brigham Young, which was still afflicting the Twelve.[3]

During George's prison term, his colleagues at the Office of the President, both the general authorities and his fellow secretaries, kept in close contact with him, always remembering him in their prayers. There was never any question about George's returning to his job after his release from the penitentiary.

After his first day back in the Office in 1881, he went each morning at 8:30 to President Taylor's house and then, beginning in January 1882, to his new official residence, the Gardo House, which was located across South Temple Street from the Office. The two "engage[d] in hunting up scriptures &c." President Taylor dictated and George Reynolds drafted the copy.[4]

After a few weeks, they finished the first piece, entitled *Items on Priesthood Presented to the Latter-day Saints*, a treatise on the Aaronic and Levitical priesthoods. "Dedicated to a stronger and better priesthood," wrote Taylor in the book's frontispiece. He also explained the book's purpose:

> As there is more or less uncertainty existing in the minds of many of the Bishops and others in regard to the proper status and authority of the Bishopric and what is denominated the "Aaronic or Levitical" Priesthood, I thought it best to lay before the brethren a general statement of the subject, as contained in the Bible and Book of Doctrine and Covenants.[5]

This work was urgently needed in the stakes, because of confusion about the role of the Aaronic Priesthood since the priesthood reorganization of 1877.

Next President Taylor and his literary-minded secretary launched into a related but more ambitious project, that of tracking the scriptural passages on the atonement of Jesus Christ and the law of sacrifice in the Bible, the Book of Mormon, the Doctrine and Covenants, and the Pearl of Great Price. Most of the resulting book, *Mediation and Atonement*, which saw many reprintings, is a compilation of scriptural passages, although there is important commentary as well. This was the first attempt by a Church president to write a theological treatise of any length or depth. Significantly, President Taylor and George Reynolds drew on the "Inspired Translation" of the Bible, a product of Joseph Smith and Sidney Rigdon. This work, although Joseph Smith had intended to publish it, was not in print until 1867, when it was published by Joseph Smith III and the Reorganized Church of Jesus Christ of Latter Day Saints. Brigham Young had not trusted this publication and refused to countenance anyone's using it. But John Taylor was of a different mind and cited it frequently in his new book. Some of the commentary in *Mediation and Atonement* also bears the marks of George Reynolds's unique literary style, thus suggesting an actual coauthorship or a ghost writing.[6]

Throughout the year 1881, while still engaged in these writing projects, George accompanied John Taylor on his travels throughout the Saints' settlements in northern Utah and southern Idaho. Once the writing projects were completed, however, the president took his son-in-law L. John Nuttall, another private secretary, on the trips. That did not disturb George, for he much preferred to stay at home. Besides, the more officious Nuttall enjoyed being part of the Church hierarchy. From 1882 to 1885, almost daily Nuttall recorded in his journal his telegraph contacts with George Reynolds regarding Church affairs. Clearly, these two secretaries helped keep Church business running smoothly during the crucial years of the federal antipolygamy crusade. George usually worked in the Gardo House office where President Taylor spent most of his mornings, and John Nuttall worked in the Office of the President, where President Taylor worked in the afternoon.

A vital service that George provided his chief during the early 1880s was recording John Taylor's revelations. George was present for at least two pivotal revelations on Church priesthood organization. Of these highly spiritual experiences, George wrote:

> It was my privilege to write from President Taylor's dictation

121

nearly all the revelations that he received. When I reported at the Gardo House in the morning I would occasionally find him writing at a table either in his bed room or in the small office on the west side of the building, occupied by myself. On my arrival, he would arise, I would seat myself where he had been sitting, and he would continue the revelation he had commenced to write by dictating it to me. While so doing he generally walked backwards and forwards along the room. When the writing was finished I read it to him, generally more than once, and he would say, "Yes, that's right." On only one occasion do I remember that he made any alteration in that which was written. There was one short phrase that did not appear quite plain. I read it over to him three times, he then slightly changed it, and when I again read it, he said, "That's right."[7]

The first known of these revelations was dictated on 13 October 1882, just a few days after the semiannual general conference of the Church. For two years the Quorum of the Twelve Apostles had had only ten members, the vacancies weighing heavily upon President Taylor's mind. In the revelation George Teasdale and Heber J. Grant were called to the apostleship, and physician Seymour B. Young, who became George's best friend in his later years, was called to be one of the Seven Presidents of the Seventy. The revelation also called for launching increased missionary work among the various Indian tribes ("Lamanites") in the intermountain West and for a general reformation among priesthood bearers and Church members. George remembered it as a privilege that he was asked by President Taylor in the General Authorities' meeting to read this revelation that brought honor to his close friends.[8]

The second known revelation to John Taylor was received six months later in April 1883. For several months the general authorities had been concerned about the ineffective organization of the seventies quorums. After a lengthy discussion with the apostles and the First Seven Presidents of the Seventy on 13 April, President Taylor withdrew with his son William W. Taylor, a member of the First Council of Seventy, and his secretary George Reynolds. To-

gether the three wrote President Taylor's views on this reorganization. The document, in Reynolds's handwriting, was then presented to George Q. Cannon and Joseph F. Smith of the First
Presidency for approval.[9]

The next morning, 14 April, the First Presidency, the Quorum
of the Twelve, and the First Council of Seventy met. Secretary
George Reynolds read the set of instructions composed the previous
day. Then he read a revelation dictated to him that morning by
President Taylor in response to his plea, "Show unto us Thy will,
O Lord, concerning the organization of the Seventies." The revelation sanctioned the instructions and added, "Thus saith the Lord
unto the First Presidency, unto the Twelve, unto the Seventies and
unto all my holy Priesthood, let not your hearts be troubled, neither
be ye concerned about the management and organization of my
Church and Priesthood. . . . I will reveal unto you, from time to time,
through the channels that I have appointed, everything that shall be
necessary for the future development and perfection of my
Church."[10]

George probably was Taylor's amanuensis for still other revelations, for he noted that "only a few of the revelations given through
[John Taylor] have been published, as the greater portion were not
addressed to the Church as a whole, or to the world, but to individuals
or special bodies of brethren."[11] George also indicated that the revelations to President Taylor bore striking resemblance to those given
to Joseph Smith and contrasted with Taylor's normal style of speaking and writing. He explained:

> On ordinary occasions the President would preface his subject
> with a somewhat lengthy introduction or argument, working grad-
> ually to the point he wished to make. In the revelations given
> through him the Lord makes no preface. "Verily thus saith the
> Lord, let my servant," or "Verily thus saith the Lord, it is my
> will"; the main subject is reached at once, and when the message
> is delivered the revelation closes without peroration or argument.[12]

During the Taylor era, George Reynolds filled other honorary and confidential assignments. In April 1881, shortly after George was released from prison, John Taylor appointed him to the exclusive Council of Fifty. One Mormon historian has noted that "the primary role of the Council of Fifty was to symbolize the otherworldly world order that would be established during the millennial reign of Christ on earth." From 1844 to 1850 this council had played a key role in the exodus of the Mormons to the West and the establishment of a civil government in Utah. But thereafter, until 1880, when President Taylor reassembled it for discussion of the federal antipolygamy crusade, its effect on Mormon society was minor. Under President Taylor the Council of Fifty met on thirty-three separate days and undoubtedly discussed tactics to counter the work of the gentiles against the Saints.[13] That he was part of such an honorary policy-making body shows again the esteem the highest Church authorities had for George Reynolds.

In 1883 President Taylor revived the School of the Prophets, an organization that had existed under both Joseph Smith and Brigham Young. On 28 April 1883, only two weeks after the revelation pertaining to the seventies was given, John Taylor received a revelation regarding the School, which was probably recorded by George Reynolds:

> Behold, I have shown unto you many things, and I will continue to make known unto you my will from time to time, on things temporal as well as Spiritual, things pertaining to my Church, my Kingdom and my Zion. . . . These things belong to my Priesthood, but more properly to the School of the Prophets. Let the School of the Prophets be organized, even all such as are worthy, but if they are found unworthy they shall not have place in my school, for I will be honored by my Priesthood; and let my laws be made known unto them as may be deemed expedient.[14]

On 25 July 1883, in compliance with the revelation, President Taylor appointed George Q. Cannon and George Reynolds to gather all information available pertaining to the Schools of the Prophets as organized by Joseph Smith and Brigham Young so that they would be in harmony with the Lord's will. The pair gave a lengthy report to the First Presidency and the Quorum of the Twelve a week later. They recommended that there be a stop to potential disclosures of what went on in the school, a problem that had undermined its effectiveness under Brigham Young. They also recommended that Zebedee Coltrin, then eighty years old and a member of the original 1833 School of the Prophets, be consulted.[15]

After more planning and consulting, John Taylor reorganized the School in October 1883. Reynolds recorded in his journal that on "the 12 Oct. the School of the Prophets was re-organized after the ancient order. We went to the Endowment House fasting, had our feet washed by the president (see Doc & Cov. Sec. 88) partook of the Sacrament &c. Thirty eight brethren were present on this occasion." The school, though projected toward a larger development, did not function after its initial organization. Lack of records makes it impossible to determine the reasons for its failure.[16]

In 1883, under President John Taylor's direction, George was elected a director of the new Church-sponsored Bullion, Beck & Champion Mining Company in Tintic, Utah. Unfortunately, this mining company became embroiled in a claims battle with the neighboring Eureka Hill Mining Company. Litigation expenses and poor financial management threatened loss of the entire property. George Q. Cannon, first counselor to Church President John Taylor, took drastic steps to save Bullion Beck, but in the process alienated Elder Moses Thatcher, an apostle who owned much of the company's stock. The operation of the Bullion Beck mine remained controversial throughout the company's stormy twenty-year history. Affairs became so entangled that George Reynolds eventually resigned from the company in 1889. George undoubtedly suffered much turmoil as he sat as secretary in crucial company meetings and in saddened Church hierarchy meetings where Elder Moses Thatcher's fate was discussed.[17]

Another assignment that came to George during President Taylor's administration was to serve on a reading committee to review books of consequence to the Church and the reading public. In 1883 he was appointed by the Salt Lake City Council (all of whom were Saints) to a committee of five to review and revise Edward Tullidge's *History of Salt Lake City*; he also acted as committee secretary. Later, in 1894, the First Presidency appointed George to a reading committee for James E. Talmage's *Articles of Faith* and for B. H. Roberts's *Succession in the Presidency* and *New Witness for God*. Finally, in 1900, the First Presidency appointed George to be on a standing committee for all Church publications.[18] Historian Davis Bitton explained:

> Quite early in the process of working up Mormon history the "reading committee" was used as a means of clearing and getting a group judgment. Since the same device was used for works of theology, it is clear that the Church leadership recognized the possibility of problems from versions of history that did not fit the image they had in mind.... The idea that nothing negative should be said about past Church leaders was a natural consequence of the position that nothing negative should be said about present leaders.[19]

Family life for George Reynolds in the period from 1881 to 1884 proved to be a laboratory in living plural marriage. Both Polly and Amelia continued to bear children, probably accepting along with George the implied Mormon doctrine of the time that the greater the number of children in this life, the greater would be the glory of the family in the hereafter. Polly bore two more sons, John and Harold; Amelia also bore two more sons, George Bruford and Edwin Don Carlos (Carl).

The Reynoldses experienced their share of rivalries between the wives. Both Polly's and Amelia's descendants today revere their respective female progenitor, but Polly's descendants indicate that Polly was becoming increasingly disturbed by the surly attitude displayed by Amelia toward Polly and her children.[20] One of George's children indicated that George often suffered migraine headaches from the pressure of keeping peace between the two families and maintaining "the appearance of a successful plural household."

> He didn't often appear in public with two wives, except at church parties where he might take [both of them]. He took his wives to concerts and plays by turns. These turns might not coincide with the time of his visits, but they worked out very well. For example, he would announce to Polly, the first wife, that he was taking Amelia, the second wife to the concert this evening. This routine was broken at times because of his headaches. One time Amelia had to be disappointed because one of his headaches came on before he could take her to the concert. He was greatly worried over this, and sorry about having to disappoint her.[21]

Certainly George cared for both of his wives and for all of his children. He was a strict father but a kind and loving one. He insisted upon obedience but was not harsh in his discipline. When he arrived home each evening, the mother at the house where he stayed that night would tell what the children had done and how they had behaved that day. If correction were needed, he administered it in a kindly manner. He would sometimes go on a walk with a child who had been disobedient. He was never known during this period to have raised his voice. It was also his practice to have a five-minute conversation with each child when he arrived at home.[22]

George naturally insisted that his children participate in Church activities. He was the successful superintendent of the Twentieth Ward Sunday School at this time, and he enrolled his children in their appropriate classes. Alice Louise Reynolds remarked, "Another factor in successful discipline, I think, is good religion. We always went to Sunday School, and that was important. Father's example was the very best, and we tried to follow it."[23]

George also continued to attend to the needs and interests of his several extended families. His own mother died in England, and he showed concern for each of his siblings, particularly those in Utah. When his brother Charles went on a mission to England, George supported him financially. His sister Julia, to whom all of his family had grown so close, became a plural wife to one of his friends and neighbors, James Evans. George also helped sponsor the immigration of Amelia's family from England and helped get them settled in Nephi, Utah. He maintained his close association with Polly's family, the Tuddenhams, and promoted their doing vicarious work for the dead for their family in the Logan Temple. His beloved father-in-law John Tuddenham, whom he always addressed as "Dad," died in 1885.[24]

George remained active in local Church affairs during these years. After George's release from the penitentiary in 1881, Bishop Sharp of the Twentieth Ward decided, as he had when George returned from the British Mission several years earlier, that he was needed as Sunday School superintendent and called him in September to that position. As he resumed leadership, typically, George fretted about the progress and success of the school, believing that his ward's program was only "about average." He noted that the greatest need was more experienced teachers.[25]

By 1883 George was basking in the success of a model Sunday School program. He recorded in his year-end journal entry: "At the close of the year the school was in a better condition than I ever recollect,—more competent teachers, better singing, large attendance, general good order."[26] In 1884, however, unprecedented problems arose in the ward Sunday School. Candidly he confided in his journal:

> I was not in good health, and became irritable, and said things that were improper. I had a misunderstanding from this cause with Sister Cecelia Sharp, one of the Sunday School Teachers, and owing to the position assumed by some of the brethren in relation thereto I resigned, but my resignation was not accepted by the Bishop, the whole matter was afterwards proven a misunderstanding of what I hastily said, and Sis. S. returned to her duties, but I lost interest in the Sunday School, and did not attend with that regularity I used to do, being glad of a reasonable excuse to stay away. This I believe had an injurious effect upon the school and it did not thrive as formerly.[27]

128

In addition to his Sunday School responsibilities, George also served again as a "home missionary." Such a person was assigned to visit wards within the stake and deliver a sermon on designated subjects in evening sacrament meeting services, much as members of stake high councils do in the Church today. In his journal George meticulously recorded where he fulfilled that calling. In October 1884, he was released from both his Sunday School and home missionary assignments, when his role as an ordained seventy was expanded.[28]

George Reynolds, as private secretary to President John Taylor, was intimately acquainted with the changing nature of the seventies' calling during the early 1880s. He was both a witness to the policy change and a participant in its implementation.

In its attempts to locate seventies for potential missionary service, in 1880 the First Council of Seventy adopted a new organizational structure to help overcome the chaotic state of the various seventies quorums by establishing ward and stake seventies presidents. As historian William Hartley explained, "A ward president, they reasoned, could become acquainted with and list all seventies residing in his ward, no matter what their official quorums were. If presidents in all wards did likewise, then practically every seventy could be located by ward and identified by quorum. A stake president of seventies could coordinate the ward presidents' work."[29] The new plan worked well, and eventually resulted in monthly ward seventies meetings and more worthy missionary candidates were supplied to the First Council. But questions remained about what to do with the existing seventy-six seventies quorums.[30]

The First Presidency under John Taylor began wrestling with the matter. As previously described, President Taylor received two revelations pertaining to the seventies' work in 1882 and 1883, with secretary and seventy George Reynolds as his amanuensis. The first of these revelations called for more seventies to be chosen to work among the Lamanites in the intermountain west. The revelation was read among the ward seventies groups and caused introspection and repentance among the quorums.[31] Having been directly involved in the revelation and given his pious nature, George was undoubtedly deeply moved by receiving this instruction from the Lord.

The second revelation, in April 1883, was more explicit about the organization of seventies quorums in the Church. It ratified the instructions drawn up jointly by President John Taylor, his son William W. Taylor of the First Council, and clerk George Reynolds. They called for a geographical method of relocating and filling existing seventies quorums. Henceforth all quorums were to be headquartered in wards or stakes. Distribution would be according to the number of priesthood holders residing in the various settlements in the Church. Vacancies in the realigned quorums were to be made only from persons residing in the same locality. Three thousand copies of this revelation and instructions were printed and distributed to seventies and stake leaders.[32]

Throughout 1883 the First Council of the Seventy hammered out the restructuring details. Salt Lake Stake with eleven hundred seventies (one-fourth of the Church's total) became headquarters for forty quorums (half the Church's total). Throughout all the reshuffling, George Reynolds remained in the same (the twenty-fourth) quorum. His quorum began meeting in the Salt Lake Sixteenth Ward meetinghouse every other Thursday "with good and prompt attendance." George became the third most senior president. "As I am the senior president in the City, when present, I take charge of the meetings," he noted. In 1884 he was designated as the senior president of his quorum when Daniel Woods of Woods Cross was ordained a high priest and Daniel Allen of Escalante was transferred to another quorum. Four of his fellow members came from the Sixteenth Ward, one from the Sixth, and one from the Seventeenth. He was the only president from the Twentieth Ward. (Interestingly each of the seven presidents, including Reynolds, had been born in either England or Scotland.) These seven presidents of the twenty-fourth quorum, with approval of bishops and the stake presidency, then proceeded to nominate new members for their quorum and to ordain them, thus bringing the quorum's total to seventy priesthood holders.[33]

The period from 1881 to 1884, following his prison term, was a time of personal satisfaction to George Reynolds. He worked daily among men whom he highly regarded as men of God and who, in turn, regarded him with tremendous respect and appreciation. His family life was stable and fulfilling, although not easy for him as head of polygamous households. He was a successful Church worker. He had also been identified as a leading Church author and proponent of Latter-day Saint doctrines and scriptural history.

Notes

1. Alice Louise Reynolds, "Biography of George Reynolds," p. 7.

2. T.Z., "Lives of Our Leaders," p. 387.

3. Diary of L. John Nuttall, vol. 1, pp. 266, 273, 277, 298–300; Leonard J. Arrington, "The Settlement of the Brigham Young Estate, 1877–79," *Pacific Historical Review* 21 (February 1952): 1–20.

4. George Reynolds Journal, vol. 6, January 1881; Ann Jardine Bardsley, "Tracing the Lore of the Gardo House," *Deseret News* 25 July 1985, p. C-1; interview with Mark Curtis, authority on the history of the Gardo House, 31 January 1986, Salt Lake City, Utah.

5. John Taylor, *Items on Priesthood Presented to the Latter-day Saints* (Salt Lake City: Deseret News Co., 1881).

6. John Taylor, *An Examination into and an Elucidation of the Great Principle of the Mediation and Atonement of Our Lord and Savior Jesus Christ* (Salt Lake City: Deseret News Co., 1882).

7. George Reynolds, "Revelation–Inspiration," *Juvenile Instructor* 37 (1 March 1902): 131.

8. A. L. Reynolds, "Biography of George Reynolds," p. 38; Francis M. Gibbons to Bruce A. Van Orden, 21 March 1983; Francis M. Gibbons, *Heber J. Grant* (Salt Lake City: Deseret Book Co., 1979), pp. 46–47; William G. Hartley, "The Seventies in the 1880s: Revelations and Reorganizing," *Dialogue* 16 (Spring 1983): 62; James R. Clark, ed., *Messages of the First Presidency*, 6 vols. (Salt Lake City: Bookcraft, 1965–75), 2:348–49.

9. Hartley, "The Seventies in the 1880s," p. 69.

10. Clark, *Messages of the First Presidency*, 2:352–54; Hartley, "The Seventies in the 1880s," pp. 69–71.

11. George Reynolds, "Revelation–Inspiration," p. 130.

12. Ibid., pp. 130–31.

13. D. Michael Quinn, "The Council of Fifty and Its Members, 1844 to 1945," *BYU Studies* 20 (Winter 1980): 163–97; George Reynolds Journal, vol. 6, 1881.

14. As cited in John R. Patrick, "The School of the Prophets: Its Development and Influence in Utah Territory," master's thesis, Brigham Young University, 1970, p. 39, and in Merle H. Graffam, *Salt Lake School of the Prophets Minute Book, 1883* (Palm Desert, Calif.: ULC Press, 1981), p. 1.

15. Patrick, "The School of the Prophets," pp. 39–40; Graffam, *Minute Book*, pp. 1–7.

16. George Reynolds Journal, vol. 6, 1883; Patrick, "The School of the Prophets," pp. 136–37; Graffam, *Minute Book*, pp. 19–56.

17. George Reynolds Journal, vol. 6, 1877; vol. 6, 1883–85. George Reynolds never revealed confidential discussions in his journal. Fellow secretary L. John Nuttall was slightly more open in his journals. Nuttall, who also was on the board of directors for BB & CM Co., repeatedly indicated some of the tensions in the company in his journal entries. For a discussion of the problems between Thatcher and Cannon in the company, including reference to participation of Reynolds and Nuttall, see Edward Leo Lyman, "The Alienation of an Apostle from His Quorum: The Moses Thatcher Case," *Dialogue* 18 (Summer 1985): 68–73.

18. George Reynolds Journal, vol. 6, 1883, 1894, 1900; *Juvenile Instructor* 34 (1 May 1899): 260–61: 40 (15 November 1905): 690.

19. Davis Bitton, "Like the Tigers of Old Time," *Sunstone* 7 (September-October 1982): 47.

20. I conducted numerous interviews with grandchildren of George Reynolds, attempting to obtain fairly the feelings from both the first and second families. Unquestionably some sore feelings were perpetuated in the first family against "Aunt Amelia," particularly to the descendants of Polly's older children, who passed on stories to their own children.

21. As cited in Kimball Young, *Isn't One Wife Enough?* (New York: Henry Holt and Co., 1954), pp. 295–96. Since Young openly used interviews with Alice Louise Reynolds for his work, it appears to me that she is the informant in this interview as well. Her prominence would also speak for her being the one.

22. Interview with Maude Ogden, 7 January 1986, Salt Lake City, Utah.

23. As cited in Young, *Isn't One Wife Enough?* p. 254.

24. George Reynolds Journal, vol. 6, 1881–85.

25. George Reynolds Journal, vol. 6, 1882.

26. Ibid., 1883; see also "Outline of Three Years' Course of Study for Twentieth Ward Sunday School," which shows the in-depth curriculum in the Sunday School superintended by George Reynolds.

27. George Reynolds Journal, vol. 6, 1884.

28. George Reynolds Journal, vol. 6, 1881–84.

29. Hartley, "The Seventies in the 1880s," p. 65.

30. Ibid., pp. 66–67.

31. Ibid., pp. 68–69.

32. Ibid., pp. 69–71; S. Dilworth Young, "The Seventies: A Historical Perspective," *Ensign* 6 (July 1976): 19.

33. George Reynolds Journal, vol. 6, 1883, 1885; First Council of Seventy Quorum Member Registers, 1876–1915; Seymour Bicknell Young Papers, LDS Church Historical Archives.

CHAPTER 14

Leading Church Author

GEORGE BUSIED HIMSELF IN THE EARLY 1880S WITH HIS OWN WRITING projects, in addition to his secretarial duties. George continued writing, especially about Book of Mormon topics. Late in 1881 he began a four-part series in the *Contributor* entitled "Objections to the Book of Mormon." "Nearly all the objections raised against the contents of the Book of Mormon, may be classed under three heads," he wrote. "They are either puerile, insincere or dishonest."[1] On the surface this frank assessment may appear narrow-minded, but Reynolds was, as a defender of the faith, responding to the harsh critics who wrote vituperative attacks against the Book of Mormon.

He proceeded to answer for his young adult readers such objections as the following: the Book of Mormon identifies the death of Christ on another day of the month than does the Bible; the Book of Mormon quotes extensively from the New Testament, even though it was written without knowledge of the New Testament; the Book of Mormon disagrees with the Bible in that it states that Jesus was born in Jerusalem; and Joseph Smith's story about the original language of the Book of Mormon plates is absurd and at variance with the discoveries made relating to the language and writing of ancient American inhabitants. Regarding the last objection, George wrote about a paper delivered at the American Philosophical Society just a year before that had demonstrated that thirteen letters of the sixteen in the Mayan alphabet resembled Egyptian signs. "Can any theory of accidental coincidences account for all this?" George asked.[2]

In 1883 the *Juvenile Instructor* published *The Myth of the "Manuscript Found," or the Absurdities of the "Spaulding Story"* consisting of fifteen essays, five of which had been already published. This work was the eleventh in the *Juvenile Instructor's* "faith-promoting series designed for the Instruction and Encouragement of young Latter-day Saints." George asserted that he had "shown that the upholders of this [Spaulding] myth are not only at variance with each other, but that all their assertions are inconsistent with the well-known facts associated with its discovery; . . . and [are] utterly unworthy of belief."[3] He offered rebuttals on just-published anti-Mormon testimonials regarding the Spaulding manuscript. He also included chapters on the Book of Mormon witnesses, including recent comments by David Whitmer; on Joseph Smith's youthful life; and on the time occupied in translating the Book of Mormon.

George's arguments regarding the Spaulding controversy – such as it is absurd to believe in a connection between Sidney Rigdon and Solomon Spaulding – were not unique but were ideas that had been advanced in the 1840s by Benjamin Winchester and John E. Page.[4] Perhaps his best original contribution was his detailed analysis of the time spent on the Book of Mormon translation. This answered the critics' claims that the alleged time of three months was too short; hence, the book must have been copied or transcribed from another book. George showed mathematically the possibility for the task's completion from April to late June 1829.[5] Ironically, in 1884, a year after Reynolds wrote this piece, a "manuscript story" by Solomon Spaulding was discovered in Hawaii, further undercutting anti-Mormon claims. This "manuscript story" bore virtually no resemblance to the Book of Mormon text.

In 1883, Reynolds began a lengthy *Contributor* series entitled "History of the Book of Mormon." His first article, "The Original Records," contained the first detailed explanation by any Church scholar on the plates of Nephi, from which most of the Book of Mormon text was taken. For the first time, George identified specific dates both before and after Christ for the numerous historians who compiled records.[6] These dates, as Reynolds refined them, became the basis for the dates that were included at the foot of each page in the 1921 edition of the Book of Mormon. In six subsequent articles he surveyed the history of the Book of Mormon peoples – the Lamanites, the Nephites, the Zarahemlaites, and the Jaredites.

In 1884 George continued his series for the *Contributor*. Using accounts by Joseph Smith, Martin Harris, Oliver Cowdery, and Lucy Mack Smith, he related the story of Joseph Smith's discovery of the plates and their translation. He added to the Saints' understanding of the translation by discussing the recent Church acquisition of some original Book of Mormon manuscripts. He noted differences in handwriting and lack of punctuation and offered an explanation, which to our ears may sound specious: "That it is not punctuated can easily be accounted for," he assured his readers. "Punctuation is a modern invention, the ancients do not appear to have had any system of stops; and the original plates, there can be but little doubt, were entirely without these aides to correct reading." He described as well the printer's manuscript, then still in the possession of the elderly David Whitmer. George was probably the first to suggest that John H. Gilbert, the compositor in the shop that printed the Book of Mormon, did the punctuation and capitalization in the printer's manuscript.[7]

Another article discussed, probably for the first time in Mormon literature, the "typographical errors" in the first edition of the Book of Mormon and their subsequent corrections.[8] The concluding article discussed American and European, including foreign language, Book of Mormon editions. Of special interest were extensive structural changes in the 1879 Orson Pratt edition. George provided a comparative chart of chapter structure for old and new editions.[9]

George enthusiastically threw himself into numerous other subjects as well. He frequently wrote articles on current events and issues. In "Thoughts on Genesis" prepared for the *Contributor*, George addressed two issues: evolution and the disputed authorship of Genesis in the Old Testament. Regarding the former, he bitingly stated, "Some scientists take an honest pride in the idea that they have descended from the ape: they consider it shows progress and development. We have no such feelings. Even if it were true, we should feel disposed to say but little regarding such a pedigree." George argued that "modern revelation" in the Book of Moses, Pearl of Great Price, clearly answers that Moses wrote Genesis. "How blessed are we in having this more sure word of revelation for our infallible guide," he confidently asserted, "which can, and does, in a few moments decide the controversies of centuries, and with truth, 'diamond truth,' makes known all that is necessary for our salvation."[10]

George recognized and appreciated advancements in science. In an 1882 article he explained, "Between real science and true religion there is no conflict; they are both important parts of one stupendous whole, harmonizing, aiding and strengthening each other; both emanating from God, the source of all truth, and both tending to His glory and to man's exaltation." But he was disturbed by "science [grown] arrogant" and "uninspired churchmen."[11]

George also wrote about current pressing political events. While Congress debated the Edmunds Bill, he commented on the controversial "anti-Mormon" legislation. He insisted that the bill, if enacted, would place "one man's conscience in the hands of another" and thereby deprive many honest citizens of religious liberty. He argued that Utah, in contrast to the states in the nation, had taxed its citizens less heavily, had more prudently and honestly disbursed public funds, and had more unanimously chosen legislators who reflected the people's will. "If our system of marriage filled the land with deserted mothers, with betrayed maidens, with fatherless waifs, or if, like prostitution and polyandry, it produced barrenness and disease, . . . there might be some excuse for moral legislation; but when the contrary is the result and well regulated polygamy fills the country with a race of bright, healthy, intelligent and bonny children, then the subterfuge of injury to the State can only be maintained by those who call evil good, and good evil."[12]

In his day many people considered George Reynolds the Church's leading authority on Mormon doctrines pertaining to the house of Israel. His *Are We of Israel?* became a classic in Mormon literature with numerous editions published during his lifetime. In 1931, more than twenty years after his death, the demand for the volume was "so urgent and continuous" that Deseret Book Company reprinted it.[13] James E. Talmage cited it in his *The Articles of Faith* in 1890. Joseph Fielding Smith and Bruce R. McConkie, two apostles and leading Mormon theologians in the twentieth century, also used *Are We of Israel?* as an authority.[14]

Reynolds began his study of the house of Israel in 1878 while waiting for his case to come before the Supreme Court. In 1883, after his prison term, George published the series as a 135-page book. His purpose was "to prove . . . from history and analogy" the Latter-day Saint belief that "the great majority of their number are of the house of Israel, and heirs to the promises made to Abraham, to Isaac, and to Jacob." Such claims had received "the ridicule of the unthinking and the contempt of the ungodly." He asserted that the Saints were of the tribe of Ephraim, who had been anciently designated as the birthright and leadership tribe. George cited an 1855 statement by Brigham Young that "Ephraim has become mixed with all the nations of the earth, and it is Ephraim that is gathering together."[15]

George's historical "authorities" included authors who espoused a movement known as "Anglo-Israelism" or "British-Israelism." Anglo-Israelism's main tenet was that the British Anglo-Saxons descended from the ten lost tribes, primarily the tribe of Ephraim, and, as such, have a divinely appointed mission to share the gospel of Jesus Christ with the world. The Anglo-Israelists never formed a separate sect but operated as "an interdenominational fellowship," retaining their affiliation with mainline Protestant denominations.

This movement emerged in the 1870s and reached its peak in the 1880s. Its philosophies were known among Protestants in the United States, Canada, Australia, and New Zealand – nations where "Anglo-Saxon" influence was considered predominant. The movement continued with many adherents until World War II, but it gradually disintegrated and by the 1980s had all but disappeared.[16]

The Anglo-Israelists taught that the British monarchy stemmed from the royal Davidic line through one of the daughters of the last king of Judah, Zedekiah. The prophet Jeremiah took her to Ireland. Furthermore, "Jacob's Stone," or pillar, was also taken to the British Isles by Jeremiah and still survives under the Coronation Chair at Westminster Abbey. They asserted that the apostle Paul and Joseph of Arimathea visited Britain and established Christianity there.[17]

A nonreligious-oriented "cult of the Anglo-Saxon" held intellectual sway in the United States during the Gilded Age, the 1880s, precisely the time when George Reynolds wrote *Are We of Israel?* Proponents held "that Anglo-Saxons were uniquely gifted with a love of liberty and a capacity for self-government."[18] Obviously, compatible secular and religious thought contributed to a mood that was right in Utah for Reynolds to write his pathbreaking book on the Israelites' origin and their whereabouts in the modern age.

Clearly, the leading Anglo-Israelists influenced George Reynolds, and he often mentioned them. He incorporated the following points from Anglo-Israelism in his work:

1. The laws, manners, customs, and languages of ancient inhabitants of northwestern Europe and those of ancient Israel are similar.

2. The lost ten tribes emigrated from the land of Media into Europe. (2 Esdras 13:39–47, from the Apocrypha, is cited.)

3. The Anglo-Saxons stem from Media.

4. *Saxon* probably means *Isaac's son*.[19]

George did not adopt all of the teachings of Anglo-Israelism by any means. He felt that some who had "made the subject of Israel's 'identification' their study, have gone almost to the verge of the ridiculous in the minuteness [of their claims]." They were "zealots," whose claims in many instances were "often strained and frequently untenable." He taught many ideas that contravened tenets of the British-Israelists:

1. Although some Israelites, mostly from Ephraim, either stayed in northern Europe or returned to Israel, most continued northward and are hidden except to the Lord.

2. Israelite remnants are found throughout Europe, not simply among Anglo-Saxons.

3. Most nations have some of Abraham's blood.[20]

Although George tempered his British-oriented bias, he still reflected the feelings of spiritual superiority that the British Church members possessed. Most adult Mormons were British converts in the 1870s and 1880s, when George shared his ideas. He was not the first Church authority to display an exuberance for Anglo-Saxons. He cited Brigham Young, who in 1863 declared:

> The sons of Ephraim are wild and uncultivated, unruly, ungovernable. The spirit in them is turbulent and resolute; they are the Anglo-Saxon race, and they are upon the face of the whole earth, bearing the spirit of rule and dictation, to go forth from conquering to conquer. They search wide creation and scan every nook and corner of this earth to find out what is upon and within it. I see a congregation of them before me to-day.[21]

In the late 1890s, twenty years after researching the house of Israel, George wrote another series of articles entitled "The Gospel in Ancient Britain." He cited a conversation between Joseph Smith and Heber C. Kimball in which the Prophet stated that biblical prophets had traveled in ancient Britain. Reynolds discussed new evidence of European and Asian migrations to Britain over a span of two thousand years. "With them [the migrants]," he asserted, "doubtless came many Israelites, either associates in their ventures or captives taken in war." Reynolds held to his earlier *Are We of Israel?* conclusion that "an admixture of Israelitish blood was infused into the population of Britain," but he was openly cautious about accepting the "Anglo-Israel" theories of all the "Old Testament worthies" who might have traveled to Britain.[22]

The Church of Jesus Christ of Latter-day Saints never officially endorsed Anglo-Israelism ideas. Church authorities stated that Israelites were to be gathered from the entire world, not from Britain alone.[23] Nevertheless, connections between Anglo-Israelism and Mormonism reappeared in the twentieth century. James H. Anderson, who as a young man assisted Reynolds with the publication of *Are We of Israel?* produced in 1937 *God's Covenant Race.* This work hailed the "inspired" teachings of Anglo-Israelism and praised the Anglo-Israel Federation of America and its periodical *Destiny.* Anderson cited his colleague from the Utah Genealogical Society and counselor in the First Presidency, Anthony W. Ivins, who reported in the April 1926 general conference that the British-Israel movement in England had "great scholars and statesmen" who as "British seers" were proclaiming the earth's end. He charged Church members to heed their counsel.[24] In 1939 Elder John A. Widtsoe of the Quorum of the Twelve Apostles discredited Anderson's ideas and the British-Israel movement.[25] Two other Latter-day Saint writers, Ernest L. Whitehead and Francis M. Darter,[26] supported Anglo-Israelism tenets, but their writings never gained popularity. Darter was excommunicated for fanaticism.

The Anglo-Israel bias continues in Mormon theological discussions and beliefs, but present-day Church teachings emphasize the existence of the blood of Israel and of Ephraim throughout the world.[27] Elder Bruce R. McConkie of the Quorum of the Twelve Apostles directed a volley against the Anglo-Israel philosophy:

> This illusion postulates that the British people are identical with the Ten Tribes of Israel . . . [that] all of the ancient prophecies relative to the restoration of Israel have been or will be fulfilled in and through Great Britain as a nation. There is not one chance in a million, or in ten thousand million, that any of the historical assumptions are true; and if they were, it would not make one

particle of difference—the doctrinal view would still be false. . . .
Providentially, this British Israel concept, once so prevalent in the
British Isles and elsewhere, has gone pretty much out of vogue
and is not taken as seriously as it once was.[28]

George Reynolds also directed attention in his writings to the
Jews. "He had a very keen sympathy for the Jews," wrote Alice
Louise Reynolds. "From my early recollections I recall we had
among other informative magazines in the home the *Jewish Chron-
icle.*"[29] Reynolds, like most Mormons, felt a kinship for two reasons—
Jews are relatives of Mormons as fellow members of the house of
Israel, and both Mormons and Jews have suffered affliction from
intolerant national governments.

Following the passage of the Edmunds Act in 1882, which out-
lawed polygamy and provided easier means to enforce the law than
had the Morrill Act of 1862, George wrote a piece for the Church's
Contributor. He compared the "same barbarous treatment" then
being inflicted upon the Jews in Russia with what was, at the same
time, being advocated against Mormons. "There is a marked simi-
larity also in the action of the governments in both countries," he
wrote:

> It is openly charged that in Russia the government officials are
> at the bottom of these troubles, that where they do not secretly
> egg the populace on, they at any rate fail to protect the Jews or
> adequately punish their barbarous persecutors. In this country it
> is well understood that the destruction of the Mormon Church is
> recognized in political circles as an "administration measure," and
> all the power of the party lash has been applied to those Repub-
> licans who ventured to express their disapprobation of the violent
> measures sought to be used against the members of that church.

George Reynolds linked Jews and Mormons as Israelite co-
sufferers. He attributed the simultaneous assaults "on the two representative branches of the house of Israel—Judah and Ephraim" to
Satan's latter-day plan preventing "the rapid growth of these two
branches of Jacob's favored race."[30] In other contexts Reynolds

lauded Jewish accomplishments, ascribing successes "to the mental strength and activity of the Jewish race, which, when given opportunity, soon outstrips its fellows."[31]

Simultaneously with this research and these writings, George also researched Abraham's background. The Church had just published a revised Pearl of Great Price. The Pearl of Great Price contained the book of Abraham, which was derived from ancient Egyptian papyri. And "as but very little has ever been said by the Elders of the Church in advocacy of its [the Book of Abraham's] claims as an inspired record," wrote Reynolds, "we think that a few chapters written to prove its genuineness and divine origin, will not be without value to the Latter-day Saints, and to the world at large."[32] Thus began *The Book of Abraham: Its Authenticity Established As a Divine and Ancient Record*, the first Church commentary on the Book of Abraham.

In telling the story of Joseph Smith's acquisition of the Egyptian mummies and papyri, George simply recounted what was thought to be their origin—that they were discovered by a Mr. "Sebolo" (actually Lebolo) who, before he died in the 1830s, deeded them to his "nephew," M. H. Chandler.[33] George also presented evidence from apocryphal and mythological sources of Abraham's faithful works, including his visits to Egypt and teachings there. In his analysis, George was a forerunner of Hugh Nibley, who attempted to justify the Book of Abraham using the same methods, although with more sophistication.[34]

George's most unusual argument in his discussion of the book of Abraham was his carefully organized claim that Cheops, the builder of the Great Pyramid at Giza, was actually the Egyptian pharaoh whom Abraham visited. He cited several Anglo-Israelist authorities on the pyramids, calling them "modern scientists." He asserted that Abraham taught Cheops principles of astronomy and then "superintended the erection of the building of the pyramid." The pyramid was designed to be an astronomical observatory "built upon mathematical principles, and designed to perpetuate, through all succeeding time, a correct knowledge of heavens and the earth" and to contain "a prophetic history of the world."[35] Modern readers would consider such pyramidology and the linking of Abraham to Cheops as superstitious, pseudoscientific, and fabricated history, yet it reflected a method many fundamentalists used to justify theology with pseudo-historical evidence.[36] That George's work on the book of Abraham during the 1880s had the aura of official sanction is clear from his acknowledgment of President John Taylor, Franklin D. Richards, Joseph L. Barfoot, John R. Howard, and David McKenzie for their suggestions and valuable information in compiling the commentary.[37]

By 1884 George Reynolds was a highly respected person in the Church's capital, Salt Lake City. Well-read Saints studied his continuous stream of writings. The First Presidency relied on him heavily for staff support. These were troubled times for the First Presidency and the Church as a whole as the United States federal government marshalled its forces for another crushing blow against Utah in its increasingly fierce antipolygamy crusade. How would George Reynolds be affected by these new events?

Notes

1. George Reynolds, "Objections to the Book of Mormon," *Contributor* 3 (December 1881): 81. The four articles under the same title, "Objections to the Book of Mormon," can be found in *Contributor* 3 (December 1881): 81–83; 3 (January 1882): 105–8; 3 (February 1882): 134–37; 4 (October 1882): 4–6.

2. George Reynolds, "Objections to the Book of Mormon," *Contributor* 4 (October 1882): 6. These articles, although not mirroring the stricter demands of present-day scholarship for stronger scientific evidence, nevertheless demonstrate that George Reynolds read more widely than many and that he drew from contemporary secular literature for many of his conclusions.

3. George Reynolds, *The Myth of "Manuscript Found," or the Absurdities of the "Spaulding Story"* (Salt Lake City: Juvenile Instructor Office, 1883), preface.

4. Lester E. Bush, Jr., "The Spaulding Theory Then and Now," *Dialogue* 10 (Autumn 1977): 55–56.

5. George Reynolds, *The Myth of "Manuscript Found"*, pp. 71–75.

6. George Reynolds, "The Original Records," *Contributor* 5 (October 1883): 1–5.

7. George Reynolds, "Translation of the Records," *Contributor* 5 (July 1884):

361–67. Just where Reynolds obtained his information about Gilbert's role is uncertain. It was not until 1892, eight years after Reynolds's writing (in 1884) that John H. Gilbert, then ninety years old, made out a memorandum detailing his recollection of the publication process of the Book of Mormon, including the fact that he provided the punctuation for the text. See Wilford C. Wood, *Joseph Smith Begins His Work* (Salt Lake City: Deseret News Press, 1958), introductory pages.

8. George Reynolds, "Translation of the Records," *Contributor* 5 (August 1884): 401–8.

9. George Reynolds, "History of the Book of Mormon," *Contributor* 5 (September 1884): 441–47.

10. Geo. Reynolds, "Thoughts on Genesis," *Contributor* 3 (October 1881): 16–17.

11. G.R., "The Conflict between Science and Superstition," *Juvenile Instructor* 17 (15 January 1882): 18–19.

12. Geo. Reynolds, "The Edmunds Bill," *Contributor* 3 (April 1882): 204–5.

13. "Are We of Israel?" *Improvement Era* 34 (October 1931): 744.

14. James E. Talmage, *Articles of Faith* (Salt Lake City: The Church of Jesus Christ of Latter-day Saints, 1890), pp. 513–14; Joseph Fielding Smith, *The Way to Perfection*, 12th ed. (Salt Lake City: Deseret Book Co., 1963), pp. 138–39; Bruce R. McConkie, *Mormon Doctrine*, 2d ed. (Salt Lake City: Bookcraft, 1966), pp. 456–57.

15. George Reynolds, *Are We of Israel?* 2d ed. (Salt Lake City: Geo. Q. Cannon & Sons, 1895), pp. 5–13; *Journal of Discourses*, 26 vols. (Liverpool: Latter-day Saints Book Depot, 1855–86), 2:268.

16. Bryan R. Wilson, *Magic and the Millennium* (London: Heinemann Educational Books Ltd., 1973), pp. 31–32; Bryan R. Wilson, *Religious Sects: A Sociological Study* (New York: McGraw-Hill, 1970), pp. 210–11; John Wilson, "British Israelism: The Ideological Restraints on Sect Organisation," in *Patterns of Sectarianism: Organisation and Religious Movements*, Bryan R. Wilson, ed. (London: Heinemann Books Ltd., 1967), p. 345; Bruce A. Van Orden, "Anglo-Israelism and Its Influence on Mormon Theology," paper delivered 28 August 1982 at 1982 Sunstone Theological Symposium, Salt Lake City, Utah.

17. Van Orden, "Anglo-Israelism and Its Influence on Mormon Theology," pp. 1–3.

18. Paul F. Boller, Jr., *American Thought in Transition: The Impact of Evolutionary Naturalism, 1865–1900* (New York: University Press of America, 1981), pp. 199–226.

19. Reynolds, *Are We of Israel?* pp. 13–14, 23–32, 38–40, 48–51. Two of the Anglo-Israelists that Reynolds most frequently cited were John Wilson and Edward Hine.

20. Ibid., pp. 19, 41–46, 51, 55.

21. *Journal of Discourses*, 10:188.

22. George Reynolds, "The Gospel in Ancient Britain," *Juvenile Instructor* 33 (15 April 1898): 295–300.

23. Van Orden, "Anglo-Israelism and Its Influence on Mormon Theology," p. 7.

24. Ibid., pp. 7–10; James H. Anderson, *God's Covenant Race* (Salt Lake City: Deseret News Press, 1937); Conference Report, Apr. 1926, p. 16.

25. John A. Widtsoe, "Evidences and Reconciliations," *Improvement Era* 42 (January 1939): 6–7.

26. Ernest L. Whitehead, *The House of Israel* (Independence, Mo.: Zion's Printing and Publishing Co., 1947); Francis M. Darter, *The Kingdom of God, the U.S.A., and British Empire* (Salt Lake City: Utah Printing Co., 1941).

27. See Bruce A. Van Orden, "The Seed of Abraham in the Latter Days," *The Old Testament and the Latter-day Saints* (Sandy, Utah: Randall Book Co., 1986), pp. 51–67.

28. Bruce R. McConkie, *A New Witness for the Articles of Faith* (Salt Lake City: Deseret Book Co., 1985), p. 517.

29. Alice Louise Reynolds, "Biography of George Reynolds," p. 35.

30. George Reynolds, "Mormon and Jew — A Modern Parallel," *Contributor* 3 (April 1882): 247–48.

31. George Reynolds, "A Wonderful School," *Contributor* 10 (March 1889): 176–77; Geo. Reynolds, "What We Owe the Jews," *Contributor* 16 (January 1895): 186–87. In all this Reynolds was not alone. During the last twenty years of the nineteenth century, he was only one of many Mormon leaders who frequently praised the Jews for their noble history, their current resilience to persecution, their stirrings to establish colonies in Palestine, and their bright prophetic future. See Bruce A. Van Orden, "Mormons and Jews: Persecuted Israel," paper delivered 28 April 1984 at annual conference of the Rocky Mountain/Great Plains Region of American Academy of Religion — Society of Biblical Literature, Denver, Colorado.

32. George Reynolds, *The Book of Abraham: Its Authenticity Established As a Divine and Ancient Record* (Salt Lake City: Deseret News Printing and Publishing Establishment, 1879), p. 1.

33. Since the rediscovery of the Joseph Smith Papyri in 1967, there has been much new research on the background of the book of Abraham that makes some previous information obsolete. See Jay M. Todd, *The Saga of the Book of Abraham* (Salt Lake City: Deseret Book Co., 1969) and H. Donl Peterson, *The Pearl of Great Price: A History and Commentary* (Salt Lake City: Deseret Book Co., 1987).

34. Hugh Nibley, *Abraham in Egypt* (Salt Lake City: Deseret Book Co., 1981).

35. George Reynolds, *Book of Abraham*, pp. 27–44.

36. See George M. Marsden, *Fundamentalism and American Culture: The Shaping of Twentieth-Century Evangelicalism 1870–1925* (New York: Oxford University Press, 1980), pp. 55–62.

37. George Reynolds, *Book of Abraham*, p. 49.

CHAPTER 15

On the Underground

T HE REYNOLDS SUPREME COURT DEFEAT DID NOT STOP THE LATTER-day Saints from practicing plural marriage. To the contrary, numbers of plural marriages actually increased. It became obvious to Eastern antipolygamy crusaders that they would need to take tougher actions against the Mormons.[1]

United States President Rutherford B. Hayes visited Utah in September 1880. The Liberal Party, a party created by gentiles in Utah to counter Mormon political domination, monopolized Hayes's time in the territory and convinced him that stricter federal anti-polygamy measures must be enacted. He urged the Congress in December of that year to pass new legislation. President Hayes's successor in office, fellow Republican James A. Garfield, urged similar action before his assassination in 1881. President Chester A. Arthur continued to exert pressure on Congress.

Citizens flooded the 1881–82 congressional session with petitions on the Mormon question, and a score of bills and amendments was introduced. The only proposal to become law was the Edmunds Act of 1882, which in reality was a series of amendments to the Morrill Act of 1862. The law declared polygamy a felony with a penalty of up to five years' imprisonment. It also tacitly acknowl-edged that polygamy would be hard to prove, so "unlawful cohabi-tation" was declared a misdemeanor punishable by six months' imprisonment. The law disfranchised polygamists and declared them ineligible for office and jury duty. The president was authorized to appoint a five-member Utah Commission to administer all further elections in the territory. Finally there were real teeth in the law that easily allowed Latter-day Saint men to be prosecuted for polygamy and the Saints in general to suffer for their beliefs.

The federal court system in Utah readied itself for action. District attorneys and federal marshals rallied behind newly appointed and strong-minded judges to seek out "co-habs": men who could easily be convicted of polygamous living. The first case to come to trial was that of Rudger Clawson, a recently returned missionary to the southern states, in October 1884. Presidents John Taylor and George Q. Cannon were required to testify in the trial. After Clawson's second wife was discovered by marshals and forced to testify of her marriage, the all-gentile jury found Clawson guilty of the felony polygamy and sentenced him to three and a half years' imprisonment, a sentence the United States Supreme Court subsequently upheld. By the end of 1884 three more Latter-day Saint men had been convicted.

The First Presidency began taking steps to protect themselves and other men involved in plural marriage. Early in January 1885, President John Taylor and many other Church officials, including secretary George Reynolds, went to Arizona, New Mexico, and northern Mexico to find new places to settle the harried polygamists. Soon the prophet authorized Arizona members to settle in the Mexican state of Chihuahua to avoid arrest. In March, after the Supreme Court first upheld the Edmunds Act provisions, President Taylor set the pattern of passive resistance by going on the Mormon "underground." He disappeared from public view to live among loyal friends, first in the Salt Lake City vicinity and later northward in Davis County. To elude arrest, most polygamists followed suit and devised ingenious hideouts for their own "underground." The Underground, as it came to be known in the local culture, also developed

Mary Gulliford Goold
at the time of her marriage

highly successful communications systems that took advantage of locally controlled telegraph, railroad, and police systems.[2]

George Reynolds, the first polygamous prisoner for conscience' sake, had been convicted under the provisions of the Morrill Anti-bigamy Act of 1862 and was liable for a second arrest under the provisions of the Edmunds Act of 1882. In April 1885 papers were served for his arrest, and he and his pregnant second wife, Amelia, had to go into hiding. He noted in his journal that Church authorities did not want him arrested, "as my second imprisonment could be used as a precedent for the same course to be taken towards other brethren."[3]

To further complicate his life, but in response to what he referred to as "direct revelation," George secretly married a third wife, Mary Gulliford Goold, in the Endowment House on 26 April 1885. With the general authorities in hiding, George turned to his stake president, Angus M. Cannon, to seal the marriage. Mary Goold, an English immigrant, was twenty-six-years old at the time of this union. She had been hired by John Taylor as a maid in his official residence, the Gardo House, where George and she became acquainted. President Taylor heartily encouraged the marriage between his trusted assistant, George Reynolds, and Mary.[4] The marriage was probably kept secret from most of George's family for some time, for to this day most of his descendants believe that she was married to him after the death of Polly in December 1885.

For his part, George hid first in the Gardo House, next in the Social Hall, and then in the Deseret Museum. Many other polygamists also hid out in the Gardo House in 1885. Whenever deputy marshals came to the front door, signals were quickly sent to each man to hide. The men would hide behind false wooden panels, in hollowed-out spaces under the bed mattresses, and in the tower of the Gardo House above a false ceiling. Amelia went into hiding first at the University of Deseret but went back home in the summer to deliver her baby, Willard (Bish), on 26 June. In July her home was raided by government officials. With the help of George's oldest daughter, Millie, Amelia was secreted in the cellar of the family shanty and was not found. Polly by this time was living in East Millcreek. "Finding neither myself nor wives the Deputies did not subpoena any of the children," George recorded in his journal.[5]

Amelia and her children then moved to rented quarters in the Nineteenth Ward and in September moved again to the Seventeenth Ward. Later they moved yet again to the George Q. Cannon complex in west Salt Lake City. "This hiding up is a very irksome irritating, and withall expensive arrangement," George noted wryly in his journal. Only rarely was George able to visit with his family.[6]

Polly became very ill again with another pregnancy during this year of much moving around. Much of the children's care fell to her oldest daughter, Millie, now seventeen years old. When the youngest child, Harold, received serious injuries, Millie knelt in prayer with the other children and then proceeded to care for his wounds. Maggie C. Shipp, one of Utah's leading doctors, saw the child and noted how successfully Millie had nursed Harold's wounds. That inspired Millie to pursue a career in nursing and midwifery, and she later took training from Shipp at Cook's College of Nursing in Salt Lake City.[7]

Polly suffered from her typical dropsy and pleurisy during her pregnancy, and her condition worsened as she drew nearer to delivery. George was hardly able to see her to comfort her. On 11 December, when she was eight months pregnant, in great suffering she delivered a little boy, Herbert, who died twenty-four hours later. According to George, "the dropsical waters in my wife appear to have overflowed her chest, producing or causing the premature confinement, and afterwards pneumonia."[8] It appeared that she might die, and George was called to her bedside. He encouraged her to exercise faith and a positive attitude, so that she might recover. She responded that she had no more intention to live. The body of baby Herbert was kept outside the window in the chill winter air to await burial with his mother.[9]

One of Polly's nurses during her last days was George's third wife, Mary. Few, if any, knew she was married to George, or she would have had to hide as well. On the evening before her passing, Polly called her mother, brother, and each child in turn to her side and gave each her parting advice. "She was fully satisfied she was dying and prayed to go, apparently being anxious to depart," related George. She gave her children to the care of her daughter Millie and to the third wife, Mary, who solemnly promised to care for them. Polly died on 17 December 1885. George could not openly attend her funeral, because deputies were conspicuously in attendance at the Twentieth Ward meetinghouse. He disguised himself as a woman and hid his beard with a shawl when he visited her casket before the funeral. Elders Franklin D. Richards and Orson F. Whitney spoke at the services. Little Herbert was buried with Polly in the Salt Lake City cemetery in the family plot.[10]

At the loss of her mother, Alice Louise (who was twelve at the time) recounted, "This was the most serious trouble that came to me in early life, and to this day is one of the keenest losses that I have ever felt. . . . I felt her loss as keenly on account of the other children, particularly the younger ones, as on my own account."[11] Polly's children remember her as "an ideal homemaker and devoted mother" and as one who "never became cross no matter how hard her trials were." By others she was considered "an English gentle-woman of high principles and rare refinement" and noted "for her gentle, unselfish, and affectionate nature."[12] Much later in life, Alice Louise recalled George Q. Cannon telling the children that their mother "would have a watch-care over us, and I think we all feel she has."[13] According to her obituary in the *Deseret News,* Polly possessed "naturally a nervous temperament." The anxiety she felt for her husband during all his legal battles "preyed upon her health." She expired, the account continued, more from "the troubled con-dition of her mind" rather than from her dropsical condition.[14]

The marshals sought George until May 1886, when he learned it would be safe to come out in the open again. The Supreme Court was studying the case of Lorenzo Snow and whether it was legal to arrest a man more than once for a polygamous offense. In June George received a blessing from William J. Smith. He was promised that his posterity would become as "numerous as the sands of the sea" and that they would bring his name "in honorable remembrance from generation to generation." He was further promised that his testimony would cause the hearts of thousands to rejoice.[15]

Now that he was free to go back to work, George Reynolds went each day to the Office of the President to help care for Church business. The entire First Presidency and most of the Quorum of the Twelve Apostles were in hiding. By this time John Taylor was secreted in a Kaysville, Utah, home. Secretary and son-in-law L. John Nuttall was constantly beside President Taylor, whose health was failing. From short entries in Nuttall's journal, we learn that George Reynolds helped run Church business and prepare dis-patches that were regularly delivered at night by couriers to Pres-idents Taylor and Cannon. (President Smith was in hiding in Hawaii.)

During this time of relatively little administrative work, George proceeded vigorously on his Book of Mormon concordance project at home and occasionally during working hours. "After [the prison stay] until the completion of the work [on the concordance in 1899] he was at his desk each morning from 5 to 7 or 7:30," reported George's daughter Alice Louise. "In the evening he frequently checked passages. We were checking and double checking all the time. He was always examining into my spare time and was always delighted if I had an hour or two either in the afternoon or evening that I could give him." The other Reynolds children also assisted their father.[16]

Because of his previous voluminous writings, in 1886 George Reynolds was recognized as the leading living Church authority on the Book of Mormon, Orson Pratt having died in 1881. His friends urged him about this time to compile his writings to be used as a Sunday School and religion class textbook.[17] Liberally drawing on articles already composed for Church periodicals but including some original material, George produced *The Story of the Book of Mormon*, which was eventually published in 1888 by his next-door neighbor, Joseph Hyrum Parry.

The first half of *The Story of the Book of Mormon* gives a running narrative; the second half contains sociological and ethnological essays, many taken from his prison writings for the *Juvenile Instructor*. *The Story of the Book of Mormon* was the Church's first complete commentary of the Book of Mormon text. It also contained the first forty-two illustrations of Book of Mormon subjects, drawn by Utah's most prominent artists, George M. Ottinger, William T. Armitage, John Held, and W. C. Morris.[18]

The book was widely advertised and highly recommended. "I recommend this work to all academies, church schools, teachers and friends of the Book of Mormon," wrote Karl G. Maeser, president of Brigham Young Academy.[19] Elder Moses Thatcher of the Quorum of the Twelve Apostles added, "It is written in forcible yet simple and unambitious style, and is well calculated to inspire faith in the hearts of the young. To the student of inspired history the work cannot fail to prove of great value."[20]

152

The Story of the Book of Mormon met with immediate success, largely because the Church's educational arm adopted it for textbook use. Eventually more editions were published, some in special bindings. George was grateful for royalties and in time purchased the copyright from Joseph Parry.[21] This volume provided a generation of the Church's youth with their initial training in the Book of Mormon.

"For many years we have taken great pleasure in perusing its sacred pages and studying its truths," George wrote of the Book of Mormon in the preface. "The more we read it the more we found it contained. . . . From reading it we turned to writing of it; and much that this volume contains has been penned at various intervals, from the days we were in prison for conscience sake, where portions were written, to the present."[22]

The opening passage of the book reveals undeviating faith and reverence before God:

> The story that we are about to relate is a true one. It is the history of the races who lived on this broad land of ours long, long ago. From it we shall learn many lessons of God's great love for man. We shall also learn how often his love has been spurned, how apt his favored children have been to walk in ways of sin, and how prone to disobey his holy law. It is a story full of light and shade, one which it will be well for all of us to take to heart, for by so doing our faith in God will increase, and we shall be prompted to strive the more earnestly to avoid the evils that others by their misdeeds have brought upon themselves and their posterity.[23]

George's work is remarkably detailed and clear, as evidenced by this passage on domestic life among the Nephites:

> In the midst of a people guided or reproved through their entire national life by an almost continuous succession of inspired teachers, it is but reasonable to conclude that the domestic virtues were assiduously cultivated, and all departures therefrom severely rebuked. Industry, economy, thrift, prudence, and moderation in dress were evidently as much the subject of the prophet's com-

153

mendation then as in these latter days. Zeniff and others directly refer to the labors and toils of the Nephite women in spinning and making the material with which they clothed themselves and their households. . . .

The materials of which the clothing of this race were made are frequently mentioned in the inspired record. Fine silk, fine twined or twisted linen, and cloth of every kind are often spoken of. In one place good homely cloth is mentioned. By the word homely we must not understand the writer to mean ugly; the word is there evidently applied in its original significance, as it is used to-day in England, for homelike or fit for home — such material as was suited to the everyday life of an industrious, hard-working people.[24]

George Reynolds was the first to seriously analyze Book of Mormon proper names. Many of his pioneering efforts were not considered valid by later scholars, but he set the stage for subsequent work. In a chapter entitled "Nephite Proper Names," he dealt with the critics' objections to so many biblical names in the text. He wrote at length about the nonbiblical names, asserting Old World derivation:

Nephi is another very remarkable name. Its roots are Egyptian; its meaning, good, excellent, benevolent. From very ancient times the Egyptians believed that all who died had to have their acts upon earth scrutinized by a council of inquisitors, before they could be proclaimed fit to enter the eternal abodes of bliss and stand in the presence of the god Osiris, the chief lord of the land of the departed. One of the names given to this god, expressive of his attributes, was Nephi or Dnephi (the D being silent, as in Dniestre, Dniepher, etc.), or the good, and the chief city dedicated to him was called N-ph, translated into the Hebrew as Noph, in which form it appears in Hosea, Isaiah, and Jeremiah. . . . From these facts we conclude that Nephi was a common name in the Egyptian tongue; and, as far as the founder of the Nephite nation was concerned, most applicable to his character, which was pre-eminently good and benevolent.[25]

The Story of the Book of Mormon gives the first major attention to Book of Mormon geography. Although his study included personal speculation, much of which is questioned today, George attempted a detailed description of every city, valley, hill, land, and river mentioned in the Book of Mormon. He argued that to the ancient Nephites, the entire North American continent was known as the land of Mulek and the South American continent was known as the land of Lehi; South America had two grand divisions, the land of Zarahemla and the land of Nephi; except in times of war, the Lamanites occupied the land of Nephi and the Nephites the land of Zarahemla; the narrow neck of land was the Isthmus of Panama; the river Sidon was the Magdalena River in Columbia; Lehi landed at thirty degrees south latitude in Chile; the descendants of Lehi spread over both continents of the western hemisphere; the Hill Cumorah (also Ramah to the Jaredites) is located in New York State; the Jaredites crossed the central Asian plateau, thence to the Pacific seaboard, probably the coast of China; the barges of the Jaredites landed in Central America.[26]

George's geographical theories motivated study of the Book of Mormon throughout the Church in subsequent years. President George Q. Cannon reported in January 1890: "We have heard of numerous lectures, illustrated by suggestive maps, being delivered on this subject [the geography of the Book of Mormon] during the present winter, generally under the auspices of the Improvement Societies and Sunday Schools. We are greatly pleased to notice the increasing interest taken by the Saints in this holy book." Cannon noted that those lecturing on geography did not offer united conclusions, which led to contention and confusion. He explained that although the First Presidency had been asked to prepare a map of Nephite geography, they refused on account of the scarcity of information in the Book of Mormon text.[27]

George's final contribution in *The Story of the Book of Mormon* was his detailed "Book of Mormon Chronology." This useful piece lists in short paragraphs major Book of Mormon events, with corresponding dates B.C. or A.D. in one column and in another the year in the Book of Mormon story (for example, 621 meant 621 years since Lehi left Jerusalem).[28] Elder James E. Talmage used this chart when he added chronological dates in the 1921 edition of the Book of Mormon.

On the home front during this period, George's life as a polygamous husband and father went through several phases. His older children were preparing to leave home. One by one they went away to school, on missions, or married. Amelia continued to live in the "north house." She gave birth to her eighth child (the seventh living), Nephi, on 13 August 1887. George's third wife, Mary, cared for the children of the first family in the "south house" and began a large family of her own.

Mary was by all accounts a remarkable woman. "She has been very much the heart of the family," wrote Alice Louise.[29] Mary was meticulous with her grooming, and George referred to her as "my girl with the golden hair." Unselfishly she cared for Polly's younger children, treating them as her own. The eldest child, Millie, assisted with this care until she was married in 1888. Throughout the rest of their lives, the relationship between Mary and Millie was sisterly and extremely close. Polly's children revered "Aunt Mary," and their children always referred to her as "grandmother." Amelia, too, respected Mary, although she was somewhat jealous of the attention George gave her, and Amelia's children were also fond of "Aunt Mary."

Mary was a bundle of energy. Early in her marriage to George, she had three miscarriages. Finally she gave birth to Georgia on 10 July 1886. Later she suffered two more miscarriages.

Mary's younger sister, Amelia Ann, planned to marry George also when she became old enough. But Amelia Ann contracted typhoid fever and died at age fifteen. She was sealed to George in 1888 in the Logan Temple with Mary standing in for her as proxy.[30]

George enjoyed the increasing maturity of his older children and was proud of their many accomplishments. He was happy that his emphasis on their education and religious training was paying dividends. "My Father and I were companions," remembered Alice

156

Louise. "We talked of many things together. He was always alive to what was going on in the world, and his conversation was of never failing interest, but the finest thing about him was his character. . . . He had just that combination of qualities that inspire high regard and deep respect and to that, in my case, was added the loyalty and love of a daughter who enjoyed his scintillating mind and congenial companionship."[31]

George remained active as the senior president of his seventies quorum. A letter from President John Taylor on the Underground indicates some of George's activities at this time: "You ask if an offending member of a quorum of Seventies who has been deprived of his Priesthood by the action of his quorum, has the right of appeal, and if so, to whom." Apparently the twenty-fourth quorum had had occasion to deprive of their place in the quorum recalcitrant members who were not abiding the Word of Wisdom. This purifying of the seventies quorums was going on throughout the Church. President Taylor answered George: "He [the offender] has the right of appeal to the Seven Presidents [of the First Council of Seventy], who preside over the whole body of Seventies."[32]

Meanwhile President John Taylor's health continued to decline, and he passed away in Kaysville on 25 July 1887, still on the Underground. George immediately took on significant assignments for the new ruling Church body, the Quorum of the Twelve Apostles. He served on the committee consisting of Wilford Woodruff, George Q. Cannon, Joseph F. Smith, and L. John Nuttall to plan the funeral services of President Taylor. Next he served as confidential secretary to the Twelve during the transition period and in one of their private meetings read the epistle of the Twelve that was to be delivered in October 1887 general conference. At a preliminary meeting of all the general authorities before the dedication of the Manti Temple, George was asked by the president of the Twelve, Wilford Woodruff, to read the dedicatory prayer that Woodruff had dictated to him. In 1888 George became secretary to the new General Church

157

Board of Education.[33] Clearly George Reynolds was one of the Church's most trusted and honored men.

Notes

1. Federal antipolygamy efforts are chronicled well in Gustive O. Larson, "The Crusade and the Manifesto," in *Utah's History*, ed. Richard D. Poll, et al. (Provo, Utah: Brigham Young University Press, 1978), pp. 257–74.

2. Ibid., 1885. The best sources on the Underground era are Gustive O. Larson, *The "Americanization" of Utah for Statehood* (San Marino, Calif.: Huntington Library, 1971), pp. 115–206; Kimberly Jensen James, "'Between Two Fires': Women on the 'Underground,'" *Journal of Mormon History* 8 (1981): 49–62; and Martha Sonntag Bradley, "'Hide and Seek': Children on the Underground," *Utah Historical Quarterly* 51 (Spring 1983): 133–53.

3. George Reynolds Journal, vol. 6, 1885.

4. Ibid.

5. Ibid.; interview with Mark Curtis, an authority on the history of the Gardo House, 31 January 1986, Salt Lake City, Utah; Ann Jardine Bardsley, "Tracing the Lore of the Gardo House," *Deseret News*, 25 July 1985, p. c-1.

6. George Reynolds Journal, vol. 6, 1885; George Reynolds to Amelia Reynolds, 2 July 1885, 20 July 1885; 25 July 1885; 21 August 1885, Special Collections, Harold B. Lee Library.

7. George Reynolds Journal, vol. 6, 1887; interview with Emily Jensen, 29 November 1985, Provo, Utah; interview with Haroldeane Rasmussen, 29 November 1985, Provo, Utah.

8. George Reynolds Journal, vol. 6, 1885.

9. Ibid. According to an interview with Maude Ogden (daughter of Millie), 7 January 1986, Salt Lake City, Utah, Polly indicated in this discussion with her husband that she had no more intention of living around that other woman (Amelia), who had caused her so much grief. According to Grant Reynolds Hardy, one of the most informed descendants of the Reynolds family, this story is commonly rumored among the first and third family descendants.

10. Ibid.

11. "Autobiography of Alice Louise Reynolds," p. 3.

12. Amy Brown Lyman, *A Lighter of Lamps: The Life Story of Alice Louise Reynolds* (Provo, Utah: Alice Louise Reynolds Club, 1947), p. 4.

13. Ibid., p. 14.

14. Haroldeane Rasmussen, "History of Mary Ann Tuddenham Reynolds, My Grandmother," an unpublished three-page typescript in the possession of Haroldeane Rasmussen.

15. George Reynolds Journal, vol. 6, 1886. For a thorough discussion of the Lorenzo Snow case, see Edwin Brown Firmage and R. Collin Mangrum, *Zion and the Courts: A Legal History of The Church of Jesus Christ of Latter-day Saints, 1830–1900* (Urbana, Ill.: University of Illinois Press, 1988), pp. 178–83.

16. Alice Louise Reynolds, "Biography of George Reynolds," p. 24.

17. Journal of George Reynolds, vol. 6, 1888.

18. George M. Ottinger's role as a pioneer artist in Utah is told in Madeleine B. Stern, "A Rocky Mountain Book Store: Savage and Ottinger of Utah," *BYU Studies* 9 (Winter 1969): 144–54.

19. Cited on a broadside advertisement on *The Story of the Book of Mormon,* in the LDS Church Historical Archives.

20. Ibid.

21. "Memo regarding Books written by George Reynolds," typescript, located in a collection of George Reynolds papers owned by Jane Reynolds Collection; *Circular of the Story of the Book of Mormon,* printed advertisement, n.d., Jane Reynolds Collection; J. H. Parry notes and assignment, Jane Reynolds Collection.

22. George Reynolds, *The Story of the Book of Mormon* (Salt Lake City: Jos. Hyrum Parry, 1888), p. iii.

23. Ibid., p. 17.

24. Ibid., pp. 313–14.

25. Ibid., pp. 377–78. Certainly Reynolds would have been well read to have come up with such information as displayed in this quotation and in many other examples throughout *The Story of the Book of Mormon.* It appears from his correspondence that many of his linguistic conclusions were drawn after consultation with his scientific friend and curator of the Deseret Museum, Joseph Barfoot.

26. Ibid., pp. 382–416. Noted Latter-day Saint anthropologists John L. Sorenson and Joseph L. Allen have produced the most scholarly and up-to-date evaluations of geography and the Book of Mormon in *An Ancient American Setting for the Book of Mormon* (Salt Lake City: Deseret Book Co., 1985) and *Exploring the Lands of the Book of Mormon* (Orem, Utah: S.A. Publishers, 1989). Their conclusions differ dramatically from those of Reynolds. Nevertheless these experts and others are indebted to Reynolds for his path-breaking studies on the subject.

27. "Editorial Thoughts," *Juvenile Instructor* 25 (1 January 1890): 18–19.

28. George Reynolds, *The Story of the Book of Mormon* (Salt Lake City: Jos. Hyrum Parry, 1888), pp. 472–87.

29. Lyman, *Lighter of Lamps,* pp. 14–15.

30. Information for these two paragraphs was drawn from numerous interviews and numerous entries in George Reynolds Journal, vol. 6.

31. "Autobiography of Alice Louise Reynolds," pp. 25–26.

32. John Taylor to George Reynolds, 1 November 1886, Jane Reynolds Collection; Hartley, "The Seventies in the 1880s," pp. 76–77.

33. Diary of L. John Nuttall, vol. 2, pp. 123, 132, 134, 152, 155; George Reynolds Journal, vol. 6, 1888; Arthur M. Richardson and Nicholas G. Morgan, Sr., *The Life and Ministry of John Morgan* (Salt Lake City: n.p., 1965), p. 449.

CHAPTER 16

Secretary to
President Wilford Woodruff

THE CHURCH OF JESUS CHRIST OF LATTER-DAY SAINTS WAS GOING through one of its worst crises in late 1887 and throughout 1888. Most of its leaders, including its presiding officer, Wilford Woodruff, president of the Quorum of the Twelve Apostles, were forced to remain in hiding to avoid arrest. The Edmunds-Tucker Act, passed in March 1887, had strengthened the federal government's power to squeeze the Saints' resolve to continue practicing their principle of polygamy. The law took away the Church's influence over the territorial militia, the educational system, and organized immigration. It even declared the Church itself disincorporated and authorized all Church property valued above fifty thousand dollars to be turned over to the government to benefit Utah's public schools. The law also further restricted the civil and voting rights of all Latter-day Saints. Immediately after President John Taylor's funeral in July 1887, the federal government implemented the escheatment provisions of the Edmunds-Tucker Act by filing suits against the Church and the Perpetual Emigrating Fund Company. Complex legal maneuvering followed.[1]

The Church's crisis was heightened by the leaders' inability to communicate well among themselves because of conditions on the

Underground. Wilford Woodruff ardently desired to reconstitute the First Presidency and call as his counselors George Q. Cannon and Joseph F. Smith, the same counselors who had served under President John Taylor, but was stifled by disagreement among the Twelve Apostles over President Cannon's role as surrogate leader in 1886–87 during President Taylor's illness and incapacity.[2]

George Reynolds, who now was free from potential arrest, assisted the presiding authorities of the Twelve in preparing documents, taking minutes of infrequent quorum meetings, and conducting correspondence. From time to time he met with President Wilford Woodruff and Elders George Q. Cannon and Joseph F. Smith at their hiding places. These brethren were grateful for his accessibility, loyalty, dependability, and productivity. They never forgot his service during the Church's time of dire need.

A vacancy in the First Council of the Seventy occurred in September 1888 with the death of Horace S. Eldredge. President Woodruff, who could not attend the soon-to-be-convened October general conference, wrote to the remaining six presidents of the First Council, requesting them to present their recommendations of ordained seventies for consideration to fill the vacancy. George Reynolds's name topped the list, followed by that of Job Pingree, B. H. Roberts, and Joseph W. Summerhays. George Q. Cannon vetoed the choice of Reynolds at this time, on the grounds that his service as a secretary was still too valuable for him to be called to the First Council. Thirty-one-year-old B. H. Roberts, who had recently received public adulation for his bold work as mission president in the southern states, received the call instead.[3]

So George Reynolds continued his vital role as secretary to the leading apostles. By summer 1889, political events and decisions made it possible for most Church authorities to come out from the Underground, and the Quorum of the Twelve resolved its internal divisions. Finally the apostles were prepared to sustain Wilford Woodruff, George Q. Cannon, and Joseph F. Smith as the new First

Presidency. This action took place publicly in the 1889 October general conference.

After Wilford Woodruff became the fourth president of the Church in 1889, both L. John Nuttall and George Reynolds served as his private secretaries. To help Nuttall restore his failing health by freeing him from a sedentary life-style, President Woodruff sent him twice to Washington, D.C., to serve as secretary to Utah's territorial delegate to the Congress, John T. Caine, and other Mormon lobbyists, including President Joseph F. Smith. In such a capacity Nuttall could obtain more exercise and enjoy more frequently the open air. During the first of these lobbying efforts in Washington in the winter of 1889–90, Reynolds directed the office staff in Salt Lake City in researching material in the *Millennial Star* and the *Journal of Discourses* that would demonstrate the loyalty of the Church to the United States.[4] The Church at this time was in an unprecedented conflict with the federal government. A special churchwide fast was called for 23 December 1889, the anniversary of Joseph Smith's birth. The Saints were enjoined to pray that the plots and schemes of those who sought to destroy the Saint's civil rights and liberties would be confounded. George Reynolds took part in fasting and praying with Church leaders in the Office of the President.[5] All their efforts came to nothing. The gentile Liberal Party in February 1890 swept into political power in Salt Lake City, and as the year proceeded, it appeared that all Latter-day Saints would soon lose their right to vote unless polygamy was denounced.

Gradually Wilford Woodruff became convinced by events and through discussions with his closest advisers that he should consider halting the practice of plural marriage. After much solemn prayer, he finally decided in September 1890 to draft a manifesto stating that no more plural marriages would be performed and that the Church would abide the laws of the land. During the months leading up to the now famous "Woodruff Manifesto," Nuttall was still in Washington and George Reynolds shouldered the burden of work in Salt Lake City. Furthermore, he had been called in April of that year to be a general authority—a member of the First Council of the Seventy. This latter calling required additional traveling and meetings. He confided in his journal that he was "much overworked" and that he had extreme difficulty in tending to all his duties. But he was not alone. All Church leaders were feeling considerable stress.[6]

Unquestionably, as President Woodruff's private secretary, Reynolds participated in the confidential discussions leading up to the publication of the Manifesto. During the celebrated Reed Smoot hearings in the United States Senate fourteen years later, George testified that he, together with Charles W. Penrose and John R. Winder, assisted with the writing and editing of the Manifesto after President Woodruff had drafted it and before it was made public. The First Presidency charged George Reynolds to send the Manifesto over the telegraph as an official announcement.[7]

After the Manifesto, the Church's conflict with the federal government gradually diminished. The Church thus entered a new era of accommodation with the larger American society. George Reynolds's roles also changed. By 1890 George was forty-eight years old and was considered more a Church senior statesman than an up-and-coming leader. As one of the First Seven Presidents of Seventy and as a senior member of the Deseret Sunday School Union Board, he traveled frequently to the stakes of Zion and promoted the cause of both the seventies quorums and the Sunday Schools. He was no longer constantly available to the president of the Church as private secretary. L. John Nuttall's health also gradually limited his effectiveness as private secretary. In 1892 George F. Gibbs, a son-in-law of Lorenzo Snow and a long-time employee in the Office, became the Church president's private secretary and closest aide. He served in that post until 1923.[8]

During this period, George Reynolds also found opportunity to continue his beloved Book of Mormon scholarly projects. He pressed forward, almost daily, in adding new passages to his Book of Mormon concordance. He was anxious to finish it but was even more anxious that the work be absolutely accurate. By February 1889, George had finished tabulating all the passages, a total of 154,000, in the Book of Mormon. Then the second, but shorter, stage of the project began: checking the entries for accuracy. With the aid of two young assistants in the Office of the President, George enthusiastically undertook the task, finishing more than half of the checking by year's end.[9] When new duties came to him in 1890 as private secretary to President Wilford Woodruff and as a general authority, he shelved this project again.[10] When opportunity arose, however, he doggedly pressed on, checking and rechecking his work.

George took the "Book of Mormon Chronological Chart" that was in his book *Story of the Book of Mormon* and with his publisher prepared a six-foot-long chart that came out in 1890. The Deseret Sunday School Union general board promoted the chart as a tool for the classroom and the home at a price of twenty-five cents on paper and one dollar if mounted on rollers. Fully extended, the chart was more than six feet long and had lines crossing at every inch. The mounted version was wound on two sticks, replicating Hebrew scriptures. As described in the *Young Woman's Journal*, "The events and dates of the world's history are printed on one side, while the corresponding dates and events of Nephite history are given on the opposite side. The colored streams representing the various peoples, flow down the center of the chart and give a most comprehensive view of the respective strength or numbers of each." The chart also included the name of each Nephite historian, the time he wrote, and the names and the length of the rule of the various chief judges.[11]

In 1931, when another edition of George's "Book of Mormon Chronological Chart" was published by his son Harold, leading Mormon educator John Henry Evans noted: "George Reynolds was the most thorough-going student of the Nephite record we have had in a hundred years. And the Chart embodies, in a form that appeals to the eye, not only the chronological details of the Book of Mormon itself, but also such contemporary data as help one to understand the narrative. I consider the Chart of the greatest value in the study of the Nephite record. There is nothing that compares with it in its grasp of events, in its accuracy, or in its illuminating details."[12] Although the chart has not been reprinted recently, other Book of Mormon chronology charts published by the Church have followed George's basic pattern.

Another book on the Book of Mormon was in the works as well: George's *Dictionary of the Book of Mormon* appeared in 1891. This volume was immediately implemented in Church schools as a textbook, and George gave gift copies to 354 Church Sunday Schools.[13] When the books were advertised, George wrote, "If you find a customer undecided between the Story and the Dictionary, push the Dictionary."[14] The *Millennial Star* urged readers to purchase the *Dictionary:* "It comprises all the biographical and geographical, as well as all other proper names, in the history to which it refers; and accompanying each is much valuable information in a comprehensive form."[15]

This dictionary, printed in several editions, emphasizes detail. For example, an entry on the Amalekites reads:

> A sect of Nephite apostates whose origin is not given. Many of them were after the order of Nehor. Very early in the days of the republic they had affiliated with the Lamanites and with them built a large city, not far from the waters of Mormon, which they called *Jerusalem.* They were exceedingly crafty and hard-hearted, and in all the ministrations of the sons of Mosiah among them only one was converted. They led in the massacres of the Christian Lamanites or people of Anti-Nephi-Lehi; and in later years the Lamanite generals were in the habit of placing them in high command in their armies, because of their greater force of character, their intense hatred to their former brethren, and their more wicked and murderous disposition. In the sacred record they are generally associated with the Zoramites and Amulonites.[16]

Every Book of Mormon person, city, valley, hill, land, and river mentioned received thorough treatment. This is George Reynolds's most enduring book. Today its most dated portions are the geographical identifications with known map locations. Modern Book of Mormon geography students might take issue with those identifications, such as George's assertion that the land Bountiful "extended southward from the Isthmus of Panama."[17] According to Reynolds, the Isthmus of Panama was the "narrow neck of land" in the Book of Mormon, a point disputed by many Book of Mormon scholars today.

George Reynolds continued maintaining his two separate polygamous households during this stressful time. He diligently saw to it that his growing families received the best possible opportunities for education, and he constantly checked on their progress. His oldest child at home, Alice Louise, was intellectually gifted, so George negotiated with his friend, Brigham Young Academy Principal Karl G. Maeser, for Alice to attend the Provo academy and receive the best available personal tutoring. The same opportunity soon followed for Florry.

At home Amelia gave birth to Nephi on 13 August 1887 and Ethel Georgina on 23 August 1889. Mary delivered her second child, Polly, named after George's first wife, on 11 May 1888 and Philip (Phil) on Pioneer Day, 24 July 1890. After the Manifesto of October 1890, George Reynolds followed the general practice of living with his plural wives and having children by them. Both Amelia and Mary bore several children in the post-Manifesto period.

Notes

1. Gustive O. Larson, "The Crusade and the Manifesto," in *Utah's History*, ed. Richard D. Poll, et al. (Provo, Utah: Brigham Young University Press, 1978), pp. 266–68.

2. Scott G. Kenney, ed., *Wilford Woodruff's Journal*, 9 vols. (Midvale, Utah: Signature Books, 1983–85), vol. 8, clearly demonstrates the tension existing in the Quorum of the Twelve Apostles (see especially 8:489–91). It started in the first meeting of the quorum following President Taylor's death (see 8:450–51) and continued over the next several months. George Reynolds took minutes during these meetings (see 8:482).

3. Notes in the William G. Hartley file at Brigham Young University of the First Council of Seventy Minutes obtained from LDS Church Historical Archives (these minutes are no longer open to scholars, according to interview with Elder

Jack H. Goaslind, member of the presidency of the First Quorum of the Seventy, Salt Lake City, Utah, 6 November 1985); Abraham H. Cannon Journal, 3 October 1888, typescript in Special Collections, Harold B. Lee Library, Brigham Young University; interview with Adrian W. Cannon, grandson of George Q. Cannon, who has studied the Cannon diaries, Salt Lake City, Utah, 17 July 1985; Truman G. Madsen, *Defender of the Faith: The B. H. Roberts Story* (Salt Lake City: Bookcraft, 1980), p. 180.

4. Joseph Christensen Journals, August 1889 to December 1889, in LDS Church Historical Archives. Christensen was a young, temporary secretarial aide to Reynolds.

5. Ibid. James R. Clark, ed., *Messages of the First Presidency,* 6 vols. (Salt Lake City: Bookcraft, 1965–75), 3:176–79; George Reynolds Journal, vol. 6, 1889; David John Journal, vol. 3, 23 December 1889, Special Collections, Harold B. Lee Library, Brigham Young University; Arthur M. Richardson and Nicholas G. Morgan, Jr., *The Life and Ministry of John Morgan* (Salt Lake City: n. p., 1965), pp. 478–79.

6. George Reynolds Journal, vol. 6, 1890.

7. *Proceedings Before the Committee on Privileges and Elections of the United States Senate, Reed Smoot Case,* 2 vols. (Washington: Government Printing Office, n.d.), 2:51–53. Frank J. Cannon, who was prominent in the negotiations leading up to the Manifesto, also acknowledged the possibility that Reynolds helped edit the document. See Frank J. Cannon and Harvey J. O'Higgins, *Under the Prophet in Utah* (Boston: C. M. Clark Publishing Co., 1911), p. 100. D. Michael Quinn in "LDS Church Authority and New Plural Marriages, 1900–1904," *Dialogue* 18 (Spring 1985): 44–45 submits further evidence of George Reynolds's assisting with the writing of the Manifesto. Richard S. Van Wagoner provides an excellent summary of the question of the authorship of the Manifesto in *Mormon Polygamy: A History* (Salt Lake City: Signature Books, 1986), pp. 261–62.

8. I have discussed the roles of all the secretaries in the Office of the President, including the private secretary, in more detail in "Close to the Seat of Authority: Secretaries and Clerks in the Office of the President of the LDS Church, 1870–1900," a paper delivered at the annual meetings of the Mormon History Association, Provo, Utah, May 1984.

9. Journal of George Reynolds, vol. 6, 1889.

10. Ibid., 1890.

11. "Book of Mormon chronological Chart, by George Reynolds," p. 188; "Editorial Thoughts," *Juvenile Instructor* 35 (1 May 1900): 281–82; Guide to Reynolds's chronological chart of Nephite and Lamanite History, broadside advertisement, located in Jane Reynolds Collection. A copy of this large chart was displayed at the George Reynolds Reunion, Salt Lake City, 31 August 1985.

12. "Are We of Israel?" *Improvement Era* 34 (October 1931): 744.

13. Journal of George Reynolds, vol. 6, 1891; "Sunday Schools to which I have given dictionaries of the Book of Mormon," memo book, Jane Reynolds Collection.

14. "Memo regarding Books written by Geo. Reynolds," Jane Reynolds Collection.

15. *Millennial Star* 54 (22 February 1892): 121–22.

16. George Reynolds, *A Dictionary of the Book of Mormon* (Salt Lake City: Jos. Hyrum Parry, 1891), p. 47.

17. Ibid., p. 352.

CHAPTER 17

Called as a General Authority

O<small>NE OF THE GREATEST HONORS THAT CAN COME TO A</small> L<small>ATTER-DAY</small>
Saint male during his lifetime is a call to be one of the Church's
general authorities. George Reynolds received such an honor in the
April 1890 general conference when he was called and sustained as
a member of the First Council of Seventy (or First Seven Presidents
of Seventy, which was a more frequently used title at that time).
Other general authorities were the three members of the First Presidency, the Quorum of the Twelve Apostles, the patriarch to the
Church, and the three members of the presiding bishopric. The
presidents of the Seventy were experts on missionary work, acting
under the direction of the First Presidency and the apostles, and
they directed the affairs of the numerous seventies quorums
throughout the Church in 1890.

Members of the Church have always been fascinated by their
general authorities, often looking upon them with awe. Faithful
Saints are expected to follow their counsel as coming from God. One
reason these men are known as "general" authorities is that their
assignments extend to all the world, not just to local wards and
stakes as subordinate positions do. Since the period when George
Reynolds served as a general authority, the number of such authorities has expanded. Not only are there seven presiding presidents (now referred to as the Presidency of the Seventy), but there

are numerous members of both the first and the second quorums of the Seventy. Since October 1986 no lay members of the Church have served as seventies, only general authorities. Most seventies today function as members of area presidencies for the Church in various locations throughout the world. They also serve in executive positions supervising departments at Church headquarters. Today's critical and expanding work of the quorums of the Seventy has some roots in the period when George Reynolds was first an active seventy and later one of the First Seven Presidents of Seventy.

The first reference to seventies in the Church's history was in February 1835, when Joseph Smith announced an unrecorded revelation establishing the seventy as a new Melchizedek priesthood office (along with elder, high priest, and apostle — the latter having just been added itself) and created a distinctly structured quorum of seventy men. The Prophet taught that the seventies were "to constitute traveling quorums, to go into all the earth, withersoever the Twelve Apostles shall call them."[1] A month later a "revelation on priesthood" (Doctrine and Covenants 107) provided further details of the responsibilities of all priesthood offices in both the Melchizedek (higher) and the Aaronic (lower) priesthoods, including the seventies. Clearly the calling of the seventy was similar to that of the apostles in preaching the gospel and in being "especial witnesses" (Doctrine and Covenants 107:25) and traveling ministers to all the world. But always the seventies were to act under the direction of the Twelve, never independently.[2]

During Joseph Smith's adminstration, three seventies quorums were established. After his death, the Quorum of the Twelve Apostles, under the direction of Brigham Young, envisioning as they did a vast expansion of proselyting the nations of the earth, gave even more emphasis to the seventies and formed a total of thirty-five quorums. Through the Church's exodus to the Rocky Mountains and subsequent colonization of many different valleys, seventies retained membership in their originally numbered Nauvoo quorums. This situation created record-keeping problems as well as difficulty for quorum members to hold meetings. Practically speaking, seventies existed from 1850 to 1880 primarily as a resource pool for potential missionaries who could be called into the Church's various missions. Approximately two-thirds of all missionaries called to foreign missions came from the seventies quorums.[3] George Reynolds was ordained a seventy in 1866 and retained that priesthood office throughout his call as one of the First Seven Presidents of Seventy in 1890. Unlike today's practice, George as a presiding seventy was not ordained to the office of high priest.

George Reynolds's call as a general authority came in April 1890 after Abraham H. Cannon was called to be an apostle. Some of the pressure from federal authorities had abated, and none of the general authorities was in hiding. Again the First Council submitted recommendations. Again the Council made George Reynolds their first choice. This time he was called, although he still was serving as private secretary to President Wilford Woodruff and would continue in that capacity for two more years. After general conference sessions, in which George's name was presented for a sustaining vote, Lorenzo Snow, president of the quorum of the Twelve Apostles, set apart the forty-eight-year-old George Reynolds as one of the First Seven Presidents of Seventy.[4]

His six colleagues were Henry Harriman, eighty-five; Jacob Gates, seventy-nine; Seymour B. Young, fifty-two; Christian D. Fjelsted, sixty-one; John Morgan, forty-seven; and B. H. Roberts, thirty-three. Harriman and Gates died within two years of George's call; Seymour B. Young became the senior president and remained as such throughout the rest of George's life. Others who became members of the First Council during George's tenure were J. Golden Kimball, Rulon S. Wells, Edward Stevenson, Joseph W. McMurrin, and Charles H. Hart. This group met each Wednesday in the Templeton Building on South Temple Street across from Temple Square. As would be expected, these men grew close. During the last two decades of his life, George considered his best friends to be Seymour Young, B. H. Roberts, J. Golden Kimball, and Rulon Wells of the

First Council as well as his other close associates on the Deseret Sunday School Union Board, of which he also was a member.[5]

George's fondness for his colleagues is revealed in a letter to B. H. Roberts, written while Roberts was struggling to hold onto his seat in the United States House of Representatives in 1899. Roberts was under attack for being a polygamist. George wrote his friend, "Last week the Council wrote you a letter, but, so far as I was concerned, at least, it was not entirely satisfactory. It did not fully convey our feelings, which are much warmer." Comfortingly he added, "I know that one man with God on his side is in the majority; and God has not deserted you, neither have many of your brethren. . . . You are standing in the gap where in a somewhat different manner, I once stood. The crowd are not fighting you or I; it is God's law they are warring on."[6]

During George's service on the First Council, it was common for the seven presidents to have "general" callings in addition to their work as seventies. This general calling enabled them when they toured or visited the various stakes to meet not only with seventies quorums but with other appropriate Church workers. John Morgan was second assistant general superintendent of the Sunday Schools, and Seymour Young and George Reynolds were members of the Sunday School general board. George eventually served in the general superintendency as well. Beginning with J. Golden Kimball, each new member of the seven presidents was also called to serve on the general board of the Young Men's Mutual Improvement Association.

On average George visited some twenty stakes per year from 1890 to 1906. Many of these were in such distant locations as Canada, Oregon, Wyoming, Arizona, and Mexico and required several weeks away from home at a time. Almost always he met with both seventies and Sunday School conferences, or faculty meetings, to instruct them in their duties. On his visits he often called and set apart new seventies quorum presidents and ordained new seventies. With his interests in history, geography, and geology, George took advantage of the opportunity to learn new things on his trips. For example, in a report to the *Juvenile Instructor* of his visit to Church branches in the Tintic mining district in Juab County, Utah, George related, "True to his perceptive instincts, the next morning, Elder Reynolds was climbing the hills of Mammoth, viewing the landscape o'er and taking in the general topography of the country for present and future information and use."[7]

Nothing was more important to the seven presidents during these years than educating prospective missionaries throughout the Church. Most of the First Council were educated men themselves and valued education as a most significant part of the gospel. As George and some of his colleagues traveled to the stakes, educating the youth became a prime topic of discussion. For example, Teancum Pratt of rural Carbon County recorded the visit of Elders Reynolds and Wells of the First Council to a conference: "We were met by Brother Reynolds and Wells, who talked mostly upon the subject of saving and educating the rising generation, and this subject is very much talked of now."[8]

The First Council planned a general seventies conference in Salt Lake City to be held for two days in January 1894. The theme for the gathering was " 'the necessity of the Elders of Israel to acquire knowledge in all branches of learning whereby they may be made efficient as ministers of the Gospel and witnesses of the work of the Almighty of this age.' During the meetings Elder B. H. Roberts' new book *Outlines of Ecclesiastical History* was launched with a 'practical illustration of how to conduct a class.' " The *Deseret News* failed to identify the main speaker at the conference, but perhaps it was George Reynolds, for the sentiments expressed certainly reflected his attitudes. The speaker stated, "All truth emanated from the same source, from God." He added, "A mind well sorted with facts and filled with the Holy Spirit is a mind that exercises influence on the world for good."[9]

In those years, serving as a member of the seven presidents was not a full-time calling and no salary was drawn for performing

173

this priesthood work. Each member of the First Council was required to earn a living and support his family. Seymour Young, the senior member of the group during all but two years of George's tenure, was a physician who still maintained his practice and made a comfortable living. Young was so compassionate that he often performed medical work for others without charge, particularly while on the road in his ministry. Others of the First Council were not so well off financially. The most colorful among them, B. H. Roberts, was perpetually poor, supporting his plural families as best he could with royalties from lecturing and writing. John Morgan was an administrator of both a local hotel and a business college, both of which suffered terribly in the Panic of 1893. George Reynolds, of course, was employed by the Church, and his daily work was in harmony with his priesthood calling. But in 1904 he made it clear before the United States Senate that there was a distinction between his "business" in the Office and his "calling" in the priesthood. Because he labored at Church headquarters, George often assisted Seymour Young in blessing and setting apart missionaries as they prepared to depart on their assignments.[10]

From the time of his release as private secretary to President Woodruff in 1892, George Reynolds served in a number of vital secretarial capacities in the Office. None of these, however, required hourly or daily attention. Hence he could travel, write, and carry out his responsibilities as needed on a more flexible schedule.

One of his duties was to process requests for divorce and cancellation of temple sealings. On occasion he summoned individuals who applied for divorce to sign papers. Alice Louise Reynolds recounts one story: "One day a man came in where the evidence was especially bad so far as he was concerned. Had that man known my Father he would have signed that paper and walked out but he stammered something about having his wife in eternity. At this Father became infuriated and said: Don't you ever think it. I should like to help kick you to hell myself."[11]

In 1893 the construction of the Salt Lake Temple was completed, and the holy edifice was dedicated in multiple ceremonies over a month's period. George attended most of these dedicatory sessions and participated in some, either speaking or praying. President Wilford Woodruff had been the Church's greatest advocate of ordinance work for the dead, and in 1894 he organized the Utah Genealogical Society to promote genealogical research among Church members. George Reynolds, who had researched his family tree and had arranged for the ordinance work to be done, became the Genealogical Society secretary.[12] He continued in that position until 1902.

By the 1890s the First Presidency (not just the Church president alone, as was generally the case with Joseph Smith and Brigham Young) had become the composite ruling entity of the LDS Church. The president was the prophet and had the final say on most matters, yet counselors increasingly exerted more influence. During the Underground era, when John Taylor was in hiding and in ill health, first counselor George Q. Cannon directed Church affairs by default. Under the aged Wilford Woodruff, formidable counselors George Q. Cannon and Joseph F. Smith played nearly an equal role with Woodruff in Church administration. Important edicts came from the First Presidency as a body after this group discussed matters and came to a joint conclusion. During the last two decades of his life, George Reynolds handled a great deal of First Presidency correspondence. For example, in 1893 George wrote in behalf of the First Presidency to E. D. Woolley, the stake president of Kanab, on a matter about which the First Presidency had heard complaints:

> I am directed by the First Presidency to say that a letter has been received at this office complaining of the habit to which some in Kanab, (and among them local authorities in the priesthood) are giving way to, of training race horses on the Sabbath day, in disregard of the commandments to keep the day holy, and to the injury of the morals of the youth of the settlement. This not being the first complaint that has been received on this matter, the Presidency would be pleased to learn from you how much there is to it, and what steps you are taking to remedy the evil, supposing it to exist.[13]

Many times local Church leaders wrote to the First Presidency at the then-famous "Box B" in Salt Lake City asking difficult doctrinal questions. Apparently Reynolds, well versed as he was in theology and the history of the Church, was often charged to answer the questions. Sometimes he stated clearly what the First Presidency had authorized him to say and then added his own opinion. At other times he wrote reasoned, concise responses that seem to have been on his own authority. One such example follows:

> There are various opinions held with regard to the Apostleship of Paul; but I know of nothing in the Scriptures to warrant the idea that he was one of the Twelve. Some imagine that he was a Seventy. My opinion is that he was an apostle, as in this dispensation, Oliver Cowdery and others have been ordained apostles yet never belonged to the Quorum of the Twelve. The same may be said of Bros. Daniel H. Wells and John W. Young. They were counselors to the Twelve they never belonged to the Quorum of the Twelve, yet they were both Apostles, for they belonged, at one time, to the First Presidency of the Church. In the eyes of many the fact that Paul was especially called by Jesus from heaven made him an Apostle; but until he was ordained to the Priesthood by one holding proper authority his administrations in the ordinances of the church would not have been legal. Paul himself, if we may judge by some of his utterances, esteemed himself equal in authority to those Apostles who belonged to the Twelve.[14]

Another assignment that came to George and his colleagues was to speak in the Church's general conferences. George was not an orator, and he knew it. He preferred not to be called upon in the conference and much preferred to offer a prayer than to speak. Elders Seymour B. Young, B. H. Roberts, and J. Golden Kimball of the First Seven Presidents were well-liked public speakers and addressed conference sessions more frequently than did Elder Reynolds. Perhaps, with his close association with the First Presidency, he was able to persuade them not to call on him to speak as often.

In his first recorded address in general conference, in October 1897, seven and a half years after he was called as a general authority,

George made public his lifelong, ardent desire for the arrival of the peaceful, millennial reign of Jesus Christ. "And these things I know will be brought about," he testified, "under the direction of those who hold the keys of power in the midst of His people, to whom He reveals His mind and will." He added, "And I am doubly thankful to know that there is not one key of the Holy Priesthood, not one power belonging to God's kingdom, not one key of authority, not one principle pertaining to the building up of righteousness upon the earth, that God has withheld from His people, in these the latter days."[15]

Beginning in 1890, with the First Presidency's permission, George gave weekly lectures at both LDS College, Salt Lake City, and Brigham Young Academy, Provo, until 1902, when his increased responsibilities with the Deseret Sunday School Union made the weekly lectures impossible. Most of his college lectures dealt with Book of Mormon topics. Related to these lectures were eleven articles on "Lessons from the Life of Nephi" and twelve articles on "The Jaredites" published in the *Juvenile Instructor* in 1891 and 1892, respectively.

In 1896 George wrote in his journal, "I delivered my usual series of lectures at the B.Y. Academy, Provo, and Latter-day Saints College, Salt Lake City. This series was a new one treating on the Evidences of the Divinity of the Book of Mormon. Articles on the same subject (being the main argument of the lectures) appeared in the *Contributor*, commencing with January. This new course cost me a great amount of study."[16]

These five articles had indeed demanded considerable research. Drawing from recently published studies, George argued that "external evidences" increased the veracity of the Book of Mormon. He examined ancient American codices containing similar Book of Mormon traditions; rings binding ancient records; the discovery of Hebrew writings and metal plates in the Americas; the ties to the Book of Mormon of ancient Mexican and Peruvian traditions as independently recorded by the chroniclers Lord Kingsborough, Sahagun, Las Casas, Torquemeda, and Montesinos; and geological evidences of cataclysmic events in the Americas. The *Millennial Star* reprinted these articles a year later. The study of external evidences pointing to the historicity of the Book of Mormon increased considerably in the Church after George's research was published.

The latter part of the nineteenth century has been identified by historians as the Age of Science. George's attempts to justify the Book of Mormon in light of the flood of scientific discoveries are commendable. A plethora of others in the Church, notably B. H. Roberts, soon followed his lead. George's professorship at Brigham Young Academy also prompted an enthusiastic determination by faculty and students to obtain firsthand scientific evidence to substantiate the Book of Mormon. The academy's president, Benjamin F. Cluff, Jr., organized an expedition to Central and South America in 1900. One of Cluff's ambitions was to discover Zarahemla in Colombia, which George Reynolds taught was on the River Magdalena.[17]

George Reynolds continued a devoted father and husband during the 1890s. One of his most impressive habits was never to leave his family in suspense about where he was, what he was doing, or when he would be home in the evening. "All his life he turned to his wife or wives as he was leaving in the morning," Alice Louise wrote, "and said, 'I shall be home at my regular time, if anything interferes I shall let you know.' And if anything interfered, he did let them know. Before the time of telephones he used a messenger." He never failed to remember wedding anniversaries and birthdays, quite a feat for a man with three wives and more than thirty children.[18]

Although George was an exemplary family man, he suffered from the weakness that many with his temperament and talents have also had. "If his reputation was particularly good [in relation to his love for his family]," Alice Louise recorded, "it was not so good when it came to putting up stoves, hanging doors, and pulling down carpets. Any wife he had could beat him at such jobs."[19]

After Alice Louise began teaching at Brigham Young Academy, she once returned home for Christmas and, as usual, went straight from the railroad depot to her father's desk in the Office of the President. "There he sat with a picture book and a doll on his desk," she recounted.

> As I came in he said, "Alice, there is a little girl in the L.D.S. hospital who is afraid Santa Claus won't know where she is. Sidney has bought the book. I have bought the doll" and I finished his sentence by saying, "and I will buy the dishes." The mere incident of this man who had 32 children of his own and staggering responsibility every day of his life taking it upon himself to see that the child at the hospital was not forgotten is not the important thing, but rather that there could be no Christmas for him unless the little girl at the hospital was provided for.[20]

In 1894, George Reynolds moved his combined first and third families to a house on Wall Street near the present state capitol building. His two families were separated by more than a mile. George was very busy with being a secretary in the Office of the President, a ranking member of the Deseret Sunday School Union Board and general treasurer, and a member of the First Council of Seventy (which meant being away from Salt Lake City almost every weekend). He was in the last years of his project of collecting the data for his monumental Book of Mormon concordance. Furthermore he was more than fifty years old and had lost the energy of his earlier years. So he chose to spend most of his evenings at the home of his third wife, Mary, where he had an office upstairs. He got in the habit of going to Amelia's house only every Thursday night. Otherwise he was generally at his home on Wall Street in the Nineteenth Ward.[21]

Most evenings he went home and spent an hour with the family, which included family prayer and time for the children to talk with their father. After dinner he retired to his office to work on his concordance, prepare his lectures, write other articles, or simply relax. Mary assiduously kept the little children and their noise away from him. Then in the mornings all the children were expected to arise early and eat breakfast with their father. The younger children did not become as acquainted with George, particularly with his happy and tender personality, as did his older children. Their memories of him are not as pleasant as those of the first children.

Amelia generally did not mind that George did not stay often in her home. She was tired of bearing children (her last one, her twelfth, was born in 1898) and did not want to have any more. But she insisted on having equal amounts of things provided her children, and George attempted to do that. Amelia's younger children suffered from lack of positive exposure to their father, although in 1902, when Amelia had a bad spell with rheumatism, he spent several months living at her house. He was also anxious to help Amelia whenever he could with her family's genealogy and temple work.

The children of the second family knew the children in the first and third families well. They often visited each other and went on outings together. The children in the first and third families were just like brothers and sisters to each other. They responded to the children from the second family not as cousins but still not quite as close as brothers and sisters.

Notes

1. Joseph Smith, Jr., *History of the Church of Jesus Christ of Latter-day Saints,* ed. B. H. Roberts, 7 vols. (Salt Lake City, Utah: Deseret Book Co., 1957), 2:202.

2. Doctrine and Covenants 107:25–26, 34, 38, 93–98.

3. S. Dilworth Young, "The Seventies: A Historical Perspective," *Ensign* 6 (July 1976): 14–18; Hartley, "The Seventies in the 1880s," pp. 62–63; James N. Baumgarten, "The Role and Function of the Seventies in L.D.S. Church History," master's thesis, Brigham Young University, 1960.

4. George Reynolds Journal, vol. 6, 1890; Abraham H. Cannon Journal, 1 April 1890; *Deseret Semi-Weekly News,* 8 April 1890, p. 3; Arthur M. Richardson and Nicholas G. Morgan, Jr., *The Life and Ministry of John Morgan* (Salt Lake City: n.p., 1965), p. 485.

5. Seymour Bicknell Young Papers; Alice Louise Reynolds, "Biography of George Reynolds," p. 30.

6. George Reynolds to B. H. Roberts, 27 November 1899, Jane Reynolds Collection. See also B. H. Roberts to George Reynolds, 8 December 1899 and J. Golden Kimball to George Reynolds, 13 September 1892, Jane Reynolds Collection. For other evidence of Reynolds's closeness to Roberts, see Truman G. Madsen, *Defender of the Faith: The B. H. Roberts Story* (Salt Lake City: Bookcraft, 1980), pp. 226, 229, 233.

7. *Juvenile Instructor* 36 (1 August 1901): 464; 27 (1 August 1892): 465–68.

8. Edna Romano, ed., "Teancum Pratt, Founder of Helper," *Utah Historical Quarterly* 48 (Fall 1980): 351.

9. *Deseret Semi-Weekly News,* 2 February 1894, p. 4; Richardson and Morgan, *The Life and Ministry of John Morgan,* pp. 565–66.

10. Seymour Bicknell Young Papers; "Lives of Our Leaders. – The First Council of the Seventy. President Seymour B. Young," *Juvenile Instructor* 36 (15 April 1901): 224–27; Madsen, *Defender of the Faith,* pp. 182–83; Richardson and Morgan, *The Life and Ministry of John Morgan,* pp. 567–68; *Reed Smoot Hearings,* 2:51–53.

11. A. L. Reynolds, "Biography of George Reynolds," pp. 33–34.

12. George Reynolds Journal, vol. 6, 1893–1894.

13. George Reynolds to E. D. Woolley, 1893, Edwin Dilworth Woolley Papers, LDS Church Historical Archives.

14. George Reynolds to J. D. Call, 24 December 1897, Jane Reynolds Collection. Other letters that I have seen from the Office of the First Presidency written by Reynolds on doctrinal questions are G. R. to W. B. Torrey, 27 November 1900 (on who the "Lamanites" are today and the success of missionary work among them); G. R. to John F. Sharp, 26 August 1898 (on observing the Sabbath day on Sunday); G. R. to J. C. Ferrin, 7 March 1899 (on whether the Old Testament prophets possessed the Melchizedek Priesthood); G. R. to Hugh J. Cannon, 5 May 1902 (on a proposed wording change in the Book of Mormon text); and G. R. to R. Ballantyne, 28 September 1897 (on how the Joseph Smith Translation of the Bible helps one understand the Old Testament passages on the Lord hardening the Pharaoh's heart), all in the Jane Reynolds Collection.

15. Conference Report, October 1897, p. 49. Reynolds discussed this same theme in his next recorded address, according to Conference Report, October 1898, pp. 18–21.

16. Journal of George Reynolds, vol. 6, 1896. This series, entitled "Evidences of the Book of Mormon: Some External Proofs of Its Divinity," is found in *Contributor* 17 (January 1896): 164–68; 17 (February 1896): 231–38; 17 (March 1896): 271–78; 17 (April 1896): 361–68; 17 (May 1896): 417–24.

17. Accounts of the Cluff expedition are found in Ernest L. Wilkinson, *Brigham Young University: The First Hundred Years,* 4 vols. (Provo, Utah: Brigham Young University Press, 1975), 1:289–329; Gary James Bergera and Ronald Priddis, *Brigham Young University: A House of Faith* (Salt Lake City: Signature Books, 1985), pp. 10–13.

18. A. L. Reynolds, "Biography of George Reynolds," pp. 30– 31.

19. Ibid., p. 32.

20. Ibid., p. 33.

21. Information for this and subsequent paragraphs on the Reynolds family comes from a composite of numerous interviews and discussions with Reynolds family descendants including an interview with George Gordon Reynolds, 31 August 1981, Salt Lake City. At that time, Gordon was Reynolds's sole surviving son. Also, some information comes from entries in George Reynolds Journal, vol. 6.

CHAPTER 18

Sunday School Administrator

In ADDITION TO ALL HIS OTHER DUTIES, GEORGE REYNOLDS CONTINUED
to labor through the years with his beloved Sunday School program.
Under George Q. Cannon, Reynolds had been a pioneer Sunday
School worker as a contributor to the *Juvenile Instructor*, treasurer
of the Deseret Sunday School Union, chairman of the publications
committee, and a writer and promoter of the Union's *Faith Promoting
Series* booklets. In the Twentieth Ward, George served three lengthy
terms as Sunday School superintendent, during which many inno-
vations in recruitment, activities, music, and curriculum were implemented. After 1885 he no longer served on the local level.

In 1883 George aided the Union in preparing the Church's first
Sunday School hymnal, *Deseret Sunday School Union Music Book*. A
year later he and Union co-worker Levi W. Richards compiled a
serial article, "Historical Review of the Deseret Sunday School
Union," for the *Juvenile Instructor*.[1] This effort presaged a much
larger project, *Jubilee History of Latter-day Saint Sunday Schools*,
which George Reynolds and Levi Richards co-authored in 1899. The
latter publication drew heavily, even in exact language, from the
1884 article. The 1884 sketch concluded with the following glowing
assessment:

> To say that [the Deseret Sunday School Union] has been a

potent instrument of religious culture, of social refinement, and moral worth, a factor in the development of God's purposes, a bond of union among His people, a source of strength to the Church, and an aid to the Priesthood would, we submit, not be claiming too much; and this position is all the more gratifying when we consider how vast has been the labor performed and how slight has been the cost in dollars and cents, to the community.[2]

In April 1889, the executive board of the Deseret Sunday School Union was formed. Before that time executive power rested with the general superintendency alone, but with the growth of the Union throughout the expanding Church and with General Superintendent Cannon's frequent absence on account of his other duties, six men were added to the executive board. George Reynolds was named the senior member of that additional six. In August that year George began serving in his new calling by going on a three-week "Sunday School mission" to small settlements in northern Utah and southern Idaho.[3]

Also in 1889 the publications committee promoted a new teaching methodology by issuing thirty-one "Sunday School Leaflets" on the life of Christ. They were written by George Reynolds and two emerging young and brilliant educators in the Church, James E. Talmage and Willard Done. Throughout the 1890s this committee, which was expanded to include Karl G. Maeser and Bertha Irving, continued to produce more leaflets until there were 212 in all. For many years the leaflets provided the basic curriculum in the Deseret Sunday School Union. They contained seventy-four lessons on the Old Testament, twenty on the life of the Prophet Joseph Smith, fifty-one on the Book of Mormon, and forty on the Articles of Faith. Each of the leaflets contained texts from the scriptures and helps for the teachers in preparing their lessons. The sections were entitled "Lesson Statement," "Questions on the Lesson," and "What We May Learn from This Lesson."[4]

After George's call to be a general authority in 1890 at age forty-eight, his work with the Sunday Schools took a new turn. Henceforth he traveled many times each year in his dual role as an executive member of the Deseret Sunday School general board and as a member of the First Council of Seventy. More often than not he conducted both Sunday School and seventies' business in the stakes and missions he visited.

In 1893 a proposal of the Deseret Sunday School Union that each stake hold annual Sunday School conferences received approval from the First Presidency. Hence, in 1894 George went in company with George Goddard of the general superintendency on an extended four and one-half month "mission" to stake and mission Sunday School conferences and meetings in California, Arizona, Mexico, Idaho, and Utah. "During my travels on S.S. Conference business [in 1894] I traveled about 11,700 miles, nearly 2,000 of which was by [horse] team," he recorded. "While visiting the stakes we not only attended the public conference meetings, but held meetings with the teachers and with the Stake Presidency & Superintendency."[5] In these settings, the general board members exhibited methods of conducting class exercises, answered questions about Sunday School matters, and gave encouragement.[6] George attended a number of such conferences in subsequent years, although he was not again absent from home for such an extended period of time.

In September 1898, George visited Rock Springs, Wyoming, and then traveled eastward to Omaha, Nebraska, where he attended meetings of the Trans-Mississippi Sunday School Congress as one of several delegates from the Deseret Sunday School Union. Obviously Latter-day Saint Sunday School leaders felt they could learn new ideas from the Protestant Sunday Schools. On the train home, George suggested to his colleagues that they propose to George Q. Cannon that a huge general Sunday School convention be held in Salt Lake City. Cannon readily accepted the idea and appointed George Reynolds, Joseph Summerhays, and George Pyper to a committee to plan and conduct the conference.[7]

The conference was held in the Assembly Hall on Temple Square, 28 and 29 November. Three sessions were held each day for the delegates, who came from each stake throughout the Church. Elder Reynolds outlined the objectives of the convention at the beginning of the conference and gave other instruction throughout. "The proceedings of the convention were considered of such practical value and importance to Sunday School workers that they were published in full by the Union."[8]

Nearly a year later, in October 1899, after the regular general conference sessions, the Deseret Sunday School Union hosted a spectacular fiftieth-year anniversary jubilee. Surviving members of the original class taught by Richard Ballantyne fifty years earlier were honored. Sunday School children from various ancestries recited the Church's Articles of Faith in different languages to symbolize the growth of the Church internationally. To commemorate the activities, Elder Reynolds and Levi W. Richards compiled the *Jubilee History of the Latter-day Saint Sunday Schools.*[9]

In company with Thomas C. Griggs of the general board, George went on a typical visit in the summer of 1900 to outlying stakes on Sunday School business. The *Juvenile Instructor* published the details of the visit as "specimenic" of experiences of general board members "when visiting distant stakes of Zion in their official capacity." The two men traveled by rail to the terminus at Belknap in southern Utah and then were conveyed first by stage and then by team to Panguitch, where they conducted sessions of a stake Sunday School conference. En route they witnessed the death of a little boy on the rails. The pair related the difficulties of reaching the isolated settlements of Tropic, Escalante, Cannonville, Hillsdale, Long Valley, and Orderville—having to be their own teamsters for forty miles—but also the hearty welcome they received everywhere. At each spot Reynolds and Griggs conducted Sunday School business, and Reynolds also met with the seventies of the area wherever possible.[10]

Also in 1900 George was called with Joseph W. Summerhays and George D. Pyper to prepare a second general convention of Sunday School workers to be held in Salt Lake City 12 and 13 November. Among other things George was to prepare answers to questions on Sunday School procedures that were to be sent to headquarters in advance by superintendents.[11] At an important preparatory meeting of the general board on 5 October, a discussion arose about dealing with the *Juvenile Instructor*, now that the George Q. Cannon & Sons publishing company had been disbanded. George Reynolds spoke in favor of the Deseret Sunday School Union purchasing the *Juvenile Instructor* and using it as the official publication of the Union. The idea was accepted, and board members Reynolds, Summerhays, and Griggs were appointed to negotiate terms of purchase with Cannon. By year's end the deal was concluded, and Cannon, who remained as editor of the publication, named George Reynolds, "the devoted Sunday School worker and warm personal friend," as the assistant editor.[12]

The second Deseret Sunday School Convention, held in November, was largely prepared under the supervision of George Reynolds and went superbly. There were 2,025 delegates representing 125,000 pupils and teachers from throughout the Church, who were trained in all aspects of their work. George took a leading role in answering the delegates' questions. The most important announcement of the convention was that henceforth the standard works of the Church — the Holy Bible, the Book of Mormon, the Doctrine and Covenants, and Pearl of Great Price — should serve as the basic curriculum in Sunday Schools. Other resources would be allowed, but none of a sectarian or secular nature. George Reynolds took a major role in formulating this policy, which has remained basically intact in the LDS Church to the present time.

George Q. Cannon observed about the Sunday School convention:

> [The Lord's] spirit was poured out abundantly, and if there is such a thing as being intoxicated with happiness, certainly those sensations were felt by very many. The assemblage was such as to call forth the blessings of the Lord. Outside of our Church, no gathering of men and women could be found more self-sacrificing

and more thoroughly filled with the spirit to do good to others, than those who were present at this convention.[13]

This second general Sunday School convention also marked the beginning of the last chapter in the career of George Reynolds, for he was called as the second assistant general superintendent of the Deseret Sunday School Union. George Goddard, the original first assistant to George Q. Cannon beginning in 1872 and also a good friend to George Reynolds, had died in January 1899. Cannon had not made any changes for nearly two years, retaining only Karl G. Maeser in the superintendency. Between sessions of the convention, the general board met, and Cannon named George Reynolds as second assistant, announcing that he was moved upon by the Spirit. George's name was then presented to the convention for a sustaining vote. Cannon told the delegates, "He has been intimately identified with the Sunday School movement from the beginning and has been one of our best and most active workers, and is as well acquainted with the workings of the organization as any man in it."[14]

This arrangement in the superintendency was of short duration. Three months later, in February 1901, seventy-two-year-old Karl G. Maeser died, followed two months later by seventy-four-year-old George Q. Cannon. The venerable Lorenzo Snow and his counselors of the First Presidency then decided that the president of the Church should serve as the Union's general superintendent. George Reynolds and Joseph M. Tanner were named as first and second assistants, respectively. Tanner was formerly president of Brigham Young College and of Utah State Agricultural College in Logan and soon was named superintendent of the Church schools. Reynolds's and Tanner's calling included being assistant editors of the *Juvenile Instructor*.

President Snow was then eighty-seven and in the last year of his life. His temperament and his health prohibited him from playing a major role in the Sunday School administration. Therefore, as the longest continuously serving member of the general board, George

187

George Reynolds in 1901,
age fifty-nine

Reynolds became the *de facto* chief of the Union and editor of the organization's periodical. He confided in his journal, "During the whole of the Year [1901] did the greater portion of the literary work of getting out the paper [*Juvenile Instructor*]."[15]

Most of the publication's editorials in 1901 reflect George's touch. A stickler for efficient modes of procedure and the Union's most experienced and knowledgeable advocate, he wrote such editorials as "The Word of God in Our Sunday Schools," "The New Sunday School Visiting Book," "Record Day—Minutes" on the necessity of keeping full and accurate records of the schools, "The Social Aspect of the Sunday School," "Stake Officers' Meetings," "Our [Stake] Sunday School Conferences," "Statistics and Secretaries," and "The Teaching of Chastity [in Sunday School]."[16]

George also wrote editorials eulogizing two of his most admired tutors and leaders, George Q. Cannon and Lorenzo Snow. Of the former George wrote:

> President Cannon in intellectual gifts was richly endowed beyond the great majority of his fellows. In faith, few were his equals. As a servant of the Most High, he was among that favored few who saw the face of the Lord while in the flesh and heard the Divine voice, and yet remained in mortality.[17]

This last revelation may have been confided by Cannon to his close friend Reynolds.

Reynolds likewise admired President Snow, as seen in this editorial observation:

> Lorenzo Snow was naturally a man among men, a man of high order, a man of strong convictions a man of fine intellectuality, and keen perceptions. Those who observed him walk, and have noticed the manner in which he placed his heel upon the earth, knew, if they knew aught of human nature, that he walked with the same firmness that he talked and conducted himself among his fellow-men. There have been in our Church few men possessed of a more delicate and sensitive nature than that with which President Snow was endowed. There was in his spirit an artistic, exquisite refinement rarely found.[18]

The period of George's greatest direct influence in the Sunday Schools came to an end on 7 November 1901, when new Church president, Joseph F. Smith, became the general superintendent of the Deseret Sunday School Union. President Smith took much firmer control of the Union and the *Juvenile Instructor* than had President Snow. For the rest of George Reynolds's life, Joseph F. Smith wrote and signed nearly all of the editorials in the *Juvenile*.

This is not to say that George's effect on the Union was not profound. He persisted in his normal, unassuming way to keep order and harmony in the work of the Union. But from 1902 until his debilitating illness in 1907, George was somewhat overshadowed by Joseph F. Smith, by second assistant Joseph M. Tanner, who because of his oratorical skills did more speaking to Sunday School workers in conferences until his release from the Union in 1906, and finally by youthful and dynamic David O. McKay, who became the best known of all Latter-day Saint Sunday School leaders.

As first assistant general superintendent of the Deseret Sunday School Union, George traveled to stake Sunday School conferences and other meetings throughout the Church; answered questions about Sunday School procedure, the history of the Church, and doctrine in a column in the *Juvenile Instructor*; helped conduct the semi-annual general Sunday School conferences; helped write and promote the curriculum aids known collectively as the "Outlines"; and cared for the finances of the Union, particularly through the program "Nickel Sunday."

George dutifully recorded in his journal every ward Sunday School and stake or mission Sunday School conference he attended. He was away on Church business of some kind almost every Sabbath day. Sometimes he visited Sunday Schools in Salt Lake City or nearby stakes. Other times he took extended trips to southern and northern Utah, Wyoming, Colorado, Arizona, Idaho, Oregon, and Alberta, Canada. In 1902 he attended the nondenominational International Sunday School Conference in Denver. General board visits to the stakes were generally reported in the *Juvenile Instructor*, and George's name often appears along with the results of his visits. As the years went by, George, then in his sixties, felt increased weariness from traveling and so noted in his journal. By 1906 he was exhausted and doing very little traveling.[19]

A column that appeared frequently in the *Juvenile Instructor* was "Answers to Questions." Although these columns never bore the name of George Reynolds, it is obvious that he wrote most if not all of them: they bear his distinctive style; they reflect information that it is known he researched and had previously written or spoken about; they deal often with Sunday School procedures, of which he was a master; and drafts of this column and letters to him containing questions from Latter-day Saints exist in his surviving papers. The questions that he answered in these numerous columns included the following: "Were any ordinances for the dead performed from the days of Moses to the time of the advent of the Savior?"; "Which comes first in the Gospel, faith or knowledge?"; "Did Abel the martyr hold the Priesthood?"; "What is the destiny of children that are born before their parents are married?"; "Did any of the general authorities of the Church enlist in the Mormon Battalion?"; "Did David Whitmer and Martin Harris hold the Apostleship at the time that they ordained the Twelve Apostles; if so, when did they receive it?"; "Where did the Nephites, the Mulekites and Jaredites respectively land on this continent?"; "Can the Indians rightfully be called the Jews?"; "What are the ten kingdoms or peoples representing the ten toes of the great image seen by Nebuchadnezzar in his dream and interpreted by the prophet Daniel?"; "How many Urim and Thummim are there?"; "When a Sunday School officers' and teachers' prayer meeting is held prior to the commencement of the regular school exercises, what is the proper mode of procedure?"; "What authorities or officers should be presented and sustained at the annual ward Sunday School conferences?"; "Should teachers prepare lessons during devotional exercises in the Sunday School?"[20]

George's answers were always to the point, lucid, and not condescending in their manner. For his time, George Reynolds was considered one of the most learned men in Utah about gospel doctrine, history of the Church, and appropriate Church procedure.

Elder Reynolds also aided his fellow Saints in understanding the Book of Mormon by answering questions directed to him from Sunday School classes, seventies quorums, and private individuals. He received questions on Book of Mormon geography, the translation process of the Isaiah portions, whether the Nephites held the Melchizedek Priesthood, and Martin Harris's 1828 interview with Professor Charles Anthon. Regarding Harris, George wrote:

> Personally I do not believe that Prof. Anthon said all that has been attributed to him. I believe that Bro. Martin Harris, who was

a nervous man, got slightly confused in his memory. I can readily understand that the Professor said they were true or genuine characters, but when it came to saying anything of the translation, cannot conceive how, as a scientific man, he possibly could do so. For independent of the statement of Moroni that no other people could read the reformed Egyptian of the Nephites, Egyptology itself was at that time in its infancy, and I doubt much if Prof. Anthon could have translated the characters even if no change had been made in them from the time Lehi left Jerusalem. This is my theory and you can have it for what it is worth.[21]

One who later followed in his footsteps in such scholarship and in writing answers to gospel questions in Church periodicals was Elder Joseph Fielding Smith, who married one of George's daughters, Ethel Georgina, shortly after George's death.

After George entered the general superintendency of the Deseret Sunday School Union, it was decided that general Sunday School conventions would no longer be held but that at April and October general conference time a separate Sunday School session could be held for officers and teachers in the organization. George often conducted these sessions, but the record of these conferences shows that he usually deferred to others in giving speeches. He did not feel that he had a strong pulpit posture, and he was pleased to see others who were more dynamic, such as Joseph F. Smith, Joseph M. Tanner, Horace Ensign, and David O. McKay, do the speaking.[22]

In the latter half of 1902, George Reynolds and select members of the general board met every Sunday to write for publication short curriculum guides for all age groups, which they designated the "Outlines."[23] This was yet another step in clarifying for the teachers what and how they should be teaching unitedly throughout the Church. Columns from the *Juvenile Instructor* show that many teachers needed some persuading and instructing to implement the outlines effectively.

Every October a Sunday was designated throughout the LDS Sunday Schools as "Nickel Sunday." George had begun this program a quarter century earlier as the Union treasurer. Even as a member of the general superintendency, he continued as treasurer. Beginning each fall in the pages of the *Juvenile Instructor,* George cajoled officers of the ward and stake Sunday Schools to coordinate effectively the Nickel Sunday, collect the monies, and remit them promptly to Sunday School headquarters. Through this system, George and the general board were able to cover all costs of the Union and avoid drawing upon the general funds of the Church. Surely one of George Reynolds's greatest contributions to the Sunday School program was his unsung and lengthy service as treasurer, in which position he kept the Union perpetually solvent.

Between sessions of the April general conference in 1906, President Joseph F. Smith asked Elder Reynolds if he did not think the Sabbath schools were in a better condition then than they had ever been. In his conference address Elder Reynolds reported that he had never known a time when the schools were doing a better work than at the present:

> Our schools are increasing in number; and that in regard to punctuality, the good order maintained, the methods adopted for instructing the children I believe we are growing and growing in the right direction, each year. Above all, I believe that the children in the schools are obtaining a better knowledge of the Gospel, and that they are not losing in the spirit and faith of the principles of eternal life. I have always regarded, and do today, that the first thing most important in connection with our Sunday schools, and indeed with all the other auxiliary organizations of the Church, is to make Latter-day Saints of our children, to develop within them a faith that shall grow with increasing years, an understanding faith, a faith that, while it appeals to the heart, will also appeal to the head, and be able to give a reason for the hope that is within; not a blind obedience, as it is sometimes called, but a comprehensive understanding of the revelations of God and the work that He is performing in this generation.[24]

Not long after this conference, Elder George Reynolds fell seriously ill and did not function again as Sunday School administrator.

Notes

1. George Reynolds Journal, vol. 6, 1883, 1884.
2. "Historical Review of the Deseret Sunday School Union," *Juvenile Instructor* 19 (15 November 1884): 9346–47.
3. *Jubilee History of Latter-day Saint Sunday Schools* 1849–1899 (Salt Lake City: Deseret Sunday School Union, 1900), p. 51; George Reynolds Journal, vol. 6, 1889.
4. *Jubilee History of Latter-day Saint Sunday Schools*, p. 41; George Reynolds Journal, vol. 6, 1889; *Deseret Sunday School Union Leaflets* (Salt Lake City: Deseret Sunday School Union, 1901).
5. George Reynolds Journal, vol. 6, 1894; *Jubilee History of Latter-day Saint Sunday Schools*, p. 32; *Deseret Semi-Weekly News*, 13 April 1894, p. 2.
6. *Jubilee History of Latter-day Saint Sunday Schools*, p. 33.
7. George Reynolds Journal, vol. 6, 1898.
8. Ibid., *Jubilee History of Latter-day Saint Sunday Schools*, pp. 35–40.
9. *Jubilee History of Latter-day Saint Sunday Schools*, pp. 520–34; George D. Pyper to George Reynolds and Levi W. Richards, 19 July 1899, in Jane Reynolds Collection.
10. *Juvenile Instructor* 35 (15 August 1900): 545–49.
11. Ibid., 35 (1 August 1900): 511; 35 (1 September 1900): 586–87; 35 (15 October 1900): 702–3; 35 (1 November 1900): 735–36.
12. Ibid., 35 (15 October 1900): 699–701; 35 (15 December 1900): 822.
13. Ibid., 35 (1 December 1900): 788; 36 (1 January 1901): 917–18; 36 (15 February 1901): 105–6; 36 (15 March 1901): 141; Knighton, "A Comparative Study of the Teaching Methods of the L.D.S. and Non-L.D.S. Sunday School Movements in the United States Prior to 1900," pp. 90–99.
14. Ibid., 36 (15 February 1901): 111; George Reynolds Journal, vol. 6, 1900.
15. George Reynolds Journal, vol. 6, 1901.
16. None of these editorials contains any by-line, but Reynolds's style is nearly unmistakable. Certain other editorials in 1901, usually not dealing with Sunday School procedure but rather centering on events in the Near East where Joseph Tanner had traveled, bear the marks of Tanner.
17. *Juvenile Instructor* 36 (1 May 1901): 274.
18. Ibid., 36 (1 November 1901): 656–57.
19. Information for this paragraph was drawn from numerous entries in volumes 36–40 (1901–1905) in the *Juvenile Instructor* and George Reynolds Journal, vol. 6, 1901–1906.
20. These questions were drawn from volumes 36–38 (1901–1903) of the *Juvenile Instructor*.
21. George Reynolds, to J. B. Merrill, 23 March 1899; see also Joel Ricks to George Reynolds, 28 December 1903; J. C. Ferrin to George Reynolds, 6 March 1899; A. Booth to George Reynolds, 9 September 1901; all located in Jane Reynolds Collection.
22. These conclusions were drawn from reports on the semiannual conferences as reported in the *Juvenile Instructor* and the published Conference Reports.
23. George Reynolds Journal, vol. 6, 1902.
24. Conference Report, April 1906, p. 24.

CHAPTER 19

Secretary to the
Missionary Committee

SOMETIME DURING THE 1890S, AFTER GEORGE REYNOLDS WAS CALLED
as one of the First Seven Presidents of the Seventy, the First Presidency organized the Missionary Committee of the Apostles and
called George as secretary. This committee decided where missionaries were needed and to which missions all prospective missionaries
would be called, including mission presidents. George sent out all
the formal calls from "Box B" and arranged for the missionaries'
railroad transportation, visas, and steamship passages. He also co-
ordinated all correspondence regarding missionary work. He answered mission presidents' questions, usually on behalf of the
missionary committee.[1] On one occasion, President Joseph F. Smith
indicated that Elder Reynolds had helped the First Presidency in
"selecting missionaries for the various fields and his judgment had
been invaluable."[2]

An excellent source illuminating some of George's work on the
missionary committee is Ben E. Rich, president of the Southern
States Mission from 1898 to 1901, who recorded all correspondence
between him and Church headquarters. Rich often asked for clari-
fication of matters administrative and doctrinal. George answered
his questions dealing with financial aid to impoverished missionaries,

elders accused of immorality, elders receiving temple endowments before entering the field, the length of missionary service, the washing of feet against the wicked, the purchase of clothing by missionaries, the disposition of tithing in kind, and elders falling into apostasy.

Supervising missionary work was one of the duties of the First Council of Seventy. On some of his trips, such as to Omaha for an interdenominational Sunday School congress, George visited and spoke to missionaries serving in the field. The duties of the First Council also extended to supplying missionaries needed closer to home. During a mining boom in the late nineteenth century, the town of Mercur was established in the Oquirrh Mountains in Tooele County. Most of the young miners were not members of the LDS Church. At the weekly meeting of the First Council on 9 August 1899, George Reynolds told his brethren that the First Presidency had asked him to submit to them the condition of affairs at Mercur and recommended that the First Council send two strong missionaries there. The seven presidents accordingly sent to Mercur three young missionaries who had recently returned from other fields of labor. Elder Reynolds set each apart to the assignment. One was his oldest son, Sidney, who had only recently returned from a mission in the southern states. The work of these three missionaries in Mercur was dramatically successful, and more missionaries were soon selected.[3]

George and his wives were naturally eager that their sons enter the mission field. George's oldest son, Sidney, went to the Southern States Mission in the late 1890s and then, as described, served a short-term mission to Mercur upon his return. Six of George's other eleven sons also served missions for the Church: George Bruford, John, Harold, Bish, Phil and Cliff. The last three served missions after their father died. While George was still alive, his daughter Nel began serving a "mission" as a hostess in the Church's new visitors center. Another daughter, Polly, also served a mission after the death of her father. Harold earned a strong reputation for himself as a missionary in Germany and, upon his return in 1906, was called by the First Presidency to assist his father as a secretary to the Missionary Committee. When his father became incapacitated, Harold became the chief secretary of the committee and served in that capacity until his own death in 1940. George also kept in close contact with his son-in-law John Russell, who had married his daughter Bertie and then immediately accepted a mission call to Scotland. Russell wrote missionary letters to George, addressing him as "Father."[4]

In the October 1901 general conference, Church president Lorenzo Snow, then in his eighty-eighth year, rose from his sickbed and enthusiastically delivered a message that pertained to the work of George Reynolds on the First Council and as secretary to the Missionary Committee of the Apostles. For some weeks President Snow had been agitated about the neglect of the Twelve and the seventies under them to further pursue the spread of missionary work to more nations of the earth. He was disturbed that the general authorities were spending too much of their precious time dealing with the problems in the stakes, when their main duty "is to warn the nations of the earth and prepare the world for the coming of the Savior."[5] So in conference the venerable President Snow solemnly charged the stake presidents and their subordinates to begin tackling their local problems with more vigor, thus freeing the apostles and seventies to be "special witnesses unto the nations of the earth." He promised that the apostles and seventies would be redirected to other fields of labor.[6]

President Snow died only four days after his stirring address. His successor, Joseph F. Smith, endorsed the new policy and began immediately to implement it. Valiant attempts were made to spread the gospel message to Japan, the Austrian Empire, and Russia, but with negligible success. As it turned out, no member of the First Council of Seventy, including George Reynolds, was asked in the next few years to establish new foreign missions. The idea of sending

197

leading seventies abroad was not abandoned, however, and today such is the expected role of members of the Quorums of the Seventy.

New enthusiasm was nevertheless injected into the spread of missionary work in the early 1900s. In the next general conference (April 1902) Elder Reynolds remarked, "I also know that there is a dearth of experienced men in the foreign ministry of the Church. I know it because of the requisitions that so often pass through my hands [as secretary] from the presidents of missions, asking for more experienced men to be sent to them." He testified that he knew that he would live to see greater growth in the foreign missions with a greater influx of elders to the field.[7] George also played a major role in the promotion of educating prospective missionaries in Church academies.

As a general authority, George was also empowered to perform marriages in the Church's temples. These marriages are considered by the Latter-day Saints to be not only valid for this life but also for the eternities. Elder Reynolds performed his first temple marriage in 1901 for his son Sidney and his bride Mary Maude Davis.[8]

George's schedule was a rigorous one and began to take its toll on his physical health, particularly after 1902, when he was in his sixties. George's typical schedule, even in his advanced age, was to work six days in the Office of the President, and then late on Saturday to travel, usually by rail, to a stake conference. If the stake were distant, he would travel all Saturday night and all Sunday night to save time. On Sunday he would attend "five or six conference meetings." After his breakdown in 1907, George wrote his son Sidney that he had been converted to the biblical injunction of working only six days a week and resting on the seventh.[9]

In 1906, the last year he was healthy enough to work, Elder Reynolds spoke in general conference about mission calls that he helped process. He exclaimed that "in all my lengthy experience I have never known the call for missionaries to be answered so willingly and so readily as is the present one" and that "the brethren whose names have been suggested show better preparation for that labor than I have ever known." But he was also disheartened about "the number of young men called who admit that they have not been keeping the Word of Wisdom." He added, "We often express a willingness to lay our all upon the altar of sacrifice, and at the same time these matters which in the minds of some appear to be of minor importance are forgotten or slighted."[10] This counsel came at a time when the First Presidency was launching a concerted effort to have faithful Church members conform to the Word of Wisdom, that is, to refrain from indulging in any form of tobacco, alcoholic beverages, tea, or coffee.[11]

In summing up George Reynolds's secretarial career, one must include many noteworthy qualities that he brought to assignments. Obviously these qualities attracted the Brethren and kept him close to high-level decision making for many years. Perhaps the most important quality was his ability to keep confidences. His family members reported that he rarely ever mentioned his work while at home and never divulged any secrets. A more recent secretary to the First Presidency, Joseph A. Anderson, remarked that one of the things President Heber J. Grant liked about him was Anderson's ability to keep his mouth shut.[12] George Reynolds was much like Joseph Anderson. He did not discuss private matters, nor did he write anything of a confidential nature in his journals. Alice Louise Reynolds recorded that her father was "trustworthy to the nth degree."[13]

Furthermore, George was noted for his promptness and punctuality. Adam Bennion wrote that he "was prompt always and was never more annoyed than at the failure of someone to meet an appointment. Whenever he promised a piece of work, it could be depended upon that it would be completed. He has set up many a night in order to finish tasks promised at certain hours. He was always 'there' and could be counted on."[14] George's family also confirmed his penchant for punctuality.[15]

One of his colleagues noted that "George Reynolds was a worker. He knew but little of rest, and nothing at all of idleness. If he had a fault, it was that he accepted too much work. He wore himself out too soon."[16]

George was ambidextrous. When he became tired of writing with one hand, he would use the other.[17] Existing samples show that the handwriting done in his secretarial capacities was more meticulous than that in his personal journal.

George sought constantly to be well-informed. He deplored the idea of being an "ignoramus." His associates often referred to his knowledge as encyclopedic, and his store of knowledge was often used by Church leaders. His knowledge included not only Church history and doctrine but also procedures, statistical data, finances, politics, secular history, human nature, and information about important people.[18]

Loyalty to the Church hierarchy, to each other, and to the work of the building the Kingdom of God was the watchword of all the secretaries in the Office of the President. That is what made George Reynolds and his associates valuable to the First Presidency. George's devotion to his chiefs is evident in his last public address:

> I want to bear my testimony that I have been acquainted with the Presidents of this Church intimately for many years — with Presidents Brigham Young, John Taylor, Wilford Woodruff, Lorenzo Snow and Joseph F. Smith; and though in minor particulars and characteristics they differed very materially, yet they were all the men of God's choice, the men for the hour, the men whom God selected as the leaders of His people, and they all did the work that God required at their hands. They were his mouthpieces, and they accomplished that which He placed them in the position to fulfill, every one of them. They were all prepared of God to do the work assigned them, and they all did it, and did it well. Notwithstanding the differences and peculiarities of their minor characteristics, there were some certain things in which they were all alike, namely, their love for the truth, their faith in God, their willingness to listen to His word, their uncompromising devotion and integrity to God and His work, their full belief in the divine calling of the Prophet Joseph. These characterized them all, and God was with them.[19]

During this last period of George's service as one of the Church's elder statesman his masterful research work, his Book of Mormon concordance, was finally published. He considered this work his greatest contribution to the work of the kingdom.[20] Hardly a week passed from the time of its inception in 1880 until 1899, when he took the finished manuscript to Chicago for printing on electro plates, that George was not writing and rewriting passages that composed the monumental work. "I have never ceased being astonished at the rapidity with which he checked passages; but the amazing accuracy of the book is due to this very process," reported his daughter Alice Louise. George's wives aided him in the project "by seeing that his room was comfortable at so early an hour and keeping things as quiet as possible around him so that he could work uninterrupted."[21]

A final typewritten manuscript was ready to take to Chicago in 1899. No publisher in Utah was equipped to handle either the intricate detail or the financial commitment for publication. The cost of electro plates preparation amounted to three thousand dollars, which George paid himself. He also paid for the printing and binding costs. "I have but little hope while I live of receiving this amount [for the electro plates] back through sales of the book, to say nothing of the other expenses such as printing and binding," he wrote upon finishing the publication in 1904. "The circulation will necessarily at first be small. As the Church grows the demand will doubtless increase. But such a book was needed, and I felt that it was very improbable that anyone else would attempt to prepare one."[22]

Reviewed and promoted in Church publications, the concordance met with positive response. For example, the new magazine for the Mutual Improvement Associations, the *Improvement Era,* stated, "The book should be appreciated and purchased by every person, and should have a place in every M.I.A., Sunday School, public and private library in the Church. Many students have waited long for it." The *Era* noted, "There is only one man in the Church having the patience, perseverance, and unselfish devotion for the work, necessary to accomplish such a prodigious undertaking, and that man is the author, Elder George Reynolds."[23] The *Millennial Star* identified the book as "the most stupendous task heretofore attempted and completed by any writer of the Church."[24]

George's unselfishness with regard to his "gift to the Church" is also demonstrated by his gifts of the concordance to the Church academies and to friends. James Dunn, a leading citizen of Tooele, wrote to George:

> Not for a long time have my feelings been so drawn out as your valuable present had done; the more so as your goodly gift was so unexpected by me. I will confess that I was so overcome by your remembrance of me that I did drop a few tears that are not dry as I write this note to you. Why, I cannot yet understand; but for a great man in Israel to remember your humble servant strikes me in a very tender spot. I do not flatter you when I say to you that you have won for yourself a name that will never die in the production of such a noble and useful book. Only the Spirit of God abounding in you could you have performed such a great task, and in such a short time.[25]

George's inclusion of lengthy entries to assist the reader's understanding increased the value of the concordance. His entries are more thorough than comparable entries in biblical concordances. Furthermore, he subdivided references to some important words to aid the reader in finding a sought-after passage. For example, the entry "People" is subdivided into categories of "A People," "Among the People," "Among this People," "All his People," "For his People," "Of his People," "Over his People," "Redeem his People," "That his People," "To his People," and forty-two others.[26]

Translators and later editors of the Book of Mormon relied heavily upon the concordance. For example, Alma Taylor, first translator of this book of scripture into Japanese, told Alice Louise Reynolds that he would never have completed his task without her father's concordance. Members of the committee that produced the 1921 edition of the Book of Mormon also indicated how much they used the concordance. That committee discovered only one error.[27]

One who built on the writings of George Reynolds and became even more well-known for his Book of Mormon scholarship was George's colleague on the First Council of Seventy, B. H. Roberts. Elder Roberts warmly acknowledged his debt to Reynolds:

It is a pleasure to note the work of this my brother, and fellow President in the First Council of the Seventies in this field of Book of Mormon labor. I feel myself much indebted to him because of his great achievements in this field of research.

First, for his excellent Book of Mormon Chronological Table, published now for many years in connection with the late Elder F. D. Richards' "Compendium."

Second, for his "Myth of the Manuscript Found."

Third, for his "dictionary of the Book of Mormon."

Fourth, for a series of articles in the "Contributor," (Vol. 5) on the History of the Book of Mormon.

Fifth, for a second series of articles in the "Contributor" (Vol. 17) under the title "Evidences of the Book of Mormon; Some External Proofs of its Divinity."

Sixth, and last, and greatest achievement of all, I thank him for his "Complete Concordance of the Book of Mormon." The amount of patient, pains-taking labor required for the production of this magnificent work will never be known to the general reader. Only the close student of the Nephite Scriptures will ever really appreciate it. What Cruden and Young have done for Bible students, Elder Reynolds has more abundantly done for Book of Mormon students. The Elders of the Church through all generations to come will, I am sure, feel deeply grateful to Elder Reynolds for his great work which will stand as a monument to his pains-taking habits of thorough application to a task; but what is better still, the work will stand as a monument of his love for the Book of Mormon.[28]

The unique contributions of George Reynolds to Book of Mormon scholarship, particularly for Church members in his era, include a succinct summary of the arguments discrediting the theory of the Soloman Spaulding origin of the Book of Mormon; the first thorough biographical discussion of the role, personalities, and contributions of the three witnesses — Oliver Cowdery, David Whitmer, and Martin Harris; the first commentary on the Book of Mormon narrative (*The Story of the Book of Mormon*); the first analysis of ethnological and cultural considerations pertaining to the book's peoples; the first chronological dating system (widely used by students today, though rarely acknowledged, was devised by George Reynolds); *A Dictionary of the Book of Mormon,* an alphabetically listed and detailed key to every person, valley, hill, river, city, and animal mentioned in the Book of Mormon; the first serious articles linking contemporary archaeological, anthropological, and lingual studies to the veracity of the Book of Mormon; his service as the first Book of Mormon teacher in the Church's educational system; and most importantly, the massive Book of Mormon concordance. The concordance and dictionary are enduring works that are still valuable aids to students, researchers, and translators.

George Reynolds rightly ranks among the five leading Book of Mormon scholars in The Church of Jesus Christ of Latter-day Saints. His peers include Orson Pratt, B. H. Roberts, Sidney B. Sperry, and Hugh Nibley. Orson Pratt's contributions directly influenced George Reynolds, and George's work in turn influenced the other four. While many of George's ideas have been superseded today by additional discoveries and new thinking, all dedicated Book of Mormon students are indebted to him for his pioneering efforts in geography, history, people and places, understanding the story line, ethnology, chronology, external evidences, concordance, and how the Book of Mormon was translated and published in several editions.[29]

Notes

1. Alice Louise Reynolds, "Biography of George Reynolds," p. 41; David John Papers, vol. 4, p. 145, Special Collections, Harold B. Lee Library; George Reynolds to Charles A. Callis, 13 December 1905, 23 December 1905, and 26 March 1906, Papers of Charles A. Callis, Special Collections, Harold B. Lee Library; Charles Bartlett to George Reynolds, Jane Reynolds Collection; James R. Clark, ed., *Messages of the First Presidency*, 6 vols. (Salt Lake City: Bookcraft, 1965–75), 4:48; Horace S. Ensign to George Reynolds in *Juvenile Instructor* 38 (1 December 1903): 727–28.

2. Journal History of the Church of Jesus Christ of Latter-day Saints, 12 August 1909, p. 1, LDS Church Historical Archives.

3. Hartley notes of First Council of Seventy Minutes; George Reynolds Journal, vol. 6, 1899.

4. Information for this paragraph was drawn from Hardy, "George Reynolds: The Early Years," master's thesis, Brigham Young University, 1972, p. 104; from several entries in George Reynolds Journal, vol. 6; and from several letters in the Jane Reynolds Collection.

5. Joseph F. Smith, "The Last Days of President Snow," *Juvenile Instructor* 36 (15 November 1901): 688–91.

6. Conference Report, October 1901, pp. 60–62.

7. Conference Report, April 1902, p. 7.

8. George Reynolds Journal, vol. 6, 1901, 1903.

9. George Reynolds to Sidney Reynolds, 13 April 1907, letter in possession of Sydney Skidmore, Potomac, Maryland.

10. Conference Report, April 1906, p. 23.

11. Thomas G. Alexander, "The Word of Wisdom: From Principle to Requirement," *Dialogue* 14 (Autumn 1981): 79–80.

12. Joseph A. Anderson, address to the faculty of Religious Education, Brigham Young University, 19 November 1982.

13. A. L. Reynolds, "Biography of George Reynolds," p. 29.

14. Adam Bennion, "George Reynolds," *Utah Genealogical and Historical Magazine* 1 (October 1910): 148.

15. Interview with Emily Jensen, Provo, Utah, 29 November 1985; interview with Haroldeane Rasmussen, Provo, Utah, 29 November 1985.

16. "President George Reynolds," *Juvenile Instructor* 44 (September 1909): 386.

17. Interview with Emily Jensen.

18. A. L. Reynolds, "Biography of George Reynolds," pp. 34–36.

19. Conference Report, October 1906, pp. 116–17.

20. A. L. Reynolds, "Biography of George Reynolds," p. 24.

21. Ibid., pp. 24–25.

22. George Reynolds, *A Complete Concordance to the Book of Mormon* (Salt Lake City: George Reynolds, 1900), preface; "Biography of George Reynolds," pp. 27–29; Journal of George Reynolds, vol. 6, 1899, 1904. I cannot find the number of copies of the concordance published in the first edition. If Reynolds's cost per copy were five dollars, for example, there would have been six hundred copies produced. If the price were four dollars, there would have been seven hundred fifty copies.

23. *Improvement Era* (December 1904): 151.

24. *Millennial Star* 67 (30 March 1905): 202.

25. James Dunn to George Reynolds, 6 December 1904; see also J. Summerhays to George Reynolds, 4 November 1904; Charles B. Bartlett (president of the New Zealand Mission) to George Reynolds, 1 June 1905; and Ezra Christianson (principal of Ricks Academy) to George Reynolds, 5 January 1904; all located in Jane Reynolds Collection.

26. George Reynolds, *Complete Concordance to the Book of Mormon*, pp. 536–47.

27. A. L. Reynolds, "Biography of George Reynolds," pp. 27–28. "Autobiography of Alice Louise Reynolds," typescript, p. 25.

28. B. H. Roberts, *New Witnesses for God*, 3 vols. (Salt Lake City: Deseret News, 1951), 3:560.

29. In my review of the writings of the Book of Mormon by Orson Pratt and B. H. Roberts, two scholars whom Reynolds knew intimately, I have concluded that (1) Reynolds did not write upon the same themes concerning the Book of Mormon as did Orson Pratt; (2) virtually all of Reynolds's contributions were either original to him or at least he arrived at them through discussion with others and that he, not others, published them; (3) the writings of B. H. Roberts on the Book of Mormon began during the decade of 1900 to 1910 at a time when Reynolds had completed his published contributions on the Book of Mormon; and (4) therefore, Roberts, in his considerations about evidences of the Book of Mormon, was indebted to Reynolds for his work rather than Reynolds being indebted to Roberts. See "Divine Authenticity of the Book of Mormon" in Parker Pratt Robison, ed., *Orson Pratt's Works* (Salt Lake City: Deseret News Press, 1945), pp. 107–289; N. B. Lundwall, comp., *Masterful Discourses and Writings of Orson Pratt* (Salt Lake City: by the compiler, 1946), pp. 387–424B; Breck England, *The Life and Thought of Orson Pratt* (Salt Lake City: University of Utah Press, 1985), pp. 161–63; David J. Whittaker, "Orson Pratt: Early Advocate of the Book of Mormon," *Ensign* 14 (April 1984): 54–57; Truman G. Madsen, "B. H. Roberts and the Book of Mormon," *BYU Studies* 19 (Summer 1979): 427–45.

CHAPTER 20

In Honorable Remembrance

IN THE LAST DECADE OF HIS LIFE, GEORGE REYNOLDS FELT THE EF-
fects of his advancing age. But it was not until 1906 that he decided
to lighten his schedule in any way. By then he had probably done
too much damage to the vital organs of his body.

On his sixty-fifth birthday, on 1 January 1907, George met with
all of his family for a special celebration. He was proud to sit for a
photograph with his twelve surviving sons, ranging from Sidney,
thirty-one years old, to little Cliff, three years old. He compared that
experience to that of Jacob and his twelve sons. Later that same
afternoon, he began working on a Sunday School assignment, writing
one of the "Outlines," when he suffered a stroke. For several days
he was not able to recover movement in all of his limbs or return
to work as a general authority or secretary. As it turned out, he did
not work again during the last two and one-half years of his life.

Two weeks after his stroke he was sent by Church officials to
Hawaii in the hope that he would recover. He was accompanied only
by his wife Mary. Samuel E. Woolley, who had been serving as
mission president of the Hawaii Mission and manager of the Church's
plantation in Laie since 1895, was in Salt Lake City on business.
The First Presidency assigned Woolley to look after the Reynoldses
on their trip to Hawaii. Woolley treated George with utmost deference, and George and Mary were accorded every courtesy and priv-

George Reynolds, center, with his twelve surviving sons

ilege, including first-class rail and steamship passage. Upon arriving in the islands, Woolley introduced George Reynolds to the Church members and told them of his many writings about the Book of Mormon. George spoke infrequently to the Sunday School children. Once he bore to them his testimony that he knew "that all the Presidents of the Church were men of God, especially fitted for the labors in the day and time in which each has lived."[1]

Under the pleasant surroundings and with many hours availed him for rest, George gradually recovered physically to the point where he could walk several miles each day, but his nervous tension remained. In a letter to his son Sidney, he confided some of his frustrations:

> Resting the body is one thing, resting the mind another. With
> me the first is a success, and I guess the other cannot be counted
> among the failures, but there comes a time when the body being

sufficiently rested seeks new activities, and to compel its continued inertia, begets unrest of mind; the mind finds in change, not in monotony the rest it needs. So with me, at present, I think Honolulu & Laie have done me all the good they can. What I now need is movement to give me new thoughts, new ideas, new feelings—and not compel my mind to be occupied only the tho'ts of the past, or wonderings regarding the future.

He yearned for the chance to see his other loved ones again. He also recognized that in returning to Utah he could not expect to work such an exhausting schedule again. But he felt that he had to get back or he would have another breakdown.[2]

During their last Sunday on the islands, Mary Reynolds was asked to address the congregation of Saints in Laie. President Woolley had introduced the subject of plural marriage and defended it as a righteous principle. Sister Reynolds added her confirmation, telling of her feelings of accommodating her life-style to that of a polygamous wife: "I know [plural marriage] is true, it has brought to me a loving husband whose salvation I feel is sure, and it brought to me two loveable women that I love and that love me, and it has brought to me nine beautiful children and the care of seven more that are as my own. I know it is true. I can feel it in every fibre of my being. Don't any of you dare to speak evil against it, for it is true."[3]

When they returned from Hawaii, George's tensions returned and he suffered a relapse. The authorities sent him to Portland for rest, but when he returned, he was no better; indeed, he seemed worse. He was sent to the state mental hospital in Provo for treatment, but through the auspices of Elder Seymour Young, who was a physician, he was soon taken back home. Young felt that being in the state hospital was an affront for one of George's station.

During this period George's children and grandchildren often came to visit him. The grandchildren had memories of his fondly touching their faces and saying such things as "My sweet little girl," and of their sitting on his lap and combing his long beard. The grandchildren tended to mix in with Mary's younger children, George's third family.

Mary cared for George in his deteriorating mental and physical condition as best she could. The children were kept away from him as much as possible. The little ones remember that he acted strangely. Young Gordon, who was difficult to handle, was sent away to Nephi for an extended separation. In the meantime, George's second wife, Amelia, was suffering considerably herself; she died in 1908 from Bright's disease (kidney failure). George had so far lost his mental faculties that he did not realize what was happening to her. His daughter May, from the second family, took care of the younger ones in that family.

Elder Seymour B. Young visited his seriously ill colleague most days each week. The end finally came on 9 August 1909.

The announcement of George Reynolds's death brought "sorrow to thousands who have been honored in personal acquaintance with Brother Reynolds, and to many thousands more who have known him through his work alone."[4] Charles W. Penrose, then serving a mission in Great Britain, undoubtedly echoed the feelings of many who had associated with George Reynolds when he wrote, "We bid him farewell with sadness that we shall see him in this life no more, but we have full confidence and faith that, if we are privileged to mingle with the just made perfect in the mansions on high, where the glory of the Father surrounds the mighty who have fought the good fight and have overcome, we shall behold the face of our dear departed brother George Reynolds among the foremost of the heavenly throng."[5]

The funeral for Elder Reynolds would normally have been held either in the Assembly Hall or in the Tabernacle on Temple Square. But coincidental with his death was the convening of the annual gathering of the Grand Army of the Republic, the organization for the Union veterans of the United States Civil War, in Salt Lake City. The Church had offered its large assembly facilities to the veterans. The Tabernacle was draped with flags and bunting and gleamed with electric lights. It was an awe-inspiring sight. A spendid parade with many bands was held in the city. George Reynolds had often teased his children that flags would wave and bands would play when he died.[6] Little did he know that his light-hearted prophecy would be fulfilled so literally.

Barratt Hall, part of the campus of LDS College and located on the block where the Church Office Building now stands, served as the substitute location for George Reynolds's funeral. The interior of the building was draped in white, and the platform and pulpit were wreathed in flowers. Church president Joseph F. Smith conducted the services. A number of Church officials were present, particularly George's associates in the Deseret Sunday School Union and the Seventy. On the stand also were Governor William Spry and James E. Talmage, president of the University of Utah. The services opened with prayer by Joseph W. Summerhays, George's close associate both in seventies work and in the Deseret Sunday School Union. A special choir for the occasion provided several musical numbers for the services.

The funeral speakers were fellow general authorities, each of whom had had a different association with George Reynolds. Each reflected on the various ways in which George had impressed and influenced him. The first speaker was Elder Seymour B. Young, senior president of the First Council of Seventy. He had known George Reynolds since the 1860s, when George had begun his labors in the Office of the President. Of George he said, "While he was a most talented and intelligent and cultured man, he was one of the most modest and retiring, never officious in his superiority but humble and quiet." George had reminded Young of the statement: "Oh, why should the spirit of mortals be proud." Young spoke at length of George's many literary attainments and how they had aided the members of the Church. He considered the concordance to the Book of Mormon to be the most important. Young indicated that in the sessions of the First Council of Seventy, George's "judgment was nearly always the crowning one in the sessions." Young was

211

also a member of the general board of the Sunday Schools and praised George's work in the Union for more than a quarter of a century. Young testified that Reynolds's "private life was an open book," that he had "fought the good fight," and that he "has made his calling and election sure."[7]

Elder B. H. Roberts, another of the First Seven Presidents of Seventy, added his tribute. "I loved George Reynolds for his noble qualities and respected him for his fine intellect and judgment," Roberts began. He indicated that in the First Council there was always absolute freedom of speech, and although he and George had differed widely in temperament, there had never been any disharmony between them. "He was an absolutely fearless man, a zealous and brave adherent to the truth." Roberts also commended his literary work, speaking especially of his fondness for George's treatise on the Book of Abraham and commending it to the youth of Zion.[8]

Elder Rulon S. Wells, also of the First Council of the Seventy, said that he could not conceive how anyone could do more than had George Reynolds to be worthy of eternal life. "He was sent to earth for a mission and fulfilled it in every way." Elder Joseph W. McMurrin of the same quorum said that George had lived and performed his work under the literal inspiration of God. No more noble legacy could have been left his family than the record and memory of his good life.[9]

President John R. Winder of the First Presidency next spoke and heartily endorsed the previous tributes. In the mission field he had likewise noted George's humility and devotion, spoken of so fondly by the others. Elder Heber J. Grant, a member of the Quorum of the Twelve Apostles, referred especially to George's great learning. He said he could go at any time to George with a problem and never come away disappointed. He urged members of the Reynolds family to follow in the footsteps of their father.[10]

President Joseph F. Smith was the concluding speaker. He explained that he had known George Reynolds for nearly fifty years, having first met him when George was working in the London Conference as a young missionary. He knew George best, he said, at his work in the Office of the President and indicated that he could not see how more could be done by anyone in a public vocation than George had done in his. "He was faithful to every trust and no more can be said of any man." President Smith stated that Reynolds had received every gift, every key, and every authority bestowed on the holy priesthood in any dispensation known in time. This included, he said, power to receive "dominion and power and eternal life worlds without end." He urged the Reynolds family members to live by the principles of the gospel and thus share in his glory. The services concluded with a benediction by Levi S. Richards, another long-time colleague on the Deseret Sunday School Union Board. Interment was in the Salt Lake City cemetery beside his wife Polly.[11]

George Reynolds was first and foremost a disciple with unceasing faith and the energy to commit to the building of the kingdom of God. Ever loyal to his superiors, he unflinchingly did whatever he was asked to do, including serving as the polygamy test case, and he gloried in the privilege of aiding the kingdom through his sacrifices. He never criticized nor complained about the leaders of the Church. Because he was loyal, trustworthy, and knowledgable as well as unusually competent in a number of organizational and bookkeeping skills, he was repeatedly named to positions of authority and influence in the Church—in secretarial capacities, in significant managerial posts in Church-owned businesses, in the Deseret Sunday School Union, and as one of the First Seven Presidents of Seventy. His memory "was so unusual that his friends declared that he never forgot anything he ever read, saw, or learned."[12]

All along he was a disciple with a mind of his own. Time and again he contributed original commentary and study aids to members of the Church to help them understand their scriptural storehouse. His writings also sought to defend the faith against contemporary opponents of the Church. He considered it a fault not to be increasing one's knowledge and shuddered at the thought of being an "ignoramus" about anything. "He was an inveterate reader, and so great

213

was his store of ready knowledge on all sorts of subjects that he was not only constantly consulted by his friends and associates, but also by many others who were seeking information."[13] A fellow disciple and close colleague who has been widely hailed as one of the most free-spirited intellectuals in Mormonism's history, B. H. Roberts, expressed genuine respect for George Reynolds's writings.

George's lasting legacy to his family was his good name, his unimpeachable character, and, for many of his children, a first-rate upbringing. Life was not easy for the two Reynolds families after George's death. In those years, the Church recommended against its employees' buying insurance, so there was no available cash for Mary and the children after George's death. Ten dollars a month was given her for a few years. Later the amount was increased somewhat. The younger children were required to take jobs to help bring in cash to the family. Gordon remembered having to sell newspapers at a young age and thus launched his career in the newspaper business.

Six of George Reynolds's children achieved fame in their chosen fields. Millie became a noted midwife in the Springfield, Utah, community. She delivered hundreds of babies, including those of "Aunt Mary" and those of her own daughters. Alice Louise became a respected professor of English and literature at Brigham Young University and a member of the general board of the Church's Relief Society. John was a wealthy entrepreneur who helped develop the city of Magna and its industries. Harold was a bishop for more than a decade and was the mission secretary of the Church for more than thirty-five years. Philip was an engineer who brought many of his father's writings back into publication and who compiled commentaries on the Book of Mormon and the Pearl of Great Price in the names of his father and his father-in-law Janne M. Sjodahl. Ethel worked in the Church historical archives and married Elder Joseph Fielding Smith of the Quorum of the Twelve Apostles.

George Reynolds had 104 grandchildren: thirty-seven from

Polly's family, forty-nine from Amelia's family, and eighteen from Mary's family.

George Reynolds's plural marriage relationships can be evaluated by the norms outlined by Vicky Burgess-Olson in her 1975 doctoral dissertation.[14] She learned that the average polygamous husband married plurally for the first time 11.2 years after his first marriage. George married his second wife, Amelia, eight years after his marriage to Polly. The average age of first wives was twenty-one. Polly was nineteen when she married George. The average age of second wives was twenty-five; Amelia was twenty-two at her marriage. The average age of third wives was twenty-two; Mary was twenty-six. The study showed that first wives averaged 9.1 children. Polly had nine. Second wives averaged 7.5 children. Amelia had twelve. Third wives averaged 7.6 children. Mary bore nine. Most polygamous men had only one or two additional wives, as did George. His experiences in the Church conformed to the pattern discovered by Burgess-Olson that polygamous men held much higher positions in the Church hierarchy and spent more time serving on missions away from their families than did monogamous men. She noted that polygamous families of the same husband usually lived in the same town but in separate households; some 57 percent lived at least part of the time in the same household. The Reynolds situation corresponds to this last norm exactly. It can thus be concluded that George Reynolds's experiences as a polygamous husband and father were not drastically different from those of most other polygamous men in Utah during the nineteenth century.[15]

George Reynolds's role in the *Reynolds v. United States* polygamy case is probably the main reason he is remembered in Mormon, Utah, and United States history. When the First Presidency asked Reynolds to stand in as a test case in behalf of the Church and its leaders, George did not hesitate. He was a model of decorum in the court room, although he was publicly scolded by the bench and ridiculed by members of the "gentile ring." He did not complain when the case was lost and he was required to serve a prison sentence. Instead of fretting about his unfortunate circumstances in either the Nebraska State Penitentiary or the Utah Territorial Penitentiary, he made the best of his situation and gained the respect of the government officials who watched over him. His fellow prisoners honored him as a man of God. No evidence exists that he ever murmured about his humiliating plight. His chief concerns were not for himself but for the well-being of his family and the growth of the kingdom. Concerning the latter, his faith was that all would be well in time.

In the Tabernacle, on 29 March 1885, just a few weeks after President John Taylor went into hiding from federal marshals, George Reynolds spoke comforting words to the Saints, who were frightened about current happenings: "It is by perfect confidence in the word of the Lord, and by willing humble obedience to all His requirements, accepting all His providences as for our best good, that we shall be delivered," he testified. "Judging by the experience of the Saints in the past, and judging by our own experience in this dispensation—as far as I know it—has all gone to prove that the closer we cleave to the Lord, the nearer He will draw unto us, the greater will be the manifestations of His power in our behalf, and the sooner will be our triumph over those who seek to injure us." He assured his listeners that the Latter-day Saints have no conflict with mankind. "We are sent forth to preach life and salvation to every soul who will hearken and obey. Our mission is one of good will to all men the wide world over. We seek the hurt or injury of no people upon the face of the earth."[16]

His greatest contributions to the Church he loved are his pathbreaking writings on the Book of Mormon, including his massive concordance. For each contribution he deserves to be held "in honorable remembrance," as he was promised in his patriarchal blessing.

In 1893 Elder Reynolds was asked to speak briefly at a meeting of the general authorities in conjunction with the dedication of the Salt Lake Temple, an event considered pentecostal in its significance for the Church. His geniune feelings of love toward God and gratitude

216

for His miraculous hand in blessing the Church flowed from this noble disciple:

> My brethren, I feel exceedingly happy in being with you this morning, and in standing for a few moments before you. I can say with all sincerity that I have rejoiced in the teachings that I have heard at the dedication of this Temple, and more so in the spirit that has been there; for I have rejoiced in the knowledge that God has accepted this house, and also that He has accepted His people; and furthermore, I have had a testimony from God for myself that He has forgiven my individual sins. All these things cause my heart to rejoice before Him, and to increase within me a desire that to my life's end I may serve Him with faithfulness, devotion and humility. There is another thing, too, that has greatly caused my heart to swell with gratitude before God in these meetings, and it is this—that God has magnified His servants of the First Presidency in the eyes of all Israel; that all the people who have congregated at these various meetings have seen that God is with them, that He is leading them, that His Spirit is with them, and that He accepts them. I know that some of the brethren, owing to circumstances that have occurred, have misunderstood some things that have been done. I am thankful beyond measure that that has been removed, and that we now are a united people— united in God, united in keeping His commandments. I have been one of those of whom mention has been made in the meeting, who wondered and feared and had trouble how ever, as things were going, we could be united again. I could not see how it could be done, unless God should work a miracle in our midst. That work He has performed; He has made us one, and I feel that this is a great and glorious day for God's Church here upon the earth. With regard to myself, my brethren, if I have offended any of you I humbly seek your forgiveness. As far as I am concerned myself, I have not an ill feeling toward any soul who dwells on this earth. I wish them all well. I desire to see them, as the children of our Great Father, all blessed, guided, and preserved by Him. These are my feelings. I am one with my brethren in the quorum. I have the fullest confidence in our leaders as the servants of God; and pray that His Holy Spirit may continue to guide us in the offices that we hold, that we may live to His honor and glory and the

salvation of our fellow men, in the positions we are called to occupy; through Jesus I ask it. Amen.[17]

In all important areas of his life, in his writings, in his work with the Deseret Sunday School Union, in the general calling in the First Council of Seventy, and with his family, George exercised much energy to spread the good news of the gospel and build the kingdom. Even in private acts, George personified the principles he taught. In 1905 the widow of a personal friend wrote George the following letter of appreciation:

> Permit me to sincerely thank you for your kindness and substantial aid in the hour of our distress.
> The mortage on our little home has been fully paid and a deed made direct to me. Words cannot express my feelings of appreciation.
> Our little home is a gift from you and others of our friends, and I hope to be able to keep it always, and your kindness in helping to make this possible I can never forget.[18]

During the last years of his life, George received a tender letter of commendation from one of his first acquaintances in the Church and the man who confirmed him a member of the Church, Elder George Teasdale of the Quorum of the Twelve Apostles. Teasdale wrote:

> Ever since I knew you, you have been a champion for Truth and righteousness, a patient laborer, a successful author, a wonderful worker. God bless you. You need not think that your labors are not appreciated, or your integrity. You have made a glorious record and will surely reap the recompense of reward. How wonderful have been the dealings of the Lord with us from the first time we met in the Somerstown branch unto the present time.[19]

Elder George Reynolds declared his life's motto in what turned out to be his last public sermon in general conference in October 1906: "I hope that all through my life I shall ever consider the Kingdom of God and His righteousness first, last, and all the time," he declared. Echoing what he had heard John Taylor say previously, George continued, "To me, this is the 'Kingdom of God or nothing' and the nothing is an impossibility to my mind."[20]

The annual First Presidency Christmas message in the year 1909, the year of George's death, included the following tribute:

> The past year has witnessed the calling to the other side of a number of the veterans who have done much for the cause of Zion at home and abroad. Among these stalwart and faithful elders from whom we have been called to part during the past year, the names of Lorin Farr, George Reynolds, John Nicholson, Charles R. Savage, Andrew W. Winberg, Amos Milton Musser, Samuel W. Richards and others stand out prominently. The services of these men were devoted to the welfare of humanity and were engaged in the ministry almost since the organization of the Church. They have been faithful and true through all vicissitudes, obstacles, persecutions and hardships, through which they were called to pass.[21]

Nor is George Reynolds forgotten today. In a special satellite broadcast about the scriptures in 1985, President Gordon B. Hinckley of the First Presidency addressed the members of the Church worldwide. He emphasized individual scholarship in studying the scriptures and spoke favorably about using concordances, mentioning that he valued his copy of Cruden's concordance of the Bible. "I also treasure my first edition of the *Concordance of the Book of Mormon*, which was printed in 1900," he declared, holding his copy close to his chest. "It represents twenty years of devoted labor on the part of George Reynolds. The volume which I have is now eighty-five years old. It was my father's. He used it much, as have I. I love the feel of its old leather cover. As I use it I can sense the pride of its compiler, who paid so heavy a price for his testimony of the gospel."[22]

In 1984 the Reynolds Family Organization was reestablished, and a reunion was held on 9 August, the seventy-fifth anniversary of George Reynolds's death. Plans were made for future gatherings and an even larger convocation of his descendants occurred in August 1985, during which historical sites relating to George were visited, speeches were given in his honor, and a slide-sound presentation was made of key events in his history. Members of all three families labored hand in hand for this enterprise. Truly this noble man is held "in honorable remembrance."

Notes

1. Samuel Edwin Woolley Journal, 11 January to 1 May 1907.

2. George Reynolds to Sidney Reynolds, 13 April 1907, copy in possession of Sydney Skidmore, Potomac, Maryland.

3. Samuel Edwin Woolley Journal, 21 April 1907.

4. "Elder George Reynolds," *Juvenile Instructor* 44 (1 September 1909): 355.

5. "Gone to His Rest," *Millennial Star* 71 (26 August 1909): 539.

6. Hardy, "George Reynolds: The Early Years," master's thesis, Brigham Young University, 1972, p. 84.

7. "Funeral of George Reynolds," *Deseret News*, 12 August 1909.

8. Ibid.

9. Ibid.

10. Ibid.

11. Ibid.

12. Amy Brown Lyman, *A Lighter of Lamps: The Life Story of Alice Louise Reynolds* (Provo, Utah: Alice Louise Reynolds Club, 1947), p. 2.

13. Ibid.

14. Vicky Burgess-Olson, "Family Structure and Dynamics in Early Utah Mormon Families — 1847–1885," Ph.D. dissertation, Northwestern University, 1975.

15. Ibid., pp. 123–37.

16. *Journal of Discourses*, 26 vols. (Liverpool: Latter-day Saints Book Depot, 1855–56), 26:160.

17. A typescript of this speech is in the Jane Reynolds Collection.

18. Nettie W. Puzey to George Reynolds, 23 May 1905, in Jane Reynolds Collection.

19. George Teasdale to George Reynolds, 26 August 1904, in Jane Reynolds Collection.

20. Conference Report, October 1906, p. 116.

21. James R. Clark, ed., *Messages of the First Presidency*, 6 vols. (Salt Lake City: Bookcraft, 1965–75), 4:211.

22. Gordon B. Hinckley, "Feasting upon the Scriptures," *Ensign* 15 (December 1985): 42.

Appendix A

Identifiable Writings of George Reynolds

BOOKS

1. *The Book of Abraham: Its Authenticity Established As a Divine and Ancient Record.* Salt Lake City: Deseret News Printing and Publishing Co., 1879.
2. *Are We of Israel?* Salt Lake City: Deseret News Printing and Publishing Co., 1883.
3. *The "Mormon" Metropolis: An Illustrated Guide to Salt Lake City and Its Environs.* Salt Lake City: Jos. Hyrum Parry, 1883.
4. *The Myth of "Manuscript Found," or The Absurdities of the "Spaulding Story."* Salt Lake City: Juvenile Instructor Office, 1883.
5. *The Story of the Book of Mormon.* Salt Lake City: Jos. Hyrum Parry, 1888.
6. *A Dictionary of the Book of Mormon.* Salt Lake City: Jos. Hyrum Parry, 1891.
7. *Jubilee History of Latter-day Saints Sunday Schools.* Salt Lake City: Deseret Sunday School Union, 1900 (co-authored with Levi W. Richards).
8. *A Complete Concordance of the Book of Mormon.* Salt Lake City: by the author, 1900.

BOOKS COMPILED OR REPUBLISHED BY PHILIP C. REYNOLDS

1. Reynolds, George. *Are We of Israel? and The Book of Abraham.* Salt Lake City: Deseret News Press, 1952.
2. Reynolds, George. *A Dictionary of the Book of Mormon.* Salt Lake City: Phillip C. Reynolds, 1954.
3. Reynolds, George, and Sjodahl, Janne M. *Commentary on the Book of Mormon.* Edited by Philip C. Reynolds. 7 vols. Salt Lake City: Deseret News Press, 1955–61.
4. Reynolds, George. *The Story of the Book of Mormon.* Salt Lake City: Deseret Book Co., 1957.
5. Reynolds, George, and Sjodahl, Janne M. *Book of Mormon Geography.* Salt Lake City: Deseret Book Co., 1957.
6. Reynolds, George. *A Complete Concordance of the Book of Mormon.* Salt Lake City: Deseret Book Co., 1957.

7. Reynolds, George, and Sjodahl, Janne M. *Commentary on the Pearl of Great Price*. Edited by Philip C. Reynolds. Salt Lake City: Deseret News Press, 1965.

ARTICLES IN PERIODICALS
Juvenile Instructor

1. "The Good Samaritan." 1 (1 February 1866): 9–10.
2. "Be Satisfied." 1 (15 February 1866): 14.
3. "The Story of Atlas." 1 (1 March 1866): 17–18.
4. "Esther, Queen of Persia." 1 (15 July 1866): 56.
5. "A Life in the Trees." 1 (1 August 1866): 60.
6. "The Gods of the Heathens." 1 (15 August 1866): 63.
7. "Who's Afraid?" 1 (1 September 1866): 68.
8. "The Two Voices." 1 (15 September 1866): 70.
9. "Strange Fashions." 1 (1 October 1866): 75.
10. "Jezebel." 1 (15 October 1866): 79.
11. "When the Teacher Comes." 1 (15 October 1866): 81.
12. "The Little Captive Maiden." 1 (1 December 1866): 90.
13. "Gehazi and Naaman." 1 (15 December 1866): 95.
14. "Ruth and Naomi." 1 (15 January 1867): 9–10.
15. "Roman Conquest of Jerusalem." 2 (1 February 1867): 17–18.
16. "Oracles." 2 (15 February 1867): 26.
17. "The Kangaroo." 2 (15 February 1867): 29.
18. "The Finding of Moses." 2 (1 March 1867): 33–34.
19. "What's Worth Doing is Worth Doing Well." 2 (1 March 1867): 37–38.
20. "The Passage of the Red Sea." 2 (15 March 18670:41–42.
21. "The Worship of the Golden Calf." 2 (1 April 1867): 49–50.
22. "David and Goliath." 2 (15 April 1867): 57–58.
23. "David and Goliath." 2 (1 May 1867): 65–66.
24. "The Friendship of Jonathon and David." 2 (15 May 1867): 73–74.
25. "Tobacco." 2 (15 May 1867): 77.
26. "An Appeal to the Lord." 2 (15 June 1867): 96.
27. "The Wisdom of Solomon." 2 (1 July 1867)97–98.
28. "How Two Put Ten Thousand to Flight." 2 (15 July 1867:105–06.
29. "The Prophet Who Fled from the Lord." 2 (1 August 1867): 113–14.
30. "Jephthah and His Daughter." 2 (15 August 1867): 121–22.
31. "Prophets and Their Difficulties." 2 (1 September 1867): 129–30.
32. "The Crystal Palace." 2 (15 October 1867): 153.
33. "The Drawing of Lots." 2 (1 November 1867): 161–62.

34. "Scribbling and Scrawling." 2 (1 November 1867): 168.
35. "The Great Bell of Moscow." 2 (15 November 1867): 169–70.
36. "The Elephant." 2 (1 December 1867): 181–82.
37. "Isaac and Rebekah." 2 (15 December 1867): 185–86.
38. "Christmas, Merry Christmas." 2 (15 December 1867): 188.
39. "The Ostrich." 3 (1 January 1868): 5.
40. "The Rhinoceros." 3 (15 January 1868): 13.
41. "The Tiger." 3 (1 February 1868): 21.
42. "The Sword Fish." 3 (15 February 1868): 29.
43. "Noah and His Days." 3 (1 March 1868): 33.
44. "The Crocodile." 3 (1 March 1869): 37.
45. "Mount Tabor." 3 (15 March 1868): 45.
46. "Editorial Thoughts." 3 (1 April 1868): 52.
47. "The City of Samaria." 3 (1 April 1868): 53–54.
48. "Editorial Thoughts." 3 (15 April 1868): 60.
49. "The Pool of Hezekiah." 3 (15 April 1868): 61.
50. "The Tower of Hippicus." 3 (1 May 1868): 69.
51. "The Valley of Jehosophat." 3 (15 May 1868): 73–74.
52. "The Mount of Olives." 3 (1 June 1868): 81–82.
53. "The Dead Sea." 3 (15 June 1868): 89–90.
54. "Work and Play." 3 (1 July 1868)100.
55. "The Shepherd Boy and the Wolf." 3 (15 July 1868): 109.
56. "The Sword of the Lord and of Gideon." 3 (15 July 1868): 110–11.
57. "The Camel." 3 (1 August 1868): 117.
58. "Man and His Varieties." 3 (15 August 1868): 124–25.
59. "Man and His Varieties." 3 (1 September 1868): 133.
60. "A Family of Lions." 3 (15 September 1868): 137–38.
61. "Man and His Varieties." 3 (15 September 1868): 141–42.
62. "Man and His Varieties." 3 (1 October 1868): 145–46.
63. "Man and His Varieties." 3 (15 October 1868): 157–58.
64. "Man and His Varieties." 3 (1 November 1868): 165–66.
65. "Man and His Varieties." 3 (15 November 1868): 173.
66. "Lapland and the Reindeer." 3 (1 December 1868): 181.
67. "Ocean Steamers." 3 (15 December 1868): 189–90.
68. "The Button Thief." 3 (15 December 1868): 189–90.
69. "A Few Words About the Gospel." 4 (16 January 1869): 15.
70. "Edom and the Edomites." 4 (30 January 1869): 17–18.
71. "Edom and the Edomites." 4 (13 February 1869): 25–26.
72. "Up and Down the Jordan." 4 (27 February 1869): 33–34.

73. "Jacob's Well." 4 (13 March 1869): 45–46.
74. "Nazareth." 4 (27 March 1869): 49–50.
75. "Waterspouts." 4 (27 March 1869): 53.
76. "Bethlehem." 4 (10 April 1869:57–58.
77. "Waterspouts." 4 (10 April 1869): 61–62.
78. "The Giant Cities of Bashan." 4 (24 April 1869): 65.
79. "Mount Lebanon." 4 (8 May 1869): 77.
80. "The Cedars of Lebanon." 4 (22 May 1869): 81–82.
81. "A Cubit." 4 (22 May 1869): 83.
82. "Foolish Thoughts." 4 (22 May 1869): 85.
83. "The Otter." 4 (5 June 1869): 93.
84. "Playing with Fire." 4 (19 June 1869): 100–01.
85. "Thou Shalt Not Steal." 4 (3 July 1869): 109.
86. "Giants." 4 (31 July 1869): 123.
87. "Editorial Thoughts." 4 (14 August 1869): 132.
88. "Dwarfs." 4 (14 August 1869): 132.
89. "The Flowers of the Field." 4 (28 August 1869): 141.
90. "Tyre." 4 (11 September 1869): 145–46.
91. "Joseph and Mary Fleeing to Egypt." 4 (25 September 1869): 153–54.
92. "Hunting Reindeer." 4 (8 October 1869): 165.
93. "The Elephant Fight." 4 (22 October 1869): 169–70.
94. "Editorial Thoughts." 4 (22 October 1869): 172.
95. "A Roman Mother." 4 (22 October 1869): 173.
96. "Haydn, the Composer." 4 (6 November 1869): 181.
97. "Anecdotes of Dogs." 4 (20 November 1869): 189–90.
98. "Don't Be Cruel." 4 (3 December 1869): 197.
99. "A Strange School House." 5 (8 January 1870): 5–6.
100. "Allegorical." 5 (8 January 1870): 8.
101. "Fishing for Pearls." 5 (22 January 1870): 13.
102. "The Old Basket Maker." 5 (22 January 1870): 16.
103. "An Eastern Fountain." 5 (5 February 1870): 21.
104. "The Animal Kingdom." 5 (5 February 1870): 24.
105. "Things We Should Be Thankful For." 5 (19 February 1870): 32.
106. "Bangkok." 5 (5 March 1870): 33.
107. "Tempted." 5 (19 March 1870): 40.
108. "The Vulture." 5 (19 March 1870): 45–46.
109. "The Wonders of the Deep." 5 (2 April 1870): 53–54.
110. "The Sahara." 5 (16 April 1870): 61–62.

111. "Pisa." 5 (30 April 1870): 69.
112. "Rice." 5 (14 May 1870): 77.
113. "Sacred Things Not to be Trifled With." 5 (14 May 1870): 79.
114. "The Iguana." 5 (28 May 1870): 81–82.
115. "The Agouti." 5 (11 June 1870): 89–90.
116. "Editorial." 5 (25 June 1870): 100.
117. "Our Menagerie." 5 (9 July 1870): 105–06.
118. "Our Menagerie." 5 (23 July 1870): 113–14.
119. "Our Menagerie." 5 (6 August 1870): 121–22.
120. "The People of Europe." 5 (20 August 1870): 129–30.
121. "Sunday School Hymn." 5 (20 August 1870): 136.
122. "The Kiajak." 5 (3 September 1870): 137–38.
123. "The Walrus." 5 (3 September 1870): 141.
124. "The Polar Bear." 5 (17 September 1870): 145–46.
125. "Hunting at the Cape of Good Hope." 5 (1 October 1870): 153–54.
126. "Pizarro and the Peruvians." 5 (15 October 1870): 165.
127. "From Shore to Shore." 5 (29 October 1870): 173–74.
128. "The Rest of the World." 5 (12 November 1870): 177–78.
129. "What's in It." 5 (26 November 1870): 188.
130. "John Wesley." 6 (21 January 18710:13.
131. "Stephen." 6 (21 January 1871): 16.
132. "A Frontier Fort." 6 (4 February 1871): 21–22.
133. "The Destruction of the Hosts of Pharaoh." 6 (4 February 1871): 24.
134. "The Deluge." 6 (18 February 1871): 25–26.
135. "The Metropolitan Railroad." 6 (18 May 1871): 45–46.
136. "Whales." 6 (1 April 1871): 49–50.
137. "Searching for Treasure." 6 (1 April 1871): 53–54.
138. "Child's Prayer." 6 (29 April 1871): 68.
139. "Our Father in Heaven." 6 (8 July 1871): 112.
140. "The Hippopotamus." 6 (2 September 1871): 137.
141. "Our Name." 6 (2 September 1871): 141.
142. "The Peacock." 6 (16 September 1871): 149.
143. "The Flamingo." 6 (30 September 1871): 157.
144. "The Cypress." 6 (14 October 1871): 165.
145. "Amulek." 10 (6 February 1875): 35–36
146. "Poor Little Sweeps." 10 (15 May 1875): 118.
147. "Writing on the Wall." 12 (1 May 1877): 97–98.

148. "Look at Your Own Faults." 12 (1 November 1877): 245.
149. "Intemperance." 12 (1 November 1877): 248.
150. "Recrimination." 12 (15 November 1877): 257.
151. "Reputation vs. Character." 12 (15 November 1877): 262–63.
153. "Daniel in the Lion's Den." 12 (15 December 1877): 282.
153. "The Angels and the Shepherds." 13 (1 January 1878): 9–10.
154. "Whiners." 13 (15 March 1878): 65.
155. "The Tiger." 13 (15 May 1878): 75.
156. "How a Little Boy Spends Money." 13 (1 July 1878): 104.
157. "Thou Shalt Have No Other Gods Before Me." 14 (1 March 1879): 53.
158. "There Is No wisdom, Nor Understanding, Nor Council Against the Lord." 14 (15 March 1879): 64–65.
159. "Be Sure Your Sin Will Find You Out." 14 (1 July 1879): 148.
160. "One Lord, One Faith, One Baptism." 14 (15 July 1879): 159.
161. "I Am the Light of the World." 14 (1 August 1879): 177.
162. "I Am the Bread of Life." 14 (15 Augut 1879): 182.
163. "Enter Ye In at the Strait Gate." 14 (15 August 1877): 195.
164. "Nursery Rhymes." 14 (1 September 1877): 202–03.
165. "Three Prophets in Three Distant Ages Born." 14 (15 October 1879): 238–39.
166. "Melchizedek." 14 (1 December 1879): 248.
167. "The Zoramites." 14 (1 December 1879): 272–73.
168. "Domestic Life Among the Nephites." 14 (15 December 1879): 285–86.
169. "The Laws of the Nephites." 15 (1 January 1880): 5
170. "The Laws of the Nephites." 15 (15 January 1880): 22.
171. "The Laws of the Nephites." 15 (1 February 1880): 27–28.
172. "The Laws of the Nephites." 15 (15 February 1880): 46–47.
173. "The Laws of the Nephites." 15 (1 March 1880): 59.
174. "Agriculture Among the Nephites." 15 (15 March 1880): 71.
175. "The Art of War Among the Nephites." 15 (1 April 1880): 77.
176. "The Art of War Among the Nephites." 15 (15 April 1880): 94.
177. "Science and Literature Among the Nephites." 15 (1 May 1880): 105–6.
178. "Personal Appearance of the Nephites." 15 (15 May 1880): 110–11.
179. "Language of the Nephites." 15 (15 August 1880): 191–92.
180. "Nephite Proper Names." 15 (15 September 1880): 207–8.

181. "A Nephite Enigma," 15 (15 September 1880): 216.
182. "The Moneys of the Nephites." 15 (1 November 1880): 249–50.
183. "The Lands of the Nephites." 15 (15 November 1880): 261.
184. "A Book of Mormon Enigma." 15 (15 November 1880): 264.
185. "The Lands of the Nephites." 15 (1 December 1880): 274–75.
186. "The Lands of the Nephites." 15 (15 December 1880): 286.
187. "The Lands of the Nephites." 16 (1 January 1881): 7–8.
188. "The Lands of the Nephites." 16 (15 January 1881): 22–23.
189. "The Lands of the Nephites." 16 (1 February 1881): 26–27.
190. "Only Believe." 16 (1 April 1881): 77.
191. "The Lord's Supper." 16 (15 August 1881): 184–85.
192. "The Betrayal of Christ." 16 (15 September 1881): 214.
193. "Elijah." 16 (1 October 1881): 221.
194. "An Incident in the Life of Cromwell." 16 (1 December 1881): 264–65.
195. "The Conflict Between Science and Superstition." 17 (15 January 1882): 18–19.
196. "The Lamb of God." 17 (1 February 1882): 46.
197. "Gaza." 17 (15 March 1882): 81–82.
198. "Patmos." 17 (15 April 1882): 122.
199. "Philadelphia." 17 (1 May 1882): 129–30.
200. "Overflow of the Nile." 17 (15 May 1882): 145–46.
201. "Thyatira." 17 (1 June 1882): 161–62.
202. "Pergamos." 17 (15 June 1882): 186.
203. "Thoughts About Palms." 17 (1 July 1882): 193–94.
204. "Internal Evidences of the Book of Mormon: Showing the Absurdity of the 'Spaulding Story.' " 17 (1 August 1882): 235–38.
205. "Internal Evidences of the Book of Mormon." 17 (15 August 1882): 251–52.
206. "The Originator of the 'Spaulding Story.' " 17 (1 September 1882): 262–63.
207. "The Book of Mormon and the Three Witnesses." 17 (15 September 1882): 281.
208. "Joseph Smith's Youthful Life." 17 (1 October 1882): 298–302.
209. "Cairo." 17 (1 October 1882): 314–15.
210. "Time Occupied in Translating the Book of Mormon." 17 (15 October 1881): 315–17.
211. "The Assyrian Captivity." 18 (15 January 1883): 26–28.
212. "The City of Samaria." 18 (15 February 1883): 49–50.

213. "St. Paul's Cathedral." 18 (1 May 1883): 129–30.
214. "Historical Review of the Deseret Sunday School Union." 19 (15 October 1884): 317. (Coauthored with Levi W. Richards.)
215. "Historical Review of the Deseret Sunday School Union." 19 (1 November 1884): 322–23. (Coauthored with Levi W. Richards.)
216. "Historical Review of the Deseret Sunday School Union." 19 (15 November 1884): 346–47. (Coauthored with Levi W. Richards.)
217. "Lessons from the Life of Nephi: The Preaching of Lehi." 26 (15 July 1891): 437–40.
218. "Lessons from the Life of Nephi: Lehi Leaves Jerusalem." 26 (1 May 1891): 281–84.
219. "Lessons from the Life of Nephi: Nephi Obtains the Records." 26 (15 May 1891): 297–99.
220. "Lessons from the Life of Nephi: The Return for Ishmael." 26 (1 June 1891): 348–51.
221. "Lessons from the Life of Nephi: Nephi's Wonderful Visions." 26 (15 June 1891): 373–76.
222. "Lessons from the Life of Nephi: The Liahona." 26 (1 July 1891): 406–09.
223. "Lessons from the Life of Nephi: A Ship Built in the Land of Bountiful." 26 (15 July 1891): 437–40.
224. "Lessons from the Life of Nephi: The Arrival on the Promised Land." 26 (1 August 1891): 475–77.
225. "Lessons from the Life of Nephi: Lehi Blesses His Posterity." 26 (15 August 1891): 502–04.
226. "Lessons from the Life of Nephi: The Division of the Race." 26 (1 September 1891): 536–38.
227. "Lessons from the Life of Nephi: Nephi Builds a Temple." 26 (15 September 1891): 574–77.
228. "Lessons from the Life of Nephi: Nephi Manufactures Plates." 26 (1 October 1891): 586–87.
229. "Akish, the Jaredite." 26 (15 October 1891): 631–33.
230. "Aaron, Son of Mosiah." 26 (1 November 1891): 650–53.
231. "The Jaredites." 27 (15 April 1892): 254–55.
232. "The Jaredites." 27 (1 May 1892): 282–85.
233. "The Jaredites." 27 (15 May 1892): 316–17.
234. "The Jaredites." 27 (1 June 1892): 339–40.
235. "The Jaredites." 27 (15 June 1892): 374–76.
236. "The Jaredites." 27 (1 July 1892): 411–13.

237. "The Jaredites." 27 (15 July 1892): 447–49.
238. "The Jaredites." 27 (1 August 1892): 469–70.
239. "The Jaredites." 27 (15 August 1892): 500–03.
240. "The Jaredites." 27 (1 September 1892): 524–27.
241. "The Jaredites." 27 (15 September 1892): 555–58.
242. "The Jaredites." 27 (1 October 1892): 603–04.
243. "The Gospel in Ancient Britain." 33 (15 April 1898): 295–300.
244. "The Gospel in Ancient Britain." 33 (1 May 1898): 332–35.
245. "The Gospel in Ancient Britain." 33 (15 May 1898): 364–67.
246. "The Gospel in Ancient Britain." 33 (1 June 1898): 401–05.
247. "The Gospel in Ancient Britain." 33 (15 June 1898): 446–49.
248. "The Gospel in Ancient Britain." 33 (1 July 1898): 466–73.
249. "The Gospel in Ancient Britain." 33 (15 July 1898): 505–10.
250. "The Gospel in Ancient Britain." 33 (1 August 1898): 531–35.
251. "The Gospel in Ancient Britain." 33 (15 August 1898): 574–79.
252. "The Gospel in Ancient Britain." 33 (1 September 1898): 596–99.
253. "The Gospel in Ancient Britain." 33 (15 September 1898): 628–31.
254. "The Gospel in Ancient Britain." 33 (1 October 1898): 659–63.
255. "The Gospel in Ancient Britain." 33 (15 October 1898): 684–87.
256. "The Gospel in Ancient Britain." 33 (1 November 1898): 723–27.
257. "The Gospel in Ancient Britain." 33 (15 November 1898): 754–57.
258. "The Gospel in Ancient Britain." 33 (1 December 1898): 785–90.
259. "The Gospel in Ancient Britain." 33 (15 December 1898): 822–24.
260. "Lives of Our Leaders. – The First Council of the Seventy. President George Reynolds." 36 (1 July 1901): 385–89.
261. "Hath No Man Seen God?" 37 (1 January 1902): 1–3.
262. "Revelation – Inspiration." 37 (1 March 1902): 129–31.
263. "View of the Hebrews." 37 (1 October 1902): 595–97.

In addition, George Reynolds wrote several unsigned editorials in the winters of 1873–74 and 1874–75 when editor George Q. Cannon was in Washington, D.C., as territorial congressional delegate. Furthermore as a member of the general superintendency of the Deseret Sunday School Union from 1901 to 1907, George Reynolds unquestionably authored numerous editorials in the *Juvenile Instructor* pertaining to Sunday School procedures and was likely the author of most of the many columns entitled "Answers to Questions."

Millennial Star

1. "The Real and the Imaginary." 25 (3 January 1863): 4–6.
2. "How Shall We Be Better?" 25 (4 April 1863): 213–15.
3. "First Impressions Indelible – Importance of Early Training." 26 (16 January 1864): 36–38.
4. "The Supernatural." 26 (16 July 1864): 449–51.
5. "It Must Be True, For It Was in the Papers." 26 (20 August 1864): 533–34.
6. "The Harmony of the Gospel." 26 (17 September 1864): 593–95.
7. "Extremes of Character." 26 (15 October 1864): 657–60.
8. "The Influence We Wield." 26 (26 November 1864): 756–60.
9. "Post Prophesying." 26 (24 December 1864): 819–21.
10. "I'll Ask Counsel." 27 (25 February 1865): 117–18.
11. "The Religion of Every Day Life." 27 (15 April 1865): 227–29.
12. "Wisdom and Knowledge." 27 (29 April 1865): 260–61.
13. "Prophets and Petrels." 33 (27 June 1871): 407.
14. "The Decline of Mormonism." 33 (27 June 1871): 408–10.
15. "The Gospel Before the Savior's Advent." 33 (25 July 1871): 472–74.
16. "Hints to Emigrants." 33 (1 August 1871): 488–89.
17. "The Power of the Priesthood." 33 (22 August 1871): 536–37.
18. "Signs in the Heavens." 33 (29 August 1871): 552–53.
19. "The Patience of the Saints." 33 (10 October 1871): 648–49.
20. "Be Not Discouraged." 33 (17 October 1871): 664.
21. "Open to Conviction." 33(7 November 1871): 714–16.
22. "Train Up a Child in the Way He Should Go." 33 (5 December 1871): 776–77.
23. "The Trial of President Young." 33 (19 December 1871): 808–09.
24. "Our Amusements." 34 (2 January 1872): 8–10.
25. "From Adam to Abraham." 34 (23 January 1872): 49–50.
26. "The Ignorance Regarding Utah." 34 (23 January 1872): 56–58.
27. "The Ridicule of Sacred Things." 34 (30 January 1872): 72–73.
28. "Our Sabbath School Teachers." 34 (6 February 1872): 88–90.
29. "New Tactics." 34 (20 February 1872): 120–22.
30. "Untruthful Pictures." 34 (20 February 1872): 125–16.
31. "The Weight of Our Calling." 34 (27 February 1872): 136–37.
32. "Obedience and Free Agency." 34 (5 March 1872): 152–54.
33. "Obedience to the Holy Priesthood." 34 (12 March 1872): 168–71.
34. "Presidents and Presiding." 34 (19 March 1872): 184–86.

35. "Love Letters." 34 (19 March 1872): 188–89.
36. "The Administration of the Lord's Supper." 34 (26 March 1872): 200–02.
37. "A Word of Warning." 34 (9 April 1872): 232–34.
38. "Tithing a Privilege and Blessing." 34 (16 April 1872): 248–50.
39. "Excommunication, Baptisms, Etc." 34 (30 April 1872): 280–82.
40. "The Release of President Young." 34 (21 May 1872): 312.
41. "The Emigration." 34 (21 May 1872): 328–29.
42. "Our Highest Interest." 34 (25 June 1872): 408–09.
43. "Are We of Israel?" 40 (19 August 1878): 513–15.
44. "Are We of Israel?" 40 (26 August 1878): 531–32.
45. "Are We of Israel?" 40 (2 September 1878): 545–47.
46. "Are We of Israel?" 40 (9 September 1878): 562–64.
47. "Are We of Israel?" 40 (16 September 1878): 577–79.
48. "Are We of Israel?" 40 (23 September 1878): 595–96.
49. "Are We of Israel?" 40 (30 September 1878): 609–11.
50. "Are We of Israel?" 40 (7 October 1878): 627–28.
51. "Are We of Israel?" 40 (14 October 1878): 641–44.
52. "Are We of Israel?" 40 (21 October 1878): 661–63.
53. "Are We of Israel?" 40 (28 October 1878): 686–87.
54. "Are We of Israel?" 40 (11 November 1878): 705–07.
55. "The Skeleton in Armor." 40 (25 November 1878): 737–40.
56. "The Book of Abraham – Its Genuineness Established." 41 (6 January 1879): 1–3.
57. "The Book of Abraham – Its Genuineness Established." 41 (13 January 1879): 17–19.
58. "The Book of Abraham – Its Genuineness Established." 41 (20 January 1879): 37–39.
59. "The Book of Abraham – Its Genuineness Established." 41 (27 January 1879): 53–55.
60. "The Book of Abraham – Its Genuineness Established." 41 (3 February 1879): 65–67.
61. "The Book of Abraham – Its Genuineness Established." 41 (10 February 1879): 81–84.
62. "The Book of Abraham – Its Genuineness Established." 41 (17 February 1879): 97–100
63. "The Book of Abraham – Its Genuineness Established." 41 (24 February 1879): 113–15.
64. "The Book of Abraham – Its Genuineness Established." 41 (3 March 1879): 129–32.

65. "The Book of Abraham—Its Genuineness Established." 41 (10 March 1879): 145–48.
66. "The Book of Abraham—Its Genuineness Established." 41 (17 March 1879): 161–63.
67. "The Book of Abraham—Its Genuineness Established." 41 (24 March 1879): 177–79.
68. "The Book of Abraham—Its Genuineness Established." 41 (31 March 1879): 193–95.
69. "The Book of Abraham—Its Genuineness Established." 41 (7 April 1879): 209–11.
70. "Repentance and Reformation." 41 (22 September 1879): 593–96.
71. "The Revelation of God." 41 (17 November 1879): 721–24.
72. "The Alma Family." 42 (19 January 1880): 33–37.
73. "The Alma Family." 42 (26 January 1880): 49–52.
74. "The Alma Family." 42 (2 February 1880): 65–68.
75. "The Alma Family." 42 (9 February 1880): 81–84.
76. "The Alma Family." 42 (16 February 1880): 97–101.
77. "The Alma Family." 42 (23 February 1880): 113–17.
78. "The Alma Family." 42 (1 March 1880): 129–31.
79. "The Alma Family." 42 (8 March 1880): 145–47.
80. "The Alma Family." 42 (15 March 1880): 161–64.
81. "The Alma Family." 42 (22 March 1880): 177–79.
82. "The Alma Family." 42 (29 March 1880): 193–95.
83. "The Alma Family." 42 (12 April 1880): 225–26.
84. "The Alma Family." 42 (19 April 1880): 241–43.
85. "The Alma Family." 42 (26 April 1880): 257–58.
86. "The Alma Family." 42 (3 May 1880): 278–79.
87. "Unknown Ancient Hebrew Prophets." 42 (7 June 1880): 357–59.
88. "The Lamanites." 42 (21 June 1880): 385–88.
89. "The Lamanites." 42 (28 June 1880): 400–04.
90. "The Lamanites." 42 (5 July 1880): 417–20.
91. "The Lamanites." 42 (12 July 1880): 433–36.
92. "The Lamanites." 42 (19 July 1880): 449–52.
93. "The Lamanites." 42 (26 July 1880): 465–67.
94. "Fashion and Education." 42 (18 October 1880): 657–58.
95. "The Gospel, Why Not Revealed in Dark Ages." 43 (18 July 1881): 433–34.
96. "Crime and Education." 44 (9 January 1882): 20–23. (Reprinted from *Contributor*.)

97. "Miracles." 44 (20 February 1882): 118–19. (Reprinted from *Contributor*.)
98. "Objections to the Book of Mormon." 44 (3 April 1882): 213–15. (Reprinted from *Contributor*.)
99. "Objections to the Book of Mormon." 44 (10 April 1882): 229–31. (Reprinted from *Contributor*.)
100. "Objections to the Book of Mormon." 44 (17 April 1882): 244–47. (Reprinted from *Contributor*.)
101. "Individual Responsibility and Testimony." 44 (10 July 1882): 436.
102. "Evidences of the Book of Mormon." 59 (10 June 1897): 353–58. (Reprinted from *Contributor*.)
103. "Evidences of the Book of Mormon." 59 (17 June 1897): 369–76. (Reprinted from *Contributor*.)
104. "Evidences of the Book of Mormon." 59 (24 June 1897): 385–93. (Reprinted from *Contributor*.)
105. "Evidences of the Book of Mormon." 59 (1 July 1897): 401–09. (Reprinted from *Contributor*.)
106. "Evidences of the Book of Mormon." 59 (8 July 1897): 417–29. (Reprinted from *Contributor*.)
107. "Hath No Man Seen God?" 64 (6 February 1902): 85–87. (Reprinted from *Juvenile Instructor*.)
108. "Ungodly Independence." 83 (28 April 1921): 259–61. (Reprinted from *Contributor*.)

Contributor

1. "The Nephites Under the Judges." 2 (February 1881): 139–42.
2. "The Nephites Under the Judges." 2 (March 1881): 171–74.
3. "The Nephites Under the Judges." 2 (April 1881): 205–08.
4. "The Nephites Under the Judges." 2 (May 1881): 235–38.
5. "Crime and Education." 2 (July 1881): 292–95.
6. "Influence of Outside Literature." 2 (September 1881): 357–59.
7. "Thoughts on Genesis." 3 (October 1881): 16–17.
8. "Miracles." 3 (November 1881): 44–45.
9. "Objections to the Book of Mormon." 3 (December 1881): 81–83.
10. "Objections to the Book of Mormon." 3 (January 1882): 105–08.
11. "Objections to the Book of Mormon." 3 (February 1882): 134–37.
12. "The Edmunds Bill." 3 (April 1882): 204–05.
13. "Mormon and Jew – A Modern Parallel." 3 (May 1882): 247–49.
14. "Objections to the Book of Mormon." 4 (October 1882): 4–6.
15. "Utah Statistics – Census of 1880." 4 (April 1883): 276–78.

16. "Utah Statistics – Census of 1880." 4 (June 1883): 352–53.
17. "History of the Book of Mormon." 5 (November 1883): 41–47.
18. "History of the Book of Mormon: Contents of the Records." 5 (December 1883): 81–85.
19. "History of the Book of Mormon: Contents of the Records." 5 (January 1884): 121–25.
20. "History of the Book of Mormon: Contents of the Records." 5 (February 1884): 161–68.
21. "History of the Book of Mormon: Contents of the Records." 5 (March 1884): 201–06.
22. "History of the Book of Mormon: Contents of the Records." 5 (April 1884): 241–46.
23. "History of the Book of Mormon: The Discovery of the Records." 5 (May 1884): 281–86.
24. "History of the Book of Mormon: The Translation of the Plates." 5 (June 1884): 321–27.
25. "History of the Book of Mormon: Translation of the Records." 5 (July 1884): 361–67.
26. "History of the Book of Mormon: Translation of the Records." 5 (August 1884): 401–06.
27. "History of the Book of Mormon: American and Foreign Editions." 5 (September 1884): 441–47.
28. "Thoughts on Civilization." 10 (November 1888): 11–13.
29. "A Wonderful School." 10 (March 1889): 176–77.
30. "Ungodly Independence." 10 (April 1889): 223–34.
31. "The Grandest Principle of the Gospel." 16 (August 1895): 611.
32. "Evidences of the Book of Mormon: External Proofs of Its Divinity." 17 (January 1896): 164–68.
33. "Evidences of the Book of Mormon: External Proofs of Its Divinity." 17 (February 1896): 231–38.
34. "Evidences of the Book of Mormon: External Proofs of Its Divinity." 17 (March 1896): 271–78.
35. "Evidences of the Book of Mormon: External Proofs of Its Divinity." 17 (April 1896): 361–68.
36. "Evidences of the Book of Mormon: External Proofs of Its Divinity." 17 (May 1896): 417–24.

Liahona: The Elder's Journal

1. "Miracles." 5 (6 July 1907): 76–77. (Reprinted from *Millennial Star*.)

2. "The Repentant Lawyer." 5 (27 July 1907): 154–56. (Reprinted from *Millennial Star*.)
3. "Objections to the Book of Mormon." 6 (2 November 1907): 534–36. (Reprinted from *Millennial Star*.)

Young Women's Journal
1. "The Bible and the Book of Mormon." 9 (November 1898): 490–92.
2. "Not Too Young." 15 (September 1904): 399–400.

Improvement Era
1. "The Thief on the Cross." 1 (February 1898): 225–30.
2. "He Shall Perish." 2 (September 1899): 801–06.
3. "Shiz – The Headless." 3 (June 1900): 588–89.
4. "Infant Baptism and the Sacrament." 4 (February 1901): 247–52.

George Reynolds is also known to have written unsigned editorials occasionally for the *Deseret News* and to have written unsigned articles for the Utah County *Enquirer* and the *Omaha Bee*. As a member of the publications committee for the Deseret Sunday School Union, he wrote numerous articles and lessons in *Deseret Sunday School Reader: First Book for Our Little Friends* (1879), *Deseret Sunday School Reader: Second Book for Our Little Friends* (1880), *The Intermediate Sunday School Reader for the Use of Our Little Friends* (1888), the Sunday School *Leaflets* (1890s), and the Sunday School *Outlines* (1900s).

Appendix B

The Children of George Reynolds

Order of Child	Given Names (Called)	Name of Mother (Order of child for her)	Date of Birth (Date of death)	Age at Death	Name of Spouse (Date married)	Number of Children
1	George Tuddenham (Georgey)	Polly (First child)	27 May 1866 30 Sep 1867	16 mo.		
2	Amelia Emily (Millie)	Polly (Second child)	5 Jan 1868 29 July 1943	75	Ed (John) Hogan (27 Aug 1888) Charles T. Martain (29 Aug 1896)	0 10
3	Heber Tuddenham (Heber)	Polly (Third child)	12 July 1870 3 May 1872	22 mo.		
4	Alice Louise (Alice)	Polly (Fourth child)	1 Apr 1873 5 Dec 1936	65		
5	Florence Mary (Florry or Flo)	Polly (Fifth child)	13 July 1874 26 Nov 1932	58	Benjamin Cluff, Jr. (1899)	6
6	Sidney Schofield (Sid)	Amelia (First child)	6 July 1874 3 Mar 1933	58	Mary Maude Davis (26 Jun 1901)	6
7	Amy Tautz (Amy or Am)	Polly (Sixth child)	16 Apr 1876 29 July 1955	79	Peter Neal Hood (26 May 1904) John William Donaldson (1911) Edward Anthon (about 1950)	4 0 0
8	Marion Groves (May)	Amelia (Second child)	7 Nov 1876 2 Aug 1952	76	Charles Woolfinden (1895)	5
9	Charles Hewett (Charlie)	Amelia (Third child)	6 June 1878 31 Oct 1879	16 mo.		
10	Eleanor Elizabeth (Nellie or Nel)	Polly (Seventh child)	21 Sep 1878 28 Jan 1920	42	William Harmer (10 June 1903)	6
11	Julia Durrant (Julia)	Polly (Eighth child)	17 Dec 1879 21 July 1880	7 mo.		
12	Susannah Alberta (Bertie or Bert)	Amelia (Fourth child)	9 Feb 1880 31 Mar 1941	61	John H. Russell (20 Sep 1900)	7
13	George Bruford (George)	Amelia (Fifth child)	21 Oct 1881 25 Jan 1937	56	Eleanor Jensen (18 Dec 1907)	2

Appendix B

Order of Child	Given Names (Called)	Name of Mother (Order of child for her)	Date of Birth (Date of death)	Age at Death	Name of Spouse (Date married)	Number of Children
14	John Leslie (John)	Polly (Ninth child)	11 Nov 1881 28 Nov 1933	52	Belva Fisher (25 June 1909) Elizabeth Wilson (22 June 1926)	2 2
15	Edwin Don Carlos (Carl)	Amelia (Sixth child)	28 Sep 1883 23 Jan 1937	53	Violet Goodfellow (Date unknown)	1
16	Harold Godfrey (Harold)	Polly (Tenth child)	18 Nov 1883 1 Nov 1940	56	Ann Amelia Howarth (23 June 1911)	4
17	Willard Hyrum (Bish)	Amelia (Seventh child)	26 Jun 1885 26 Nov 1939	54	Eve Pyper (June 1907)	4
18	Herbert (Herbert)	Polly (Eleventh child)	11 Dec 1885 12 Dec 1885	1 day		
19	Georgia Ann (Georgia)	Mary (First child)	10 Jul 1886 31 Jan 1966	80	Frank M. Gibson (23 Aug 1911)	3
20	Nephi Winsor (Nephi)	Amelia (Eighth child)	13 Aug 1887 20 Oct 1940	53	Bertha Hardy (17 Aug 1908)	2
21	Polly Anatroth (Polly)	Mary (Second child)	11 May 1888 5 Sep 1959	71	T. Fred Hardy (25 Sep 1914)	4
22	Ethel Georgina (Ethel)	Amelia (Ninth child)	23 Aug 1889 26 Aug 1937	48	Joseph Fielding Smith (2 Nov 1908)	9
23	Philip Caswallon (Phil or Cas)	Mary (Third child)	24 Jul 1890 12 Jan 1966	76	Lila Sjodahl King (19 Mar 1919)	2
24	Josephine Edna (Josephine or Jo)	Amelia (Tenth child)	21 Aug 1891 16 May 1960	69	Clarence W. Burningham (2 Oct 1914)	11
25	Gwendolyn (Gwen)	Mary (Fourth child)	30 Dec 1891 6 Mar 1895	4		
26	Rosalie Temple (Rosalie)	Mary (Fifth child)	5 Oct 1893 15 May 1917	24		
27	Bruford Alan (Bru)	Amelia (Eleventh child)	20 Mar 1895 16 Oct 1947	52	Zella Scott (22 Sep 1916)	2
28	Julia Adelaide (Jewell)	Mary (Sixth child)	16 Aug 1895 18 Oct 1983	88	Joseph Romney Brain (4 Jun 1915)	3
29	George Gordon (Gordon)	Mary (Seventh child)	6 Sep 1897 15 May 1983	85	Helen Winters (29 Dec 1948)	0

Appendix B

Order of Child	Given Names (Called)	Name of Mother (Order of child for her)	Date of Birth (Date of death)	Age at Death	Name of Spouse (Date married)	Number of Children
30	Olive Gertrude (Gertrude)	Amelia (Twelfth child)	24 Aug 1898 11 June 1973	74	Harlan M. Adams (Oct 1931)	0
31	Arthur Reed (Art)	Mary (Eighth child)	24 May 1900 4 Dec 1972	72	Janette Cox (27 Nov 1920)	3
					Charlotte Riter (6 Mar 1958)	0
32	Clifford Meredith (Cliff)	Mary (Ninth child)	22 June 1903 29 Aug 1976	73	Lucille Herber (1 July 1925)	1
					Gladys M. Nelson (26 Sep 1929)	2

Bibliography

Principal sources for this biography come from the George Reynolds Journal (the original is in the LDS Church Historical Archives), two contemporary articles about him ("Lives of Our Leaders" by T.Z. published in 1901 in the *Juvenile Instructor* and a biographical sketch about him by Andrew Jenson), a master's thesis about his early life by Grant R. Hardy, the George Reynolds Collection in Special Collections of the Harold B. Lee Library of Brigham Young University, oral interviews with family members, a collection of documents and memorabilia in the hands of Jane Reynolds of Salt Lake City, Utah, and Reynolds's actual writings.

I have concluded that Reynolds himself wrote the *Juvenile Instructor* sketch. The only indication of the author is the "T.Z." that appears at the end of the article. On another occasion Reynolds wrote an article under the pseudonym "T.Z." and another under "Tautz," which was his mother's maiden name. "T.Z." corresponds with "Tautz." Furthermore, the other sketches in the "Lives of Our Leaders" series had a by-line and tended to be overly complimentary of their subjects. The biography of George Reynolds stands in stark contrast to the others in its modest portrayal of the man and his accomplishments. That would have befit Reynolds's native modesty. Finally, George was the chief editor of the *Juvenile Instructor* at the time and wrote or edited many of its articles.

BOOKS

Anderson, James H. *God's Covenant Race.* Salt Lake City: Deseret News Press, 1937.

Anderson, Richard Lloyd. *Investigating the Book of Mormon Witnesses.* Salt Lake City: Deseret Book Co., 1981.

Alexander, Thomas G., and Allen, James B. *Mormons and Gentiles: A History of Salt Lake City.* Boulder, Colo.: Pruett Publishing Co., 1984.

Allen, Joseph L. *Exploring the Lands of the Book of Mormon.* Orem, Utah: S.A. Publishers, 1989.

Arrington, Leonard J. *Great Basin Kingdom*. Lincoln, Neb.: University of Nebraska Press, 1958.

Barlow, Ora H., ed. *The Israel Barlow Story and Mormon Mores*. Salt Lake City: Publishers Press, 1968.

Baskin, Robert N. *Reminiscences of Early Utah*. n.p., 1914.

Bergera, Gary James, and Priddis, Ronald. *Brigham Young University: A House of Faith*. Salt Lake City: Signature Books, 1985.

Biennial Report of the Warden of the Nebraska State Penitentiary for the Years 1879 and 1880. Lincoln, Neb.: Journal Co., 1881.

Bloxham, Ben, et al. *Truth Will Prevail*. Solihull, England: The Church of Jesus Christ of Latter-day Saints, 1987.

Boller, Paul F., Jr. *American Thought in Transition: The Impact of Evolutionary Naturalism, 1865–1900*. New York: University Press of America, 1981.

Book of Mormon. Salt Lake City: The Church of Jesus Christ of Latter-day Saints, 1981.

Bush, Lester E., Jr., and Mauss, Armand L., eds. *Neither White Nor Black: Mormon Scholars Confront the Race Issue in a Universal Church*. Midvale, Utah: Signature Books, 1984.

Cannon, Frank J., and O'Higgins, Harvey J. *Under the Prophet in Utah*. Boston: C. M. Clark Publishing Co., 1911.

Cannon, George Q. *A Review of the Decision of the Supreme Court in the Case of Geo. Reynolds vs. the United States*. Salt Lake City: Deseret News Printing and Publishing Establishment, 1879.

Clark, James R., ed. *Messages of the First Presidency*. 6 vols. Salt Lake City: Bookcraft, 1965–75.

Darter, Francis M. *The Kingdom of God, the U.S.A., and British Empire*. Salt Lake City: Utah Printing Co., 1941.

Deseret Sunday School Union Leaflets. Salt Lake City: Deseret Sunday School Union, 1901.

Deseret Sunday School Union Music Book. Salt Lake City: Juvenile Instructor Office, 1884.

Doctrine and Covenants. Salt Lake City: The Church of Jesus Christ of Latter-day Saints, 1981.

England, Breck. *The Life and Thought of Orson Pratt*. Salt Lake City: University of Utah Press, 1985.

Evans, Richard L. *A Century of "Mormonism" in Great Britain*. Salt Lake City: Publishers Press, 1937.

First Book For Our Little Friends. Salt Lake City: Juvenile Instructor Office, 1879.

Foster, Lawrence. *Religion and Sexuality: The Shakers, the Mormons, and the Oneida Community.* Urbana, Ill.: University of Illinois Press, 1984.

Gaustad, Edwin S., ed. *A Documentary History of Religion in America to the Civil War.* Grand Rapids, Mich.: William B. Eerdmans Publishing Co., 1982.

Gibbons, Francis M. *Heber J. Grant.* Salt Lake City: Deseret Book Co., 1979.

Graffam, Merle H. *Salt Lake School of the Prophets Minute Book, 1883.* Palm Desert, Calif.: ULC Press, 1981.

Jenson, Andrew. *Encyclopedic History of the Church of Jesus Christ of Latter-day Saints.* Salt Lake City: Deseret News Publishing Co., 1941.

———. *Latter-day Saint Biographical Encyclopedia.* 4 vols. Salt Lake City: Andrew Jenson History Co., 1901–36.

Journal of Discourses. 26 vols. Liverpool: Latter-day Saints Book Depot, 1855–86.

Jubilee History of Latter-day Saint Sunday Schools, 1849–1899. Salt Lake City: Deseret Sunday School Union, 1900.

Kenney, Scott G., ed. *Wilford Woodruff's Journal.* 9 vols. Midvale, Utah: Signature Books, 1983–85.

Larson, Gustive O. *The "Americanization" of Utah for Statehood.* San Marino, Calif.: Huntington Library, 1971.

Lundwall, N. B., comp. *Masterful Discourses and Writings of Orson Pratt.* Salt Lake City: N. B. Lundwall, 1946.

Lyman, Amy Brown. *A Lighter of Lamps: The Life Story of Alice Louise Reynolds.* Provo, Utah: Alice Louise Reynolds Club, 1947.

Lyon, T. Edgar, Jr. *The Life of a Pioneer Poet.* Provo, Utah: Religious Studies Center, Brigham Young University, 1989.

Madsen, Truman G. *Defender of the Faith: The B. H. Roberts Story.* Salt Lake City: Bookcraft, 1980.

Marsden, George M. *Fundamentalism and American Culture: The Shaping of Twentieth-Century Evangelicalism, 1870–1925.* New York: Oxford University Press, 1980.

McConkie, Bruce R. *A New Witness for the Articles of Faith.* Salt Lake City: Deseret Book Co., 1985.

———. *Mormon Doctrine.* 2d ed. Salt Lake City: Bookcraft, 1966.

Nibley, Hugh. *Abraham in Egypt.* Salt Lake City: Deseret Book Co., 1981.

Nichols, James Hastings. *History of Christianity, 1650–1950.* New York: Ronald Press Co., 1956.

Poll, Richard D., et al., eds. *Utah's History.* Provo, Utah: Brigham Young University Press, 1978.

Proceedings Before the Committee on Privileges and Elections of the United States Senate, Reed Smoot Case. 2 vols. Washington: Government Printing Office, n.d.

Reynolds, George. *A Complete Concordance to the Book of Mormon.* Salt Lake City: George Reynolds, 1900.

———. *Are We of Israel?* 2d ed. Salt Lake City: Geo. Q. Cannon & Sons, 1895.

———. *A Dictionary of the Book of Mormon.* Salt Lake City: Jos. Hyrum Parry, 1891.

———. *The Book of Abraham: Its Authenticity Established As a Divine and Ancient Record.* Salt Lake City: Deseret News Printing and Publishing Establishment, 1879.

———. *The Myth of "Manuscript Found," or the Absurdities of the "Spaulding Story."* Salt Lake City: Juvenile Instructor Office, 1883.

———. *The Story of the Book of Mormon.* Salt Lake City: Jos. Hyrum Parry, 1888.

Reynolds, George, and Sjodahl, Janne M. *Commentary on the Book of Mormon.* Edited by Philip C. Reynolds. 7 vols. Salt Lake City: Deseret News Press, 1955–61.

———. *Commentary on the Pearl of Great Price.* Edited by Philip C. Reynolds. Salt Lake City: Deseret News Press, 1965.

Richardson, Arthur M., and Morgan, Nicholas G., Jr. *The Life and Ministry of John Morgan.* Salt Lake City: n.p., 1965.

Roberts, B. H. *A Comprehensive History of The Church of Jesus Christ of Latter-day Saints.* 6 vols. Provo, Utah: Brigham Young University Press, 1965.

———. *New Witnesses for God.* 3 vols. Salt Lake City: Deseret News, 1951.

Robison, Parker Pratt, ed. *Orson Pratt's Works.* Salt Lake City: Deseret News Press, 1945.

Second Book for Our Little Friends. Salt Lake City: Juvenile Instructor Office, 1980.

Sorenson, John L. *An Ancient American Setting for the Book of Mormon.* Salt Lake City: Deseret Book Co., 1985.

Smith, Goldwin. *A History of England,* 3d ed. New York: Charles Scribner's Sons, 1966.

Smith, Joseph, Jr. *History of the Church of Jesus Christ of Latter-day Saints.* Edited by B. H. Roberts. 7 vols. Salt Lake City: Deseret Book Co., 1957.

Smith, Joseph Fielding. *The Way to Perfection.* 12th ed. Salt Lake City: Deseret Book Co., 1963.

Talmage, James E. *Articles of Faith.* Salt Lake City: The Church of Jesus Christ of Latter-day Saints, 1890.

Taylor, John. *An Examination into and an Elucidation of the Great Principle of the Mediation and Atonement of Our Lord and Savior Jesus Christ.* Salt Lake City: Deseret News Co., 1882.

———. *Items on Priesthood Presented to the Latter-day Saints.* Salt Lake City: Deseret News Co., 1881.

Todd, Jay. *Saga of the Book of Abraham.* Salt Lake City: Deseret Book Co., 1969.

Van Wagoner, Richard S., and Walker, Steven C. *A Book of Mormons.* Salt Lake City: Signature Books, 1982.

Van Wagoner, Richard S. *Mormon Polygamy: A History.* Salt Lake City: Signature Books, 1986.

Whitehead, Ernest L. *The House of Israel.* Independence, Mo.: Zion's Printing and Publishing Co., 1947.

Whitney, Orson F. *History of Utah.* 4 vols. Salt Lake City: George Q. Cannon and Sons, 1898.

Wilkinson, Ernest L. *Brigham Young University: The First Hundred Years.* 4 vols. Provo, Utah: Brigham Young University Press, 1975.

Williams, Charles R. *The Life of Rutherford Birchard Hayes.* 2 vols. New York: Da Capa Press, 1971.

Wilson, Bryan R. *Magic and the Millennium.* London: Heinemann Educational Books Ltd., 1973.

———. *Religious Sects: A Sociological Study.* New York: McGraw-Hill, 1970.

———. *Patterns of Sectarianism: Organization and Religious Movements.* London: Heinemann Books Ltd., 1967.

Young, Kimball. *Isn't One Wife Enough?* New York: Henry Holt and Co., 1954.

ARTICLES IN PERIODICALS

Alexander, Thomas G. "Federal Authority Versus Polygamic Theocracy: James B. McKean and the Mormons, 1870–75." *Dialogue* 1 (Autumn 1966): 85–100.

———. "The Word of Wisdom: From Principle to Requirement."*Dialogue* 14 (Autumn 1981): 78–88.

Allen, James B. " 'Good Guys' Vs. 'Good Guys': Rudger Clawson, John Sharp, and Civil Disobedience in Nineteenth Century Utah." *Utah Historical Quarterly* 48 (Spring 1980): 148–74.

"Are We of Israel?" *Improvement Era* 34 (October 1931): 744.

245

Arrington, Leonard J. "The Search for Truth and Meaning in Mormon History." *Dialogue* 3 (Summer 1968): 56–66.
———. "The Settlement of the Brigham Young Estate, 1877–1879." *Pacific Historical Review* 21 (February 1952): 1–20.
Bennion, Adam. "George Reynolds." *Utah Genealogical and Historical Magazine* 1 (October 1910): 148.
Bitton, Davis. "Like the Tigers of Old Time." *Sunstone* 7 (September-October 1982): 47.
Bitton, Davis, and Bunker, Gary L. "Phrenology among the Mormons." *Dialogue* 9 (Spring 1974): 43–61.
Bradley, Martha Sonntag. " 'Hide and Seek': Children on the Underground." *Utah Historical Quarterly* 51 (Spring 1983): 133–53.
Buerger, David. " 'The Fulness of the Priesthood': The Second Anointing in Latter-day Saints Theology and Practice." *Dialogue* 16 (Spring 1984): 10–84.
Bush, Lester E., Jr. "The Spaulding Theory Then and Now." *Dialogue* 10 (Autumn 1977): 40–69.
———. "Excommunication and Church Courts: A Note from the General Handbook of Instructions." *Dialogue* 14 (Summer 1981): 74–98.
Campbell, Eugene L., and Campbell, Bruce E. "Divorce among Mormon Polygamists: Extent and Explanations." *Utah Historical Quarterly* 46 (Winter 1978): 4–23.
Cannon, Kenneth L., II. "Beyond the Manifesto: Polygamous Cohabitation among LDS General Authorities." *Utah Historical Quarterly* 46 (Winter 1978): 24–36.
Clayton, James L. "The Supreme Court, Polygamy and Enforcement of Morals in Nineteenth Century America: An Analysis of *Reynolds v. United States.*" *Dialogue* 12 (Winter 1979): 46–61.
Conference Report. 1896–1906.
"Correspondence." *Millennial Star* 27 (30 September 1865): 621–22.
"Correspondence." *Millennial Star* 30 (11 July 1868): 443.
"Correspondence." *Millennial Star* 32 (20 December 1870): 814.
"Correspondence." *Millennial Star* 37 (6 September 1875): 573.
"Correspondence." *Millennial Star* 41 (18 August 1879): 518.
"Correspondence." *Millennial Star* 41 (29 September 1879): 621.
"Correspondence." *Millennial Star* 41 (20 October 1879): 668.
Davis, Ray Jay. "Plural Marriage and Religious Freedom: The Impact of *Reynolds v. United States.*" *Arizona Law Review* 15 (1973): 287–306.
Dyer, Robert G. "The Evolution of Social and Judicial Attitudes towards Polygamy." *Utah Bar Journal* 5 (Spring 1977): 35–45.

"Editorial Thoughts." *Juvenile Instructor* 44 (1 May 1909): 204.

"Elder George Reynolds." *Juvenile Instructor* 44 (September 1909): 386–88.

Embry, Jessie L., and Bradley, Martha S. "Mothers and Daughters in Polygamy." *Dialogue* 18 (Fall 1985): 99–107.

"George Reynolds." *Young Woman's Journal* 20 (September 1909): 463–64.

"Gone to His Rest." *Millennial Star* 71 (26 August 1909): 539.

Hartley, William G. "The Seventies in the 1880s: Revelations and Reorganizing." *Dialogue* 16 (Spring 1983): 62–89.

Hill, George R. "Deseret Sunday School Union." *Improvement Era* 59 (November 1956): 800.

Hinckley, Gordon B. "Feasting upon the Scriptures." *Ensign* 15 (December 1985): 42.

Irving, Gordon. "The Mormons and the Bible in the 1830s." *BYU Studies* 13 (Summer 1973): 473–88.

James, Kimberly Jensen. " 'Between Two Fires': Women on the 'Underground.' " *Journal of Mormon History* 8 (1981): 49–62.

Jensen, Richard L. "Without Purse or Scrip? Financing Latter-day Missionary Work in Europe in the Nineteenth Century." *Journal of Mormon History* 12 (1985): 3–14.

Linford, Orma. "The Mormons and the Law: The Polygamy Cases." *Utah Law Review* 9 (1964): 308–70.

"Lives of Our Leaders. – The First Council of the Seventy. President Seymour B. Young." *Juvenile Instructor* 36 (15 April 1901): 224–27.

Lyman, Edward Leo. "The Alienation of an Apostle from His Quorum: The Moses Thatcher Case." *Dialogue* 18 (Summer 1985): 67–91.

Madsen, Truman G. "B. H. Roberts and the Book of Mormon." *BYU Studies* 19 (Summer 1979): 427–45.

Magrath, C. Peter. "Chief Justice Waite and the 'Twin Relic': *Reynolds v. the United States.*" *Vanderbilt Law Review* 18 (1965): 507–43.

McKay, David O. "Sunday Schools of the Church." *Improvement Era* 33 (May 1930): 480–81.

Mehr, Kahlile. "Women's Response to Plural Marriage." *Dialogue* 18 (Fall 1985): 99–107.

Miller, Jeremy M. "A Critique of the Reynolds Decision." *Western State University Law Review* 11 (Spring 1984): 165–98.

Pratt, Orson. *The Seer* 1 (March 1853): 41.

Quinn, D. Michael. "Latter-day Saint Prayer Circles." *BYU Studies* 19 (Fall 1978): 79–105.

———. "LDS Church Authority and New Plural Marriages, 1890–1904." *Dialogue* 18 (Spring 1985): 1–105.

———. "The Brief Career of Young University at Salt Lake City." *Utah Historical Quarterly* 41 (Winter 1973): 69–89.

———. "The Council of Fifty and Its Members, 1844 to 1945." *BYU Studies* 20 (Winter 1980): 163–97.

———. "Utah's Educational Innovation: LDS Religion Classes,1890–1929." *Utah Historical Quarterly* 43 (Fall 1975): 379–89.

Reynolds, George. All periodical articles by George Reynolds are listed in Appendix A, "Identifiable Writings of George Reynolds."

Romano, Edna, ed. "Teancum Pratt, Founder of Helper." *Utah Historical Quarterly* 48 (Fall 1980): 328–65.

Stern, Madeleine B. "A Rocky Mountain Book Store: Savage and Ottinger in Utah." *BYU Studies* 9 (Winter 1969): 144–54.

"The First Sunday School in the British Mission." *Juvenile Instructor* 34 (1 May 1899): 283.

"The Petition for Clemency," *Millennial Star* 41 (16 June 1879): 378.

T.Z. "Lives of Our Leaders.—The First Council of Seventy. President George Reynolds." *Juvenile Instructor* 36 (1 July 1901): 385–89.

Van Orden, Bruce A. "George Reynolds and Janne M. Sjodahl on Book of Mormon Geography." *Thetean* (1982): 60–79.

Underwood, Grant. "Book of Mormon Usage in Early LDS Theology," *Dialogue* 17 (Autumn 1984): 35–74.

Washburn, J. N. "A History of the Sunday Schools of The Church of Jesus Christ of Latter-day Saints." *Instructor* 74 (August 1949): 376–77.

Wells, Junius F. "A Living Martyr." *Contributor* 2 (February 1881): 154–56.

Whittaker, David J. "Orson Pratt: Early Advocate of the Book of Mormon." *Ensign* 14 (April 1984): 54–57.

Young, S. Dilworth. "The Seventies: A Historical Perspective." *Ensign* 6 (July 1976): 14–18.

NEWSPAPERS

Deseret News. Salt Lake City, Utah. 1909, 1985.

Deseret Semi-Weekly News. Salt Lake City, Utah. 1869, 1874–76, 1879, 1890, 1894.

Omaha Bee. Omaha, Nebraska. 1879.

Salt Lake Daily Herald. Salt Lake City, Utah. 1872, 1874–76, 1879.

Salt Lake Tribune. Salt Lake City, Utah. 1874–76, 1879.

The Herald. Provo, Utah. 1985.

THESES AND DISSERTATIONS

Baumgarten, James N. "The Role and Function of the Seventies in L.D.S. Church History." Master's thesis, Brigham Young University, 1960.

Burgess-Olson, Vicky. "Family Structure and Dynamics in Early Utah Mormon Families—1847–1885." Ph.D. dissertation, Northwestern University, 1975.

Flake, Lawrence R. "The Development of the *Juvenile Instructor* under George Q. Cannon and Its Function in Latter-day Saint Religious Education." Master's thesis, Brigham Young University, 1969.

Hardy, Grant R. "George Reynolds: The Early Years." Master's thesis, Brigham Young University, 1972.

Hulett, James Edward, Jr. "The Social and Psychological Aspects of the Mormon Polygamous Family." Ph.D. dissertation, University of Wisconsin, 1939.

Knighton, Ronald Lewis. "A Comparative Study of the Teaching Methods of the L.D.S. and Non-L.D.S. Sunday School Movements in the United States Prior to 1900." Master's thesis, Brigham Young University, 1968.

McBride, Don Wallace. "The Development of Higher Education in The Church of Jesus Christ of Latter-day Saints." Ph.D. thesis, Michigan State College of Agriculture and Applied Science, 1952.

Patrick, John R. "The School of the Prophets: Its Development and Influence in Utah Territory." Master's thesis, Brigham Young University, 1970.

Quinn, D. Michael. "Organizational Development and Social Origins of the Mormon Hierarchy, 1832–1932: A Prosopographical Study." Master's thesis, University of Utah, 1973.

MANUSCRIPTS

Callis, Charles A. Papers. Special Collections, Harold B. Lee Library, Brigham Young University.

Circular No. 4 of the General Board of Education of The Church of Jesus Christ of Latter-day Saints, 1889. LDS Church Historical Archives.

Church Educational System Letterpress Copybooks, 1888–1917. LDS Church Historical Archives.

"Church Emigration." Typescript, LDS Church Historical Archives.

Dunn, Sadee G. Lecture notes from classes taught by G. Reynolds, 16 January to 15 May 1899. Special Collections, Harold B. Lee Library, Brigham Young University.

Firmage, Edwin Brown, and Mangrum, R. Collin. "Zion and the Courts: A Legal History of The Church of Jesus Christ of Latter-day Saints, 1830–

1900." Typescript manuscript soon to be published by University of Illinois Press.

First Council of Seventy Index to Seventies Ordinations, 1839–1971. LDS Church Historical Archives.

First Council of Seventy Quorum Member Registers, 1876–1915. LDS Church Historical Archives.

Hartley, William G. Notes of First Council of Seventy Minutes obtained from LDS Church Historical Archives. Hartley office at Brigham Young University. Special Collections, Harold B. Lee Library, Brigham Young University.

Journal History. Compilation of newspaper articles and historical statements on a daily basis. LDS Church Historical Archives.

"Outline of Three Years' Course of Study for Twentieth Ward Sunday School." Printed outline located in LDS Church Historical Archives.

Rasmussen, Haroldeane. "History of Mary Ann Tuddenham Reynolds, My Grandmother." Typescript in possession of Haroldeane Rasmussen.

"The Reynolds Case, Supreme Court of the United States, No. 180 – October Term, 1878, George Reynolds, Plaintiff in Error, vs. The United States." Pamphlet, Special Collections, Harold B. Lee Library, Brigham Young University.

Reynolds, Alice Louise. "Autobiography of Alice Louise Reynolds." Typescript located in Special Collections, Harold B. Lee Library, Brigham Young University.

———. "Biography of George Reynolds." Typescript manuscript in Special Collections, Harold B. Lee Library, Brigham Young University.

———. "Sketch on the Life of Grandfather George Reynolds." Typescript manuscript obtained from Joseph Fielding McConkie.

Reynolds Collection. Manuscript collection of materials related to George Reynolds in Special Collections, Harold B. Lee Library, Brigham Young University.

Reynolds, George. "Autobiographical Sketch of George Reynolds." Typescript manuscript obtained from Grant Reynolds Hardy.

———. Letterpress Book, 1871–72. In possession of Vessa Hood Johnson, Springville, Utah.

———, to Amelia Schofield Reynolds. Numerous letters, 1879, 1885–86. Special Collections, Harold B. Lee Library, Brigham Young University.

———, to "Dad" (John Tuddenham), 7 April 1870. Letter in possession of Emily Jensen, Provo, Utah.

———, to Sidney Reynolds, 12 April 1907. Photocopy in possession of Sydney Skidmore, Potomac, Maryland.

Reynolds, Jane. Collection. Papers of George Reynolds and Harold Reynolds in possession of Jane Reynolds, Salt Lake City, Utah.

Salt Lake City Twentieth Ward Historical Records. LDS Church Historical Archives.

Utah District Court Records, Record Group #21, United States of America, District of Utah, Papers and Files in Case Nos. 1631 and 2148, United States of America vs. Geo Reynolds. National Archives-Denver Branch. (Microfilm copy in possession of the writer.)

Van Orden, Bruce A. "Anglo-Israelism and Its Influence on Mormon Theology." Paper delivered 28 August 1982 at 1982 Sunstone Theological Symposium, Salt Lake City, Utah.

——. "Close to the Seat of Authority: Secretaries and Clerks in the Office of the President of the LDS Church, 1870–1900." Paper delivered at the annual meetings of the Mormon History Association, Provo, Utah, May 1984.

——. "Mormons and Jews: Persecuted Israel." Paper delivered 28 April 1984 at annual conference of the Rocky Mountain/Great Plains Region of American Academy of Religion – Society of Biblical Literature, Denver, Colorado.

——. "The Seed of Abraham in the Latter Days." Paper delivered 8 February 1986 at Sidney B. Sperry Symposium, Brigham Young University, Provo, Utah.

Woolley, Edwin Dilworth, Papers. LDS Church Historical Archives.

Young, Seymour Bicknell, Papers. LDS Church Historical Archives.

DIARIES

Cannon, Abraham H. Journal. Typescript. Special Collections, Harold B. Lee Library, Brigham Young University.

Christensen, Joseph. Journals. LDS Church Historical Archives.

John, David. Journal. Special Collections, Harold B. Lee Library, Brigham Young University.

Nuttall, L. John. Diary. Typescript in 4 vols. Special Collections, Harold B. Lee Library, Brigham Young University.

"Prisoners for Conscience' Sake." Typescript compilations of interviews and journal entries of Mormon men who were imprisoned. LDS Church Historical Archives.

Reynolds, George. Journal. Vols. 1, 3–6. LDS Church Historical Archives. (Photocopy in possession of the author.) Vol. 1 is from 8 May 1861 to 31 August 1862. Vol. 2 is missing. Vol. 3 is from 19 June 1863 to 13 June 1864; vol. 4 is from 14 June 1864 to 26 April 1872; vol. 5 is from

27 April 1872 to 20 January 1881; vol. 6 is from 20 January 1881 to 1 September 1906.

Rich, Ben E. Journal. LDS Church Historical Archives.

Woolley, Samuel Edwin. Journal. LDS Church Historical Archives.

INTERVIEWS

Cannon, Adrian W. Salt Lake City, Utah. 17 July 1985.

Curtis, Mark. Salt Lake City, Utah. 31 January 1986.

Esplin, Ronald. Provo, Utah. 27 November 1985.

Goaslind, Jack H., Jr. Salt Lake City, Utah. 6 November 1985.

Hardy, Grant Reynolds. Salt Lake City, Utah. (Interviews were conducted with Hardy on many occasions from 1981 to 1986.)

Jensen, Emily. Provo, Utah. 29 November 1985.

McConkie, Amelia Smith. Salt Lake City, Utah. 8 January 1986.

Myers, Emily. Salt Lake City, Utah. 8 January 1986.

Ogden, Maude. Salt Lake City, Utah. 7 January 1986.

Parker, Zetha. Salt Lake City, Utah. 6 January 1986.

Rasmussen, Haroldeane. Provo, Utah. 29 November 1985.

Reynolds, George Gordon. Salt Lake City, Utah. 31 August 1981.

Robbins, Evelyn. Provo, Utah. 1 February 1985.

Grant Reynolds Hardy with Margaret Russell Bennett. Salt Lake City, Utah. 18 July 1970.

Grant Reynolds Hardy with Laura Woolfinden Hastings. Salt Lake City, Utah. 1970.

Index

Index

Reynolds, Clifford Meredith, 196
Reynolds, Edwin Don (son) (Carl), 126
Reynolds, Eleanor (daughter) (Nellie), 80, 196
Reynolds, Ethel Georgina (daughter), 166, 214; marries, 192
Reynolds Family Organization, 219-20
Reynolds, Florence Mary (daughter) (Florry), 55; attends Provo academy, 166
Reynolds, George:

Childhood:
birth of, 1; conversion of, 1; education of, 3; baptism of, 3-4

Church service:
appointed outdoor missionary, 6; called as missionary, 7, 9-11; arrives in Liverpool, 16; becomes clerk of European-British Mission, 16; works on emigration of Saints, 20, 25; gathers statistics on subscriptions, 21; compiles mission statistics, 21-22; called as branch president, 23; called as a seventy, 30; employed by Brigham Young, 32; joins Nauvoo Legion, 32; assists at Endowment House, 34; becomes superintendent, 35; called as tithing clerk, 35; leaves on second mission to England, 37; third mission of, 41; appointed acting head of European Mission, 45; works in Endowment House, 52; called as superintendent of Sunday School and secretary of ward store, 53; enters polygamy, 55; joins united order branch, 74; called to presidents of Seventy, 75; becomes clerk to Quorum of the Twelve, 79; called as home missionary, 80; addresses Sunday assembly, 113; as secretary, 118-19; appointed to Council of Fifty,

124; gathers information on School of Prophets, 124-25; serves on reading committee, 125-26; on reorganizing seventies quorums, 129-30; serves on committee to plan John Taylor's funeral, 157; reads dedicatory prayer of Manti Temple, 157; as secretary to Wilford Woodruff, 162; called as general authority, 162-63, 169; set apart as one of First Seven Presidents of Seventy, 171; becomes Genealogical Society secretary, 175; and Sunday School conference, 184-85; named assistant to Sunday School Union, 187; called to Missionary Committee, 195; performs marriages, 198; speaks in general conference, 198-99; last public address of, 200, 218-19; speech of, at Salt Lake Temple dedication, 216-18

Personal/family life:
rebaptized, 29-30, 75; marries Mary Ann (Polly) Tuddenham, 30; illness of, 33-34, 50; receives patriarchal blessing, 34; builds house, 34; brothers come to America to live with, 35; buys Singer sewing machine, 38; resigns from positions, 42; contracts smallpox, 44; family of, joins Church, 53; marries Amelia, 55-56; receives blessing, 94-95; receives Pratt's edition of the Book of Mormon, 107; begins construction of new house, 117; suffers migraine headaches, 126-27; tries to keep peace between two households, 127; authority on house of Israel, 137; marries Mary Gulliford Goold, 148-49; gives

257